SANDALS, MANDALS, AND MARY JANES

SANDALS, MANDALS, AND MARY JANES

A History of Shoes

WILLIAM J. BOLEN, Ph.D.

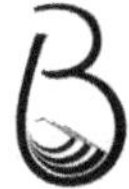

BOOKLOGIX
Alpharetta, GA

Every effort was made to make the manuscript as accurate as possible and to use primary source materials when possible. This was often rendered most difficult because of the age of the sources. In the event we have erred in any way, we welcome information that will allow us to make corrections in a future edition. Because of the complexity of copyright laws, it was difficult at times to determine whether a photograph was included in the public domain. When not sure we have made every effort to request permission to use photographs and illustrations. No copyright infringement is intended.

ISBN: 978-1-6653-0016-2 - Paperback
eISBN: 978-1-6653-0017-9 - ePub
eISBN: 978-1-6653-0018-6 - mobi

Library of Congress Control Number: 2021911676

Printed in the United States of America   1 2 1 6 2 1

⊚This paper meets the requirements of ANSI/NISO Z39.48-1992 (Permanence of Paper)

Figure 2-4: Richard Sheaff (President of The Ephemera Society of America), *Mary Jane Candy*. Photograph.

Figure 6-2: Carole Raddato, *Bronze caliga from an over life-size statue of a Roman cavalryman*. Gladiators — Death and Triumph at the Colosseum exhibition, Museum und Park Kalkriese, Frankfurt, Germany. Uploaded by Marcus Cyron, CC BY-SA 2.0, https://commons.wikimedia.org/w/index.php?curid=30370758

Figure 9-8: *Dorcus Skirt*. Photograph. https://www.vintag.es/

*This book is dedicated to the memory of Anna Maria Bolen,
loving wife and mother.*

CONTENTS

INTRODUCTION

It is often said that "we humans tend to think that what we have experienced in our lifetime is the way things always were."[1] Attitudes of clothing, including footwear, have changed dramatically over the years. What may have been very stylish in the past may today be viewed as strange, or even ridiculous. For instance, how many people would believe that the classic round-toe, single-strap Mary Jane shoe, considered by many to be a "little girl's shoe," first appeared as a man's shoe that was worn by kings and soldiers? It was only later that women became associated with the Mary Jane shoe style. Contrary to common belief, Mary Janes were not created as a child's shoe, even though boys and girls wore them.

Today, it is confusing to see some shoes marketed specifically for men, while others are just for women, and some are unisex that can be worn by either sex. Androgynous shoes, not specified for either sex, are often listed as children's shoes. This line of demarcation is further complicated by the fact that what was traditionally worn by one sex may today be more suitable for the other, or even both sexes. Styles have changed to the point that men may be called a sissy or other uncomplimentary names for wearing shoes now viewed as feminine.

It is also a myth to believe that children's shoe styles have always been a child's style. Rather, footwear worn by children before the 1800s and 1900s mimicked the styles in fashion for adults. During the nineteenth century, shoes with laces became more common for adults than footwear with straps and buckles. But strap shoes for children continued to be common, as seen in drawings, paintings, and photographs. This phenomenon may have been because it was more practical for children, especially for those who had not mastered the tying of laces, to put on or take off shoes with straps. A shoe company advertised the benefits of hook-and-loop fasteners on footwear and recommended that buyers leave their laces at home. This may be part of a paradigm shift whereby sandals and other forms of footwear may use hook-and-loop closures to the exclusion of other types of fasteners in the future.

The names advertisers assign to various styles of footwear to influence purchases, especially those linked to gender, have changed dramatically over time to affect the way people perceive footwear usage. For instance, single-strap shoes about the turn of the twentieth century were referred to as "sandals" or "slippers" in different advertisements because of the straps and openness on top.

The chapters of this book will take the reader on a historical journey to uncover the origins of sandal, mandal, and Mary Jane footwear. In North America, a single-strap-style shoe is commonly known as a Mary Jane, but in the UK it is termed a court shoe, strap shoe, or bar shoe, with other names found depending on the country of origin.

At the turn of the twentieth century, a multi-strapped shoe was called a "sandal," or more specifically a "Roman sandal." The history of multi-strap footwear as well as shoe styles with an added central T-strap are discussed in chapters 3 through 6. It was at the end of the twentieth century that multi-strapped footwear became known as "gladiator sandals," even though gladiators usually fought barefoot.

Geography has made a big difference in the classification of T-strap sandals. In North America, the double T-strap was known as a "barefoot sandal" throughout most of the 1900s. In the twenty-first century, this sandal was put into the Mary Jane category when sold to women, but was called a traditional English sandal when marketed to boys and girls. Currently, strap shoes can be found in adult sizes on the internet as *men's* Mary Janes. None of these terms have been used much in Europe. By the 2000s, the twin T-strap style is found on the internet listed as a shoe or Mary Jane Oxford, but never as a *sandal*. The term "sandal" is reserved for footwear that has thinner straps and more open space. Even the name "barefoot sandal" that for one hundred years referred exclusively to the double T-strap style has now been assigned to the open, beaded, flip-flop-style sandal. Thus, one can see that footwear names and styles have changed over time.

Rogers (2008) reports that footwear was "having an identity crisis" because of the ever-increasing number of hybrids flooding the shoe market that incorporated the best features of sneakers, boots, and Oxfords to those of sandals.[2] These hybrid shoe/sandals are a new look for feet, and could become the preferred style of footwear for the future because they allow individuals to wear sneakers that breathe.

Sandals available for today's men have also acquired the name "mandal." The increase in the popularity of this footwear is covered in later chapters. In the twenty-first century, many other fashion changes are occurring, including longer hairstyles, jewelry, and scent worn by men and boys, which would have been considered feminine not too long ago. In history, long hair was actually the preferred style by men rather than short hair. Body piercing is another example that has existed from ancient times and has become popular in recent years. Steele (1996) notes that boys had "their ears, noses, and breasts pierced, and rings inserted in them in the 1880s," so it is hardly a modern phenomenon.[3] The old saying "What goes around, comes around," with ever more frequent style revivals, is very true for footwear.

Fashion and sandals have been used to accentuate class distinctions over the millennia. Many people attempted to improve their status by copying the clothes worn by royalty and the wealthy. Some mothers even dressed their boys in strap shoes and fancy lace and velvet clothing to emulate royal families, who dressed their princes and princesses in such clothes for centuries to present a certain image of status quo and stability. This often resulted in ridicule and criticism for such mothers, especially by those of lower economic levels for trying to imitate their betters. Princess Diana dressed her sons in Mary Jane–style shoes before they went to school and then in traditional English prep school T-strap sandals. Such footwear appears strange to North American eyes, although Jacqueline Kennedy did the same to her son John-John.

It appears that the main force currently driving fashion change has been an attempt by young people to copy new styles worn by celebrities and sports figures. There has also been a conscious desire by the youth to look different from older generations, rather than copying royalty. And in the twenty-first century, styles change at a much faster pace than in the past as a result of exposure to movies, television, travel, the internet, and other visual experiences. One may not realize it, but changes in fashion occur constantly. To observe things within an historical perspective helps one to evaluate changes in class differences and gender that one might not be aware of otherwise.

Given this context of change in the world of fashion, and sandals in particular, it would seem appropriate at this point to say a word about the circumstances that led to the writing of this book. While searching for a pair of shoes on the internet, the author saw an ad for Dr. Martens double-T-strap shoes that were listed as "Men's Dr. Martens Twin T-Bar Shoes." In the UK, the horizontal straps across the instep of the foot are referred to as bars or crossbars, and the shoes as bar shoes. There was no mention of sandals or Mary Jane shoes in the ad. He showed the ad to his daughter, Valerie, who said that the twin T-bars looked to her like children's shoes, and they could not possibly be for men. They were curious about this and, following some discussion, decided to check the shoes out. They did not know at the time that their quest would eventually take them to several countries, and lead to an almost endless search in libraries, museums, and old mail-order catalogs, not to mention the countless hours researching websites on the internet over the course of several years.

The study was expanded to include the broader family of closed-toe sandals. This included Mary Jane–style shoes, as they were considered sandals on the basis of one or more straps and the broad opening on the vamp at the front of the shoe. In fact, at the turn of the twentieth century, any footwear with straps and an opening on the top was called a sandal. The more we researched, the more we encountered gender, class, and feminist issues. We felt we needed to determine how a child's shoe differs from an adult's, aside from size considerations. More importantly, what constitutes a female shoe as opposed to a male shoe when the feet of both genders are the same except for size differences? And why should a simple piece of leather used to make a shoe or a sandal have strong gender properties assigned to it, unless one considers whether the leather came from a cow or a bull? Further, who determines what is a boy's or a girl's shoe when it could fit either sex?

Questions involving gender and sandal usage are addressed in chapter 9, where an attempt is made to tie all the previous chapters together. Personal interviews and polls were conducted on the internet to collect firsthand information. In this research, the word "sissy" was encountered on numerous occasions as it relates to footwear. The author felt others might also be interested in the research findings and decided to publish this material in book form.

This study on shoes is unlike anything reviewed on the subject of footwear. This is because most scholars, whether they are shoe historians, costume, fashion, or clothing experts, usually study footwear from historical epochs. These experts may just concentrate on the relation of footwear to a specific topic such as culture, fetishism, or fashion trends in a postmodern society.

This book takes the approach of tracing back as far as possible individual closed-toe sandal styles to their point of origin to ascertain who wore them and why, as a way to gain perspective on shoe styles. A major finding from the research is that men and women wore the same or very similar footwear over the millennia until quite recently. Also, footwear fashions were initially created for adults, not children, contrary to our original premise. Another finding is that advertising and manufacturing companies have played a major role in differentiating style based on gender, perhaps for profit motives. For, after all, two distinct style lines for men and women allow for less opportunity to share footwear and hand-me-downs with siblings. This point is discussed in depth in the book as well as the fact that many people seem conditioned to masculine and feminine names associated with footwear. Colors are also assigned by gender to shoes (i.e. pink for girls and blue for boys) so that people have come to accept this as the norm over time. It would appear there is "nothing in nature that makes green the color of envy, or white the color of virginity" like humans see in shoe colors.[4]

Observation by the author in the twenty-first century found that sandal usage became more popular for men and boys. Only a few years ago, most men in the US would never have been seen in sandals. Thus, the author wondered what were the dynamics to cause this change in attitudes toward sandals, since it appeared to be a reversal of the historical pattern of styles going from male to female rather than vice versa. Were people becoming less concerned with gender in shoe styles compared to attitudes in the twentieth century?

Evidence from the research found that footwear in the past began as a male style, but as more women wore male styles, fewer men and boys wanted to wear the same shoe. Was this change a perceived loss of masculinity, or was it a fear of adverse peer comments? Could the pressure to conform for men exist because of standards imposed on men and boys by shoe companies, or was it some other factor? Discussion of the name "mandal" and its impact on the increase in sandal sales to men is discussed in chapter 8.

The question of why women seem able to more easily wear men's clothes and shoe styles without a problem is discussed. Another question looked into was the social equity allowing men to wear Mary Jane–style shoes, if they choose to, as a retro style that takes them back to the days when this style was worn by kings and soldiers.

On the other hand, would women be willing to share strap shoes with men? Thompson (2003) raises the interesting point that women wear Mary Jane shoes largely as a perceived means to reclaim their younger days of innocence. She states that women find

Mary Jane shoes "nostalgic and valuable to those who want to escape the male dominated society, while still keeping that innocence and femininity."[5] This could be the reason why Mary Janes have come to be called little girl shoes, or "baby dolls."

There are also shoe-related items that have gone from female to male and become unisex. Take the shoelace, for example, that was once considered effeminate and unfashionable for men to use in any form, for this was the period when shoe buckles like those worn by George Washington were so popular. And the more elaborate, bejeweled, or fancy the buckles were, the better. So when Thomas Jefferson was the first US president to wear shoelaces at his inauguration to the White House in 1801, he raised a lot of eyebrows.[6] In the eighteenth century, "fops" at Oxford University began wearing shoes with laces and the style eventually became popular. This is the reason they are called "Oxfords" today.[7] Following Jefferson's lead, laced shoes became increasingly popular in the US to the extent that when someone wished to purchase them, they asked for a pair of "Jeffersons" until the mid-1800s. Laced shoes were often called *corset shoes* in the 1700s because they laced up like a woman's corset, but Jefferson considered laces to be more democratic, unlike the buckle shoes associated with the old aristocracy.[8]

Thus, the critical question about shoes is, do strap shoes and sandals receive more attention vis-à-vis gender issues than lace-up Oxfords and high-top footwear that are and have been worn by both sexes? In the past, women have worn combat boots, saddle shoes, and high-top sneakers, which previously were exclusively men's footwear, with little attention paid to the person who had these shoes on. So let us look briefly at sandal morphology for some clarification of this concern.

In general, sandals can be characterized as footwear fastened to the foot by straps, bars, or thongs. The purpose of the straps is to securely hold the foot in place. Sandals are generally open at the top, rather than boots and shoes that enclose the foot. Sandals are considered one of the earliest forms of footwear, as seen in the September 2006 issue of *National Geographic* magazine that shows a picture of a fifteen-thousand-year-old sandal.[9]

Sandals can be divided into either open- or closed-toe types. Open-toe sandals have been known as Jesus sandals that date from biblical times or before. The author found Jesus sandals in his world travels worn by both sexes, and they have not changed since biblical times. The only exception was that the women's version of the Jesus sandal tends to be more colorful and have more decorations. Currently, flip-flops are an excellent example of open-toe sandals that are unisex and ubiquitous throughout the world. Flip-flops are a descendant of the sandal found in ancient Egypt and other early warm-climate civilizations.

Closed-toe sandals, on the other hand, including Mary Jane–style shoes, have shown a greater diversity of style throughout the years. Consequently, this book concentrates on the closed-toe shoe to study trends, popularity, attitudes, and myths in the chapters that follow. Changes graphically are shown by including as many illustrations and photos as possible. Further, a search was made to locate primary sources of information through catalogs and newspapers, as well as polls and questionnaires to canvass people's opinions. It is recognized that the size of the polls conducted and the number of individuals who completed the questionnaires were limited because of time and resources. But, in the opinion of the author, the polls and questionnaires provide valuable information. However, more in-depth and exhaustive research using polls and interviews on topics related to sandals could be undertaken at a future date.

In research for chapter 2, a surprise was the discovery that strap shoes with the name "Mary Jane" have only been used since just before World War I. For most of its long existence, the Mary Jane style has been referred to as a sandal, slipper, strap shoe, or bar shoe. Because of this finding, a typology was created to study these shoes according to the number of straps, or bars, and whether they had a center T-strap.

Specialized forms of Mary Janes, such as high-heel Mary Janes, Mary Jane sneaker/sandal hybrids, etc., are found in later chapters.

Sandals are fastened by buttons, buckles, or hook-and-loop fastener straps. In the 2000s, a trend by marketers was to lump footwear with straps under the heading of Mary Janes. As a result, some T-strap sandals were called "Mary Janes" while others were referred to as fisherman sandals, which tended to be unisex. Rogers (2008) reports that there was an "identity crisis" with sandals being combined with sneakers and boots.[10]

The author recognizes that it is not possible to study the thousands of varied sandal variations, but the ones included in this book give a representative sample of the changes that have occurred over time. To some it might come as a surprise that despite the seemingly endless variety of sandals, according to Young (2006), there are only four basic types[11]:

1. Thong   3. Sport sandal, including sandal/sneaker hybrids
2. Slide   4. Fisherman

In fact, all footwear can be categorized into only eight basic types:

1. Sandals   5. Pumps
2. Monk straps   6. Clogs
3. Moccasins   7. Boots
4. Mules   8. Lace-up Oxfords

This is according to shoe historian W. A. Rossi (1996), as everything else in shoes is a variation of these types.[12]

The author agrees with the idea that footwear is mysterious, and one of the more complex accessory items of wearing apparel. Shoes express a "huge range of meanings, prejudices, and tensions in society."[13] Later chapters focus on individuals' feelings toward the sandal that can be very strong or even controversial. While the overall appearance of sandals has remained the same, public opinion and feelings have changed over the centuries.

With the information collected from polls, questionnaires, and personal interviews, the writers addressed some of the social-psychological questions with respect to Mary Janes and other closed-toe sandals.

An example of the word "sissy" as it relates to shoes was found in October 2008 in the case of a photo that appeared on an online auction (Figure I-1). It was labeled "Little Boy Sissy Outfit and Shoes." Actually, the boy is dressed in a stylish Buster Brown outfit and strap shoes, very popular in the 1910s for boys. Girls, on the other hand, were never dressed in this fashion style at that time. Questions were raised to the seller about her usage of the term "sissy," and she replied that "by today's standards, [the boy] would appear to be dressed like a girl, thus, I used the word sissy, perhaps wrongly."[14]

According to O'Keeffe (1996), most female shoe styles originated as men's footwear, but with women's "properties."[15] So, why is it that as more women begin to wear a particular shoe style, men avoid that particular shoe? It could be a feeling of discomfort to see men or boys wear shoes that are perceived to be female, or fear they could be labeled as "sissy" or "girly."

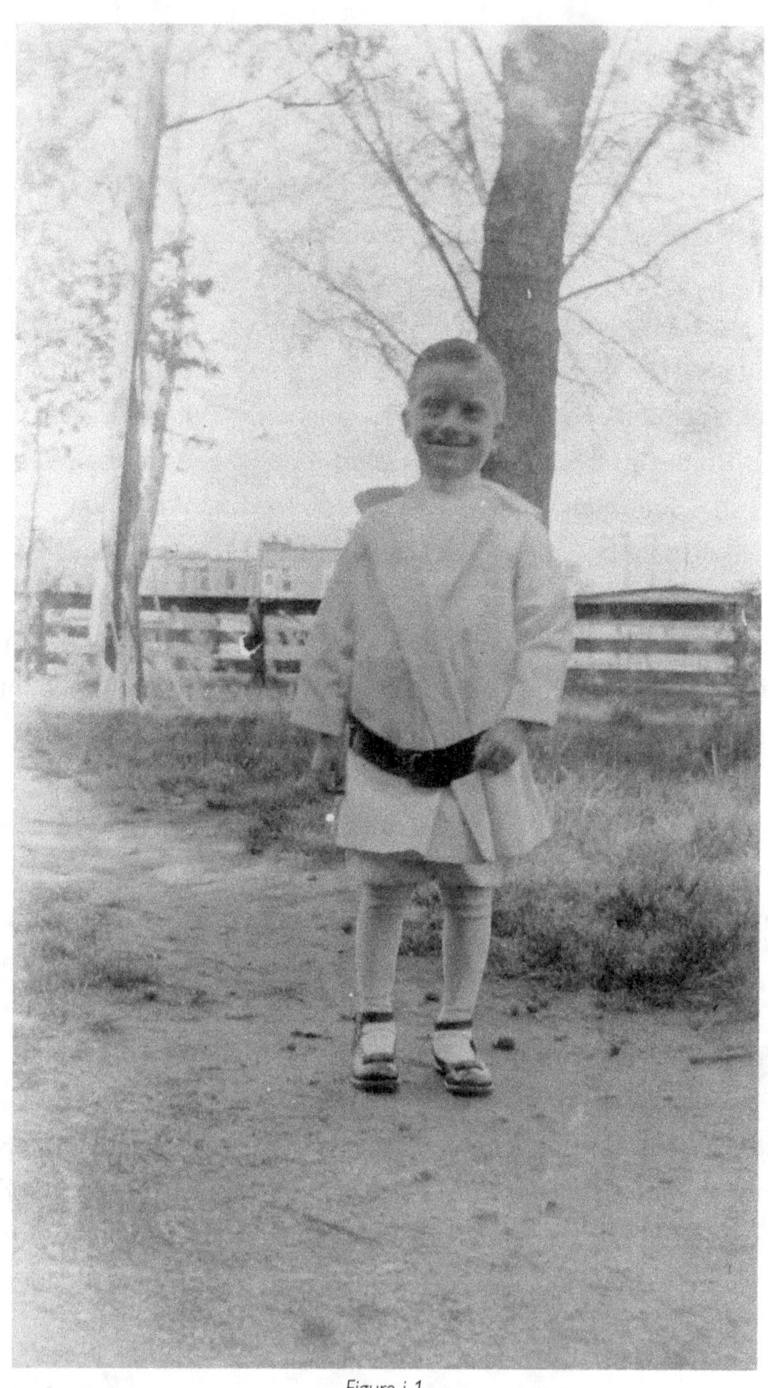

Figure i-1
Little boy "sissy" outfit and shoes, ca. 1910s

O'Keeffe reports that Mark Gottdiener, urban sociologist, notes that "women in American society have traditionally been given a weaker social position than men and the mere act of wearing women's clothing situates the person in a subordinate role."[16] This might cause some men to fear any article of clothing perceived to be female; on the other hand, women are free to wear men's shoes and clothes without any criticism.

Chapter 9 considers the term "sissy" within the context that it is not just derogatory to a man, but it also has a negative connotation toward women. The term "sissy" originated in the days when women were considered the "weaker sex." The author wonders if the term could fade away as more people wear unisex clothes, androgynous footwear, and women are treated more fairly in the workplace (i.e. equal pay for equal work). Maybe the use of genderless names or no names assigned to footwear by advertising and manufacturing companies could play a role for this to be accomplished. Only 10 percent of the people who responded to questions on an internet poll felt they could rely on gender-related names to guide their footwear purchases, while 90 percent did not. So why continue to use names or assign gender to footwear? A 2009 Payless.com ad illustrates this point. The ad shows a group of Airwalk Kicks sneakers, with two identified as men's and five as women's, which are made in smaller sizes than the men's, but are identical except for the color schemes. Would it not be simpler, easier, less confusing, and cheaper to have a single range of sizes similar to Europe (EU sizes) and Britain (UK sizes) for individuals to decide which they prefer? On the other hand, the US sizing for both sexes has been in place since the 1880s and, in the researchers' opinions, was devised to give women the impression they had smaller feet for vanity reasons. It would seem simpler to list both men's and women's sizes as a single-size system, as in the

UK and Europe. The difference in US shoe sizes is based on the old English measurement of one-third of an inch, which is the length of a barleycorn. Men's sizes are listed as one-and-a-half sizes different from a woman with the same-size foot.[17]

Consideration was given to the question that sandals could play a role in liberating men's feet from stuffy lace-up shoes. Based on medical experts' findings, sandals may actually be associated with fewer foot problems than other types of footwear. Liberation for men was observed in the twenty-first century when men began to wear more colorful footwear as opposed to dark lace-up Oxfords and high-tops that were more common in the 1900s.

Several stores and outlets in 2013 advertised a Ralph Lauren laced ankle hiking boot, Dover III, with a superimposed Mary Jane style to create a hybrid that was sold in men's sizes. The men who reviewed this hiking boot on the internet stated that it was very comfortable, but said nothing about the resemblance to the Mary Jane shoe.

While many books are available on the subject of shoes, especially children's books, research found there are few scholarly works written specifically on the subject of sandals. Rielle and McNeil (2006), shoe historian and podiatrist Kippen (2004), Weidner's Historical Boys' Clothing website, Mellish and Green's Balkan website, and Peacock (2005) are exceptions. Thompson (2003) is the only scholar to write a journal article on the history and evolution of the Mary Jane shoe style.

The author hopes this book gives the reader a perspective on sandals and that it may add to the body of knowledge on this subject. As Shari Benstock and Suzanne Ferriss (2001) state in the introduction to their book, *Footnotes: On Shoes*, may the reader "strap on your sandals and wander with us."[18]

Introduction Notes

1. Dietzen, J., *Monitor*, vol. 54, no. 11 (April 2007): 16.

2. Rogers, G., "Notes on a Sandal," *Mail Online* (July 7, 2008), www.dailymail.co.uk/femail/article-1031888/Notes-sandal-Is-shoe-Is-boot-Footwear-having-identity-crisis-season.html.

3. Steele, Valerie, *Fetish Fashion: Sex and Power* (New York: Oxford University Press, 1996), 191.

4. Ibid., 160.

5. Thompson, M. J., "Mary Janes: The Return of Innocence in a Postmodern Society," *Journal of the Utah Association of Family and Consumer Science*, vol. 9, no. 1 (2003): 10.

6. Riello, G. and P. McNeil, *Shoes: A History from Sandals to Sneakers* (New York: Berg Publishers, 2006), 106–107.

7. Kippen, C., "Foot Talk" (September 3, 2005), foottalk.blogspot.com.

8. Lawlor, L., *Where Will This Shoe Take You?: A Walk through the History of Footwear* (London: Walker Books, 1996), 38.

9. Newman, C., "The Joy of Shoes," *National Geographic* magazine, (September 2006), www.nationalgeographic.com.

10. Rogers, "Notes on a Sandal."

11. Young, E., "Making Their Mark," *Eagle Tribune* (July 16, 2006), www.eagletribune.com/lifestyle/x1876241949/Making-their-mark-Its-all-about-comfort-as-sandals-for-men-gain-ground/print.

12. Rossi, W. A., "The Brief History of Footwear," *Journal of Current Podiatric Medicine*, vol. 39, no. 6 (1990); quoted in Lawlor, *Where Will This Shoe Take You?*

13. Riello and McNeil, *Shoes*, 28.

14. Irene, eBay message to author (October 27, 2008).

15. O'Keeffe, L., *Shoes: A Celebration of Pumps, Sandals, Slippers and More* (New York: Workman Publishing, 1996), 240.

16. Rubinstein, R. P., *Dress Codes: Meanings and Messages in American Culture* (New York: Westview Press, 2001), 12.

17. Rossi, W. A., *The Complete Footwear Dictionary* (Malabar, FL: Krieger Publishing, 2000).

18. Benstock, S. and S. Ferriss, *Footnotes: On Shoes* (Piscataway, NJ: Rutgers University Press, 2001).

CHAPTER 1

ONE-STRAP MARY JANE SHOES

One might wonder why the classic Mary Jane–type shoes are included in a book on closed-toe sandals. However, many people may not know that this footwear was traditionally referred to as a sandal until the early twentieth century. In its simplest form, the footwear is characterized as having a flat heel, single strap, and a blunt toe. There are geographical differences in that the style is referred to as "Mary Janes" in North America, while older terms, such as "strap shoes," "court shoes," and "bar shoes" are more commonly used in Europe, although the Mary Jane name is increasingly being used in Europe, judging by recent ads online. These terms are used interchangeably in this book. While almost everyone is familiar with this type of footwear, most people have no idea where the style originated, nor who actually wore them in the past. Why are they often referred to as little girls' shoes in recent times? O'Keeffe (1996) believes the style has retained its popularity because it "signals a child's transition from baby to little girl or boy."[1]

Early History of Mary Jane Footwear

Paintings of King Henry VIII and others during the Renaissance period show countless people wearing single-strap shoes, which gives the impression that the style was created in the

1400s or 1500s. From a timeline perspective, the style can be traced back much further in the past. Thompson (2003) reports that Romans wore a very similar shoe as far back as 34 AD, which was made of "thick black leather and heavily decorated with a hole-punched pattern."[2] An example of such Roman footwear can be seen at the Chesters Roman Fort and Museum in the vicinity of the English town of Hexham. The fort, which guarded the wall built by Emperor Hadrian to keep the "barbarian" Scots and Picts out of Roman Britain, had a contingent of five hundred soldiers and their families, many of whom were from the province of Dacia, present-day Romania and Bulgaria.

According to information at the fort's museum, the shoe was excavated by Professor Francis Haverfield in 1903. It was found in a ditch located outside the southeast corner of the fort, where the wet peat soil had preserved it for two thousand years. The shoe had punched holes in the straps through which leather strips were passed to fasten it to the foot (Figure 1-1). These strips or laces, according to Thompson (2003), evolved into the straps and buckles of Mary Jane–type footwear.

The Museum of London had an exhibit of Roman coin makers in 2006. According to information at the exhibit, a Roman mint was established in 288 AD and operated until 388 AD for the purpose of making Roman coins to pay the Roman garrison in Britain. One of the mint workers is pictured wearing a similar type of sandal as the one found at the Chesters Roman Fort. The method of fastening is very similar to the way tap shoes are fastened, although modern-day versions use shoelaces or ribbons rather than leather strips.

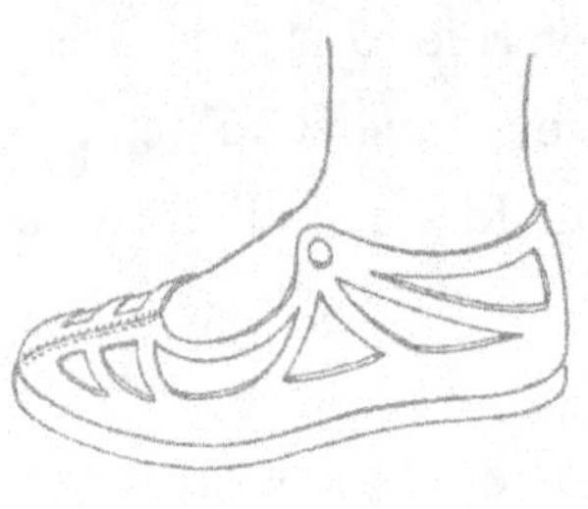

Figure 1-1
Roman Mary Jane–type sandal
100–200 AD

In his book, *The Roman Era in Britain*, Ward (1911) includes an illustration of a Roman closed-toe sandal found in Britain which has the shape of a Mary Jane, but with many cutouts on the sides and on top that create a "skeleton of slender bands reaching down to the sole."[3] It also had a pair of "lace-holes" like the Chesters Roman Fort shoe, rather than the traditional instep strap found on later Mary Janes.

Wilson (1968), in her book *A History of Shoe Fashions*, includes an illustration of a pointed-toe shoe with a single ankle strap dating from the Danish period of occupation of Britain during the period 700–1066 AD. She also includes an example of a basic Mary Jane shoe with a strap across the instep that was worn by the Normans between 1066 and 1154. She writes that the Norman version was a "simple shoe worn by the common people, made in black or brown rawhide or natural suntanned leathers." There were also shoes having other colors and more elaborate decorations, but these would have been worn by the "upper-class people." Regardless of the color or decorations, shoes were "invariably made with a round toe, flat sole, and no heel lift" at that time.[4] Neither the Danish nor the Norman footwear used buckles for fastening.

An image of a shoe from the Middle Ages that closely resembles what is generally thought of as a classic Mary Jane shoe is contained in the New York Public Library Digital Gallery collection. It is described as a French "gentleman's shoe" dating from about 1240 (Figure 1-2). This shoe was "molded exactly to the shape of the foot" and had a strap across the instep fastened by either a buckle or a button.[5] Carlson (1996) sketched a

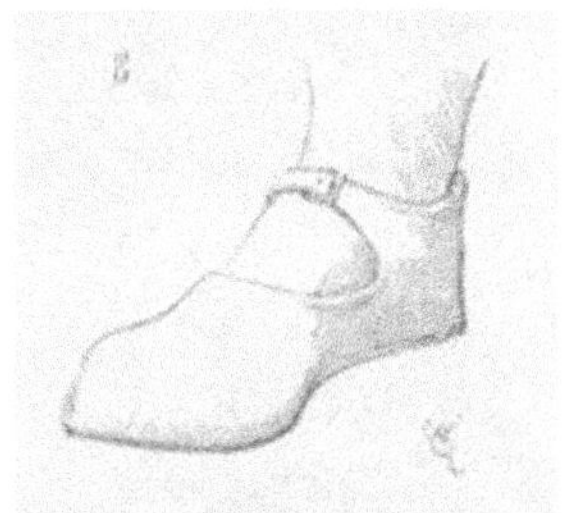

Figure 1-2
Gentleman's strap shoe, ca. 1240

pattern of a similar "Ankle Latched Shoe" showing how it was probably made during the Norman period from a single piece of leather almost a thousand years ago.[6]

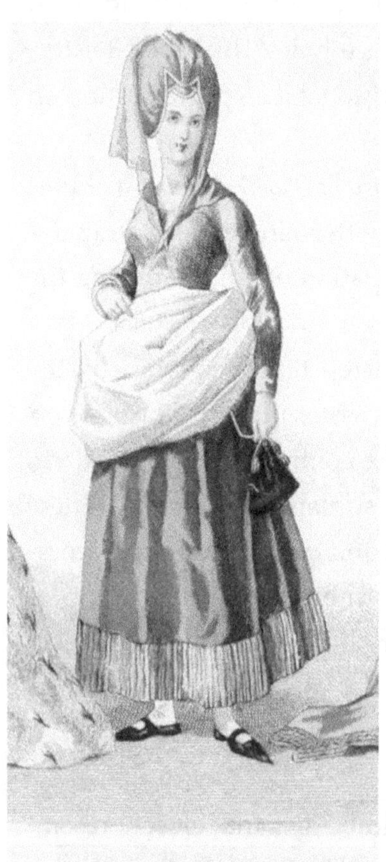

Figure 1-3
French woman, ca. 1400

Figure 1-3 is a rare image of a French woman wearing Mary Jane–style shoes dating from the period 1395 to 1423, when Charles VI was king of France. It is rare because most images through the ages show women with their feet covered, or just the toes shown, right up until the twentieth century, thus making it difficult to assess what kind of footwear they wore. They are said to have worn the same, or very similar, footwear to those worn by men. A simple brown leather shoe was displayed in a history museum in Amsterdam in 2009 dating from the period 1300 to 1350. On the basis of these and other examples, one can conclude that because of its simplicity of design and construction, the Mary Jane shoe style became very popular in medieval times in many parts of Europe.

Strap Shoes during the Renaissance and Beyond

During the Renaissance, Mary Jane, or bar shoes as they were called at that time, became very popular and were worn by both men and women of all classes. While they also were worn by children during this period, they were *not* considered a child's shoe prior to the nineteenth and twentieth centuries. Children were dressed as little adults, there being no specific children's fashions at that time. In fact, children were "supposed to look like replicas of adults."[7] Since footwear worn by children were actually miniature adult shoes, there was no provision for growing feet. Even in the 1920s, a leading trade journal, *Boot and Shoe Recorder*, stated that "juvenile styles march in the rear of adult styles."[8]

Figure 1-4 shows a portion of a Currier and Ives print done in 1892 for the Columbia Exposition in celebration of the four hundredth anniversary of Columbus landing on the shores of the New World at San Salvador in the West Indies. Columbus and his men are depicted wearing strap shoes common for this time period. Currier and Ives received this inspiration from the artist

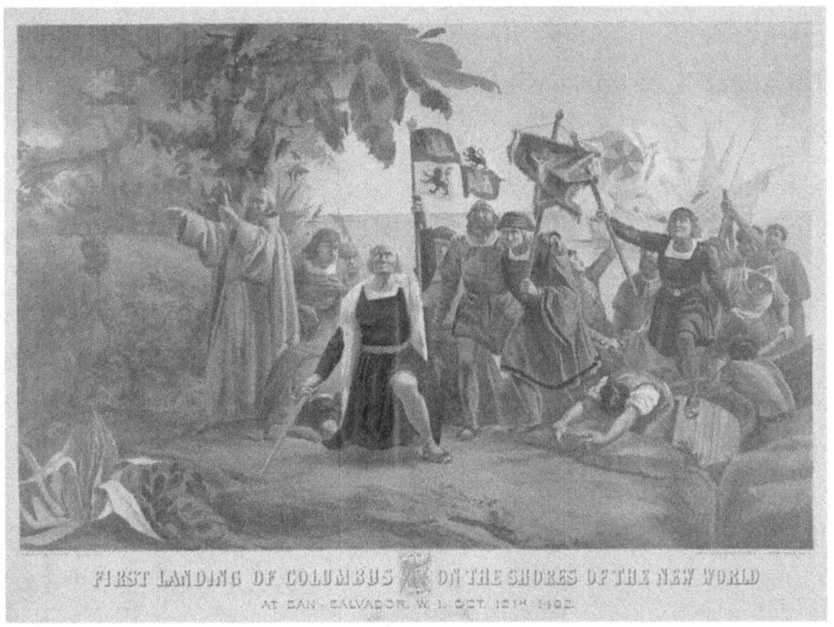

Figure 1-4
Lithograph of Columbus and his men wearing strap shoes, 1892

Dióscoro Teófilo de la Puebla Tolín (1862), who studied in Rome and Madrid and painted from a "historicism" tradition, so he would have been familiar with the clothing styles and shoes worn in Columbus's time.

It appears to have been very common for soldiers and sailors to wear strap shoes as part of their uniforms during the Renaissance, perhaps because they were simple to make and, therefore, relatively less expensive than other forms of footwear.

Boys from the 1500s to the twentieth century continued to wear tunic outfits and strap shoes because they were worn by men and were considered stylish, at least for those whose parents could afford to outfit them in such clothing. However, as girls began to wear tunics, boys lost interest in such clothing, and the wearing of Mary Janes also faded for men.

Besides paintings, the internet was another source of information to help establish the history of strap shoes, as seen in pictures of clothing and footwear worn as part of historic recreations. An example of this is soldiers (mousquetaires) who participated in the celebration of the 350th anniversary of the founding of Treyvaux, Switzerland, in 1618. The soldiers were seen wearing strap shoes with white hose as part of their "uniform," as many soldiers did at the time.

During the 1600s the classic Mary Jane style seems to have declined in popularity as clothing styles changed. At that time both men and women began wearing heavy-looking T-strap shoes with high heels, which frequently had ornate buckles and bows on the top of the shoe. Sometimes, an ornate "shoe rose" decoration made of loops of ribbons was added in the 1590s. Later, more elaborate gold and silver lace was placed on top of the shoe to create "smart" footwear for those who could afford it. Shoes worn by common folk were less ornate, and generally had lower heels.[9]

It was discovered that T-straps provided open spaces on either side of the "T" and were more comfortable because these spaces allowed the shoe to bend more easily when walking and provided ventilation for the foot to breathe.[10]

During the eighteenth century, fashion was heavily influenced by the French court. Louis XIV, known as the Sun King, ruled for seventy-two years. Because he was short in stature, he introduced the style of high heels for both men and women, but no one could wear heels higher than the king. Portraits show him wearing high-heel shoes with either a single strap or T-strap style. In Figure 1-5 he is wearing a red pair as part of a very elaborate costume. It was painted in 1701 by Hyacinthe Rigaud and is located in the Louvre Museum in Paris. Historically, red shoes conveyed a symbol of wealth, authority, and power, since red dye was very expensive, being extracted from crushed cochineal beetles. Initially, Louis "imposed a rigid protocol allowing only himself and his court to wear red heels in France."[11] The heels not only increased his height but also proclaimed his victories, because he had battle scenes painted on them. Louis may have gotten the idea from the Romans, where only the emperors could wear red sandals. Shoe styles reflected one's status and wealth in society, for aristocrats generally wore shoes made of expensive textiles and silk, whereas lower-class men and women wore leather shoes similar to one another. Thus, shoes played an important role in accentuating class distinctions rather than gender differences until very recently. There were even laws prescribing clothing which could be worn with the purpose of keeping people "in their place." But by 1792, things began to change dramatically with the effects of the French Revolution.

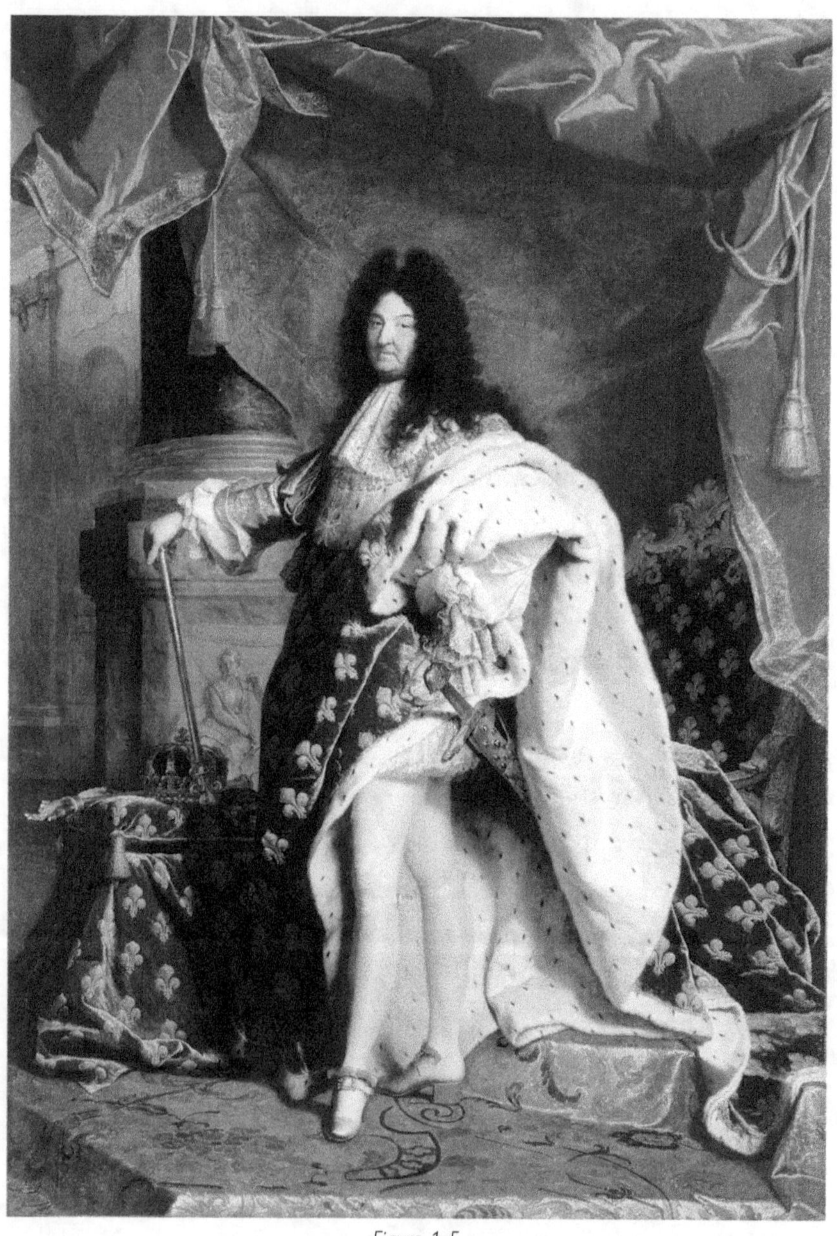

Figure 1-5
Louis XIV wearing red high heels, 1701

The French Revolution had a profound impact on clothing styles and footwear. For example, heels shrank in height and eventually disappeared in order to emphasize that all people are born on an equal level. Expensive shoes of silk were "largely replaced by more affordable and better wearing leathers." And, with the fall in the price of red dye in the nineteenth century, red shoes became very popular with the public.[12] At the turn of the twenty-first century, there was a resurgence in the popularity of red shoes worn by both sexes. Expensive shoe buckles also disappeared in France after the Revolution since they had been viewed as a symbol of wealth and wearing them could lead one to the guillotine. Thomas Jefferson also stopped wearing shoes with large buckles and switched to "democratic" laced shoes, even though these shoes were seen by many as being feminine and were actually called "corset" shoes because they laced like a woman's corset.

Prior to the Revolution, there was a tendency for both men's and women's footwear to look very similar, but by the 1790s, gender differences began to be more pronounced. Men's footwear after that time tended "toward functionality," so that their boots and stout shoes were in sharp contrast with earlier "light and flimsy neoclassical" styles.[13]

The Nineteenth-Century Strap Shoes

Low-heeled pumps with and without straps to secure them to the foot became popular after the turn of the nineteenth century. Many of these shoes had thin soles and were not suitable for outdoor use. Boys would wear them with garments called "skeleton suits" at that time. Interestingly, this is one of the first times that boys were wearing fashions that were actually different from those worn by their fathers. The skeleton suits had long pants, whereas most men were still wearing knee britches, similar to those worn by Benjamin Franklin. Skeleton suits were popular for over fifty years, from the late 1700s to the mid-1800s. They were given this strange name because the boys wearing them tended to be slender at that age.[14]

The Victoria and Albert Museum in the UK has a watercolor in its painting collection of a four-year-old boy named Alfred Fuller, who wore a blue dress, long pantalettes covering his legs, and strap shoes. The large balloon sleeves were characteristic of women's dresses in 1836 England, where the picture was painted. A girl might wear this type of dress, but with longer hair, and she definitely would not have been painted carrying a whip and playing with a hobby horse.[15]

Some authors, such as Elizabeth Browning, tried to promote a more unisex approach to clothing in the midnineteenth century. Her son, Pen, was born in 1848 and was "outfitted in dresses, pantalettes, strap shoes, and tunics."[16] His clothes were similar to clothing worn by Browning's brothers at the time (Figure 1-6).

Browning was concerned with "women's rights and social justice," believing that women and men are equal and that "there should not be such sharp distinctions in masculine and female clothes, especially children's clothes."[17] Browning's ideas may sound revolutionary, but times were changing during the Industrial Revolution, with families migrating

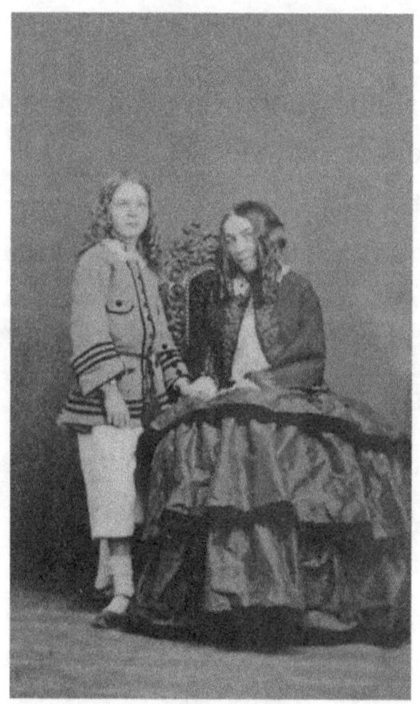

Figure 1-6
Penn and Elizabeth Browning, mid-1800s

to the cities and the beginning of the feminist movement. Women's roles began to change, which in turn affected the clothing they wore. On the other hand, Kent State University Museum's *Centuries of Childhood* exhibit noted that "Victorian materialism put girls back into crinolines and bustles, and both young boys and girls into stays, long hair, and numerous petticoats."[18]

By the midnineteenth century, slippers and sandals declined in popularity as people wanted to be more mobile. As a result, there was a demand for high-top boots and shoes with thicker soles to cope with the mud, garbage, and horse manure found on the largely unpaved roads. Slippers made of fabric would often wear out in a matter of hours when worn outdoors. Strap shoes for adults became less common, although they continued to be used for more formal occasions, or in the form of rubber overshoes such as seen in an ad found in the 1894–95 edition of the Montgomery Ward mail-order catalog. The straps held the overshoes firmly on the foot, and they were advertised not to come off in the mud (Figure 1-7). As such, they were called "safety strap sandals," and were a very practical use for a Mary Jane style. With these rubber overshoes, one could wear "indoor" shoes outdoors in any kind of weather.

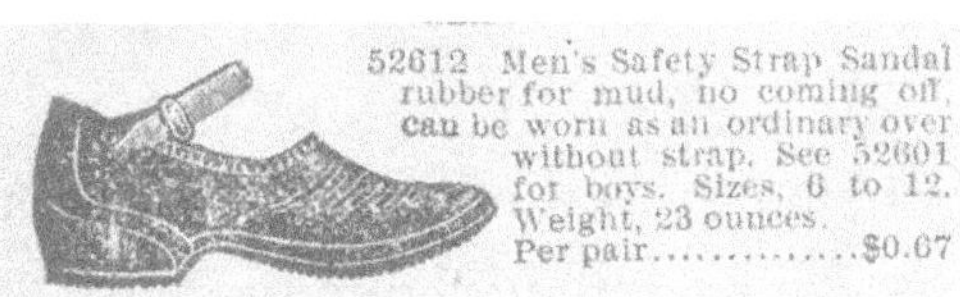

Figure 1-7

Mary Jane–type overshoes for men and boys, 1894–95

With the invention of the McKay sewing machine in 1858, mass production of boots and shoes began for the first time, which in New England created a revolution in the shoe industry. Prior to this time, footwear had been hand made by cobblers with no consideration given to gender, no matter one's age. Generally, this was also consistent during Victorian times, as there did not appear to be much distinction between girls' and boys' shoes. For the most part, almost everyone wore high-top shoes. Strap shoes were available but would be used on more formal occasions. Shoe "colors were limited to one: black, and men's and women's shoes looked alike."[19] Also, this was before the time when shoe companies assigned "names" to their footwear to steer men to styles which they said were men's shoes, and women to those they said were ladies' shoes. This resulted in the creation of two lines of shoes based on gender. Children's shoes during this time period were not usually divided into boys' versus girls' shoes until the twentieth century, when people became more gender-conscious with respect to footwear.

By the end of the nineteenth century, "women were buying shoes that looked very much like those worn by men," thus reflecting "women's growing role in a masculine world."[20] Manufacturers responded by introducing more "elaborate shoes with fancy straps" to attract women buyers.[21] According to O'Keeffe (1996), shoes eventually "became a symbol of emerging equality not only between the sexes, but among social groups as well."[22]

In the early 1900s, low-cut Mary Jane strap sandals were also offered as an alternative type of footwear, but the high-top style prevailed until well into the 1920s. It should be emphasized that low-cut shoes were a small minority of styles, especially in colder weather when the common belief was that one had to be "crazy" to wear them in winter in the cold and snow. The 1916 Montgomery Ward catalog had a Mary Jane–type "strap slipper" that was advertised as a "common sense" shoe to "wear around the house."[23] Thus, they were generally considered as "indoor" shoes at this time. Newspapers also advertised more expensive strap shoes that were worn on more formal occasions. But during the 1920s and 1930s, as hemlines became shorter, thus exposing the feet, this led to low-cut shoes, especially Mary Jane types, becoming more prevalent.

Boys and Skirted Garments in the 1800s and 1900s

During the middle of the nineteenth century there appears to have been a move toward individualized children's fashions as opposed to continuing to dress them as little adults. Queen Victoria was proud of her Scottish Stuart blood, and "popularized kilts for boys when she began outfitting the young princes in kilts." She "insisted" that her family wear kilts on occasions such as the annual visits to Balmoral Castle in Scotland.[24]

The British royal family seems to have continued this tradition even in recent years. In 1987, a photograph taken of the princes, William and Harry, shows them wearing kilts and strap shoes like their cousin, Zara Phillips, daughter of Princess Anne. Their grandfather, Prince Philip, is also shown wearing a kilt.

The boys' father, Prince Charles, while not in this photo, has also been seen wearing kilts, and even buckle brogues, a type of Mary Jane shoe that has a small decorative buckle on the toe. These are often worn as part of the formal military uniform by Scottish Highland regiments (Figure 1-8). The wearing of kilts had been prohibited in Scotland by an Act of Parliament in 1746.[25]

Queen Victoria's insistence that her sons wear kilts seems to have been a major reason for initiating the movement of small boys' fashion back from long pants, such as was worn as part of a skeleton suit, or knee pants, to skirts and tunics in the mid-1800s. This change in fashion of boys' clothing is very much in evidence

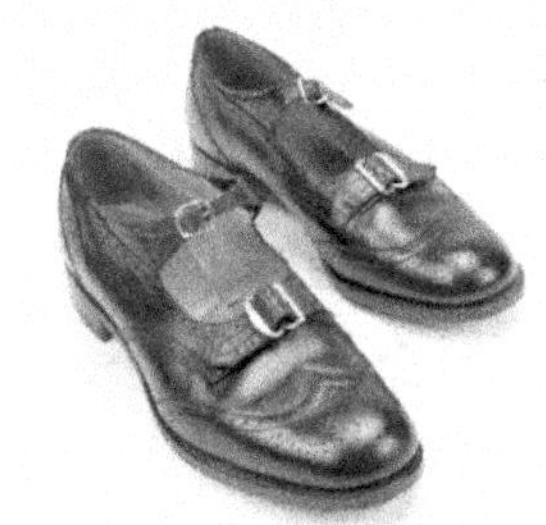

Figure 1-8
Men's buckle brogue shoes, 2009

from the photographic record and paintings dating from the later 1800s and early 1900s. Of course, it was still customary for most very small boys, generally under the age of five, to wear dresses or "petticoats" before being "breeched," the time when small boys graduated from skirts and dresses to pants, for countless generations. Actually, dress-type garments for children were considered to be more sanitary. Furthermore, in accordance with Rousseau's philosophy in the 1760s, "dresses promoted movement and ease for both sexes" in that they "allowed for children's natural development."[26] Weidner (1999) in Historical Boys' Clothing says that the "prevalence of dresses for boys comes as a great surprise to the modern boy who has no idea that young boys, until relatively recently, commonly wore dresses." Only until the 1920s "has the fashion faded."[27]

Weidner reported in 2002 that the Scottish kilt was always a male garment. American mothers used the kilt suit as an "intermediate step between dresses and outfits with knee pants, such as the Fauntleroy suit or sailor suits." These mothers may not have been ready to "fully breech" their sons, "but felt that they were becoming too old to still wear dresses."[28]

Figure 1-9 shows a boy dressed in full Scottish regalia complete with strap shoes. The photo was taken by the artist G. Grelling in Detroit, Michigan, during the American Civil War in the 1860s, as evidenced by a revenue stamp on the back of the photo that was required at that time to help pay the cost of the war. Tunic suits, which resemble a smock or a dress, might actually be worn over a boy's short pants. If one looks critically at photos of these tunics, one will see a strong similarity to garments worn by men (not women) during medieval and Renaissance times.

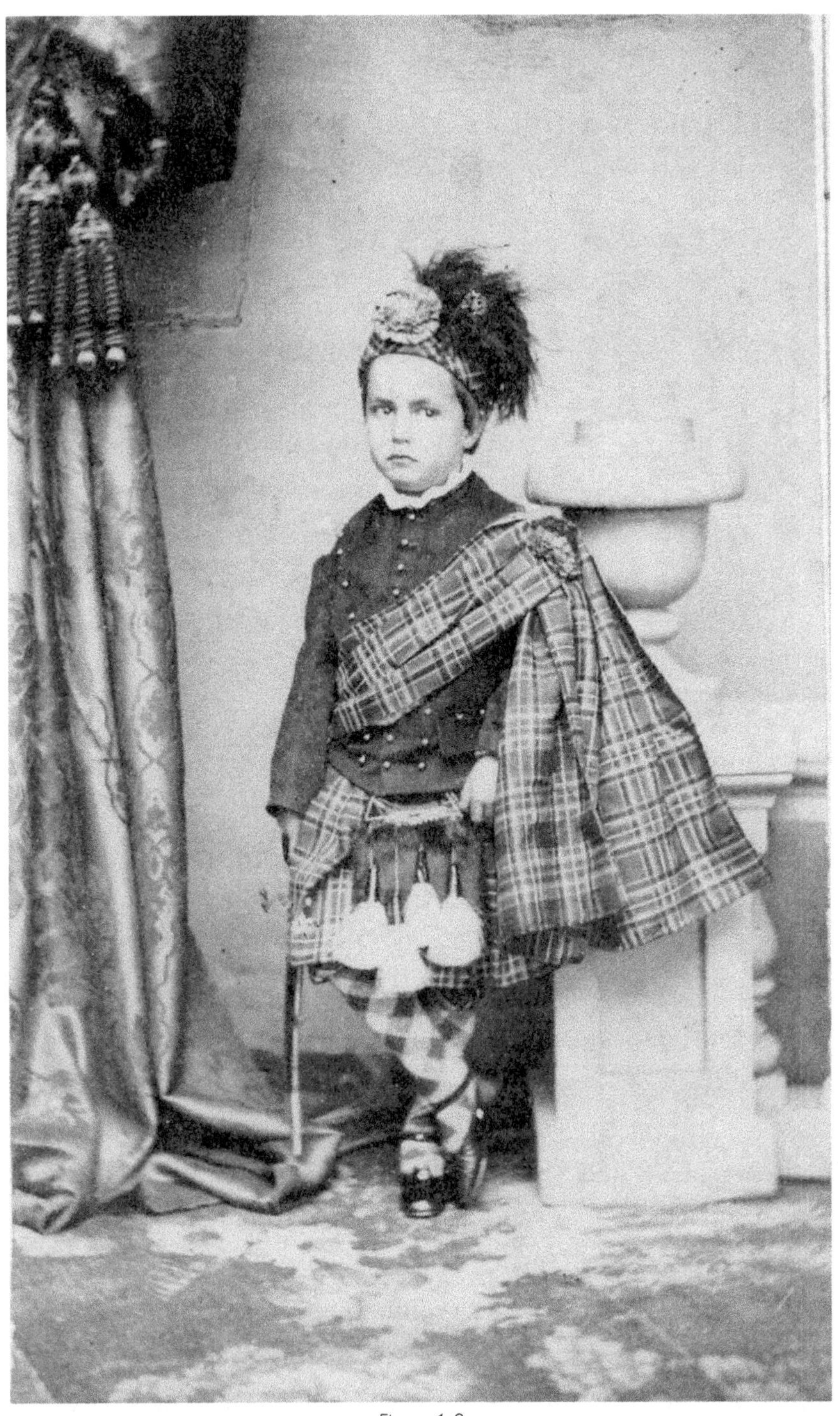

Figure 1-9
Boy in kilt and strap shoes, ca. 1862

The Fauntleroy Craze

The Fauntleroy suit was a style worn by boys in the late 1800s and well into the twentieth century. While it was never worn by girls, it often was made of fine velvet fabric and had fancy colors and cuffs. Figure 1-10 is an example of three boys elegantly dressed in Fauntleroy suits and wearing very fancy strap shoes about the turn of the twentieth century. All three boys have dark stockings, but only one has his legs fully covered. By the early 1900s white short socks became more common, with strap shoes for both boys and girls as dark Victorian colors became old-fashioned.[29]

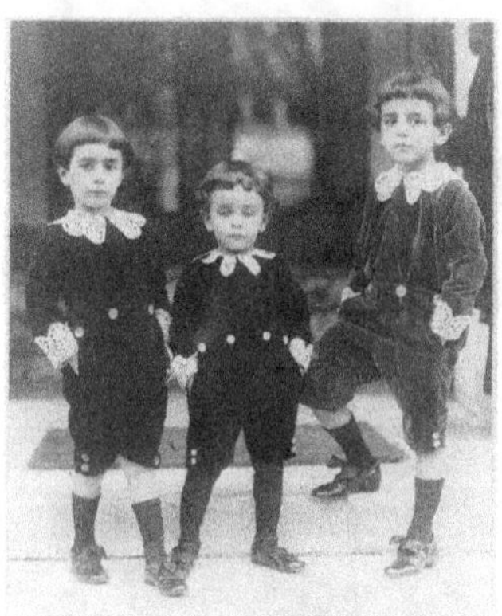

Figure 1-10

Boys wearing Fauntleroy suits late 1800s

The whole Fauntleroy craze began with the publication of a book by Frances Hodgson Burnett called *Little Lord Fauntleroy* in 1885. It contained numerous illustrations which were used to guide mothers in dressing their sons in this fashion. Even if a family could not afford the velvet suit, other fabrics could be substituted and details such as long curled hair, floppy bows, and strap shoes (Mary Janes) could be used.[30] With regard to the footwear worn with these suits, the predominant footwear for adults and children during the second half of the nineteenth century was high-top boots and shoes; however, the photographic records show that Mary Jane–type strap shoes were worn with these clothes, especially for formal occasions or in the house. The original Lord Fauntleroy wore Mary Janes, which was often copied by many mothers so their sons would become exact copies. Many mothers liked to imitate fashions worn by royalty, who dressed their children in "fancy" clothes, including Mary Jane–type shoes. However, for the most part, such clothing was expensive and not generally affordable by the majority of "common folk" at the time.[31] Strap shoes were more practical, on the other hand, especially for very small children, who had not as yet learned to tie their shoes. The old nursery rhyme "One two, buckle [or button] my shoe" would tend to indicate such popularity. They certainly were easier to put on and take off than the high-top footwear then in vogue.

Jarrott (2013) states that the Fauntleroy suit was the "most infamous style for boys to wear."[32] According to Maureen Taylor (2008) in *A Royal Look for Boys*, the style may have been popular among mothers, but not the "tormented young boys" who had to wear them. She noted that "boys subjected to the style began wearing the look as toddlers [and continued] until they were pre-teens, but in some families boys wore [Fauntleroy suits] until they were in their early teens."[33] Not surprisingly, when the *New York Times* took a poll in 1895 of boys' favorite books, *Little Lord Fauntleroy* was not on any of the boys' lists, but it was on the parents' lists.[34] When worn with a kilt, mothers could delay breeching a bit longer.

Figure 1-11 is an illustration of a boy appearing in the June 1907

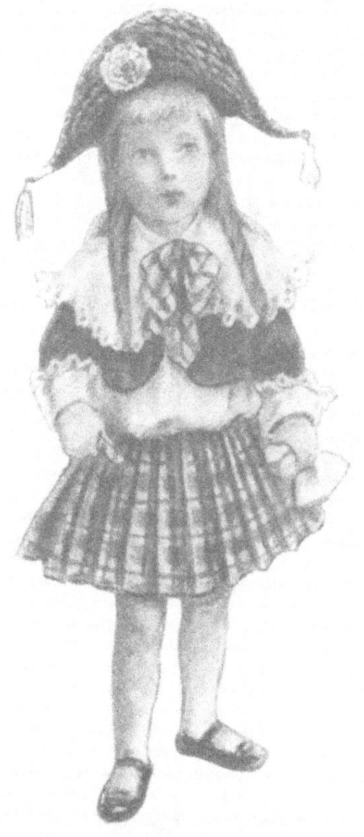

Figure 1-11
Boys' kilted Fauntleroy outfit, 1907

Ladies Home Journal, wearing such a kilted Fauntleroy outfit with a military hat. The illustration was advertised as a boys' outfit, since Fauntleroy suits and kilts were not worn by girls at the time. Even the magazine commented that the boy with his long curls looked "ridiculous" wearing such a hat and oversized collar. No mention, however, was made of the kilt or Mary Jane–type shoes that he wore since they were popular for boys at the time.[35] Paoletti (1999) states that mothers were trying to create an "ideal" image of the "perfect son" by wearing such clothing and footwear.[36] While Fauntleroy suits were not actually worn by girls, there are accounts of boys hating the style and arguing with one another as to whether the kilt or the lace collar on these suits was more "sissy." Footwear, on the other hand, was never debated, whether strap shoes or high-tops, since these were accepted as unisex.

Carrying the Fauntleroy craze to an extreme, the mother of billionaire aviator Howard Hughes thought her son was "special," and she didn't want him to be like other "rough" boys in Houston, Texas, where they lived just after the turn of the twentieth century. She wanted to set Howard apart from other boys by dressing him like a "Texas version of Little Lord Fauntleroy." As such, he had to wear ruffled shirts, black velvet knickers, and white sheer hosiery covering most of his legs. As for his footwear, only black Mary Jane shoes would do to complete the picture. In this way, he stood out from the other boys and felt very embarrassed. He pleaded with his mother to wear clothes more like the other boys in his school. Porter (2005), a biographer of Hughes, says that his mother refused to change his "dress code" and he continued to look like a dandy in the frontier town where he had to "endure the taunts of his hell-raising classmates who mocked him for 'dressing like a girl.'" In dressing this way, she wanted him to be the prettiest boy in the world. Not only did he have to wear clothes he hated, but he had to endure having to take several baths a day with strong soap because his mother feared Howard might have become infected with germs as a result of contact with other people, whom she believed were carriers of disease. He felt lonely and isolated because he was not allowed to have any friends.[37] Is it no wonder Hughes had so many problems later in life, including being a lifelong hypochondriac?

Sailor Suits and Mary Jane–Type Footwear

Sailor suits, unlike Fauntleroy suits, were actually very popular with both boys and, later, with girls. Queen Victoria is said to have started the fashion of boys wearing these garments when her eldest son, Albert Edward, the Prince of Wales, at the age of four started wearing a scaled-down version of clothes copied from crew members on the Royal Yacht in 1846. At first a boy's garment, the style was adopted by girls by the end of the nineteenth century and fondly called "middies." Eventually, more girls wore middies than boys. Today, the garment style survives and is still worn by both sexes.

In other countries, such as Japan, sailor suits and Mary Jane shoes are often worn by girls as part of their school uniforms. According to information at Historical Boys' Clothing, as more and more girls wore the garment, fewer boys did so. Eventually, sailor suits became associated with smaller boys' styles, so that older boys abandoned the style, viewing them as "childish."[38] There were country differences with boys wearing the sailor-suit style longer in Europe than in North America. The styling is different, too, and was based on the type of uniforms sailors actually wore in those countries. Figure 1-12 is an example of a typical sailor suit worn by an Austrian boy. It needs to be emphasized

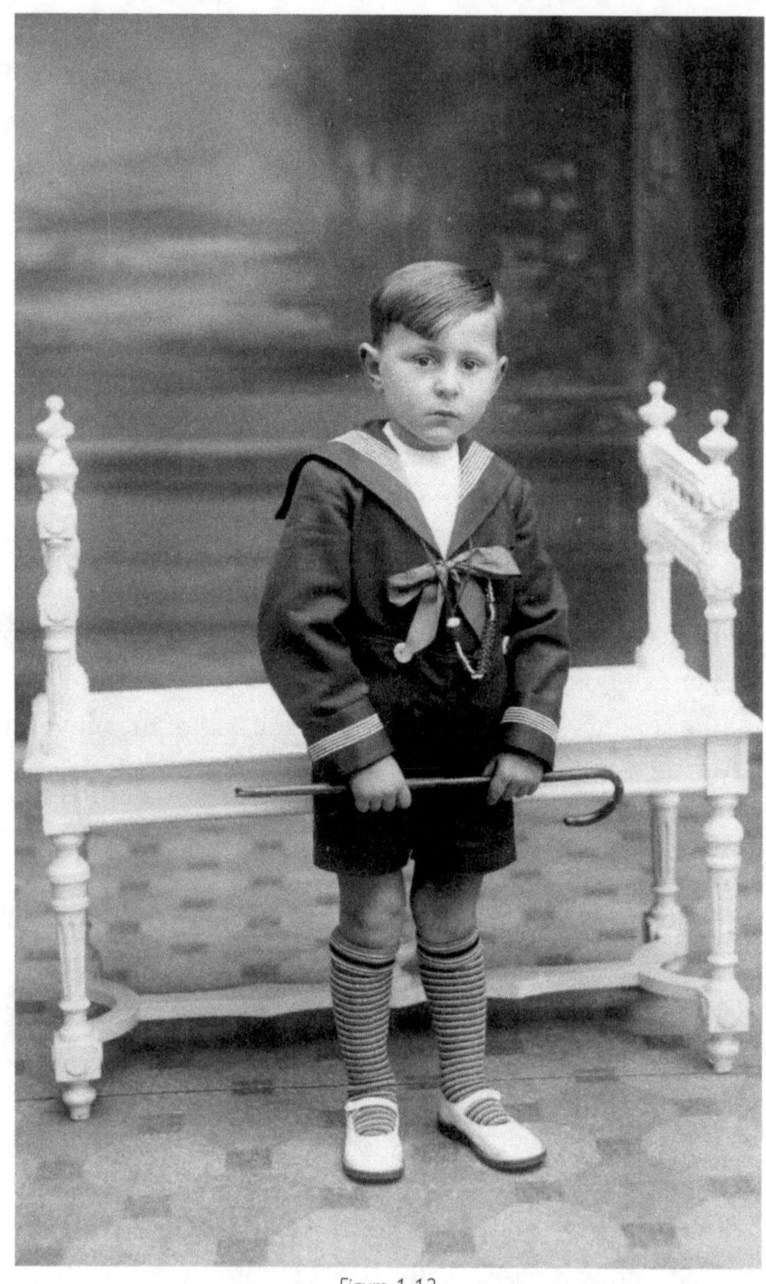

Figure 1-12

Austrian boy wearing a sailor suit and strap shoes, 1935

again that the predominant style of shoes for both sexes was the high-top until well into the 1920s, or even longer in some countries according to evidence seen in the photographic record. This image is included to show that strap shoes were an alternative type of footwear for those who wished to wear them. Likewise, Mary Jane shoes today are but one form of footwear available as an alternative to other types (i.e. athletic shoes and open-toe sandals.) Their popularity has waxed and waned with fashion trends over the years.

Adults and Strap Shoes

While strap shoes were worn by women in the 1800s as an alternative to high-top footwear, they were rarely worn by men, judging by evidence found in the photographic record. In 1885, a photograph showed an opera singer, F. Romani, wearing a pair of strap shoes as part of a Turkish costume as he performed in an opera called *Indigo*. Likewise, in a 1935 Marx Brothers film, both male and female members of the opera chorus wore classic Mary Jane shoes in one of the scenes of *An Evening at the Opera*.

The twentieth century ushered in the resurgence of these low-cut shoes for both adults and children as the use of high-tops began to decline, especially in summer months. High-top footwear continued to be popular until the 1920s as fashion footwear, especially in rural areas where roads were unpaved and sidewalks generally nonexistent. They continue to be popular in the twenty-first century for activities like hiking. Mail-order catalogs and newspaper ads about the turn of the twentieth century and thereafter verify photographic evidence. For example, there were one hundred adults' and children's shoes advertised in the 1897 Sears, Roebuck and Co. catalog. Out of this total, only five ladies' low-cut Mary Jane–type shoes were offered, and none for children.

Thus, 95 percent of the shoes were high-tops for adults and 100 percent for children. Ten years later, there were thirteen adult strap shoes called "sandals" in the 1907 Sears, Roebuck and Co. catalog, but they were still a very small minority compared to the number of high-tops offered. These strap shoes were advertised for "street or dress" occasions. Granted, there were other sources for footwear at the time, but Sears and Montgomery Ward were major mail-order distributors that reached practically every part of the country and catered to the public's shoe preferences of the day. These catalogs played a major role in providing "fashion" to the masses and a barometer of public tastes in footwear.

In the 1909 Sears, Roebuck and Co. catalog, there were still only five ladies' strap shoes listed, but in addition there were five listed in children's sizes for "boys and girls." There were also two men's twin buckle-strap "Oxfords" with the straps and buckles over the instep listed in the same catalog. These men's shoes were given the names "Adventure" and "Social Lion" by Sears. While not true Mary Jane–type shoes, these twin-strap shoes might be considered a transition to the Mary Jane style for men because two years later (1911), Sears included two single-strap men's shoes in its catalog, one of which is shown in Figure 1-13. The shoes had a rather high Cuban heel, and were available up to men's size 11, considered large for that time. It appeared under the heading "'Men's Specialties – Our Own Make' at $2.95 a pair."

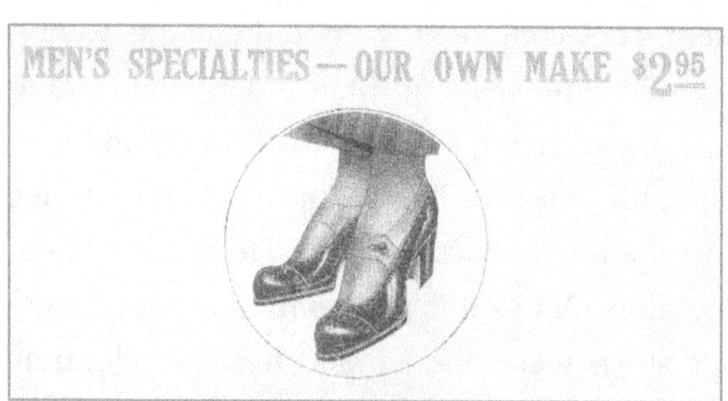

Figure 1-13
Men's strap shoe
1911

Strap shoes continued to increase in popularity for both sexes so that by 1912 Sears listed a men's "Mat Strap Pump" on its Oxford shoe page as the "latest style" (Figure 1-14). There was no reference to the name Mary Jane associated with these men's shoes or the ladies' strap shoes, either. Ladies' versions tended to have higher heels and a pointier toe than the men's strap shoes, which had a rounded bump-toe effect.

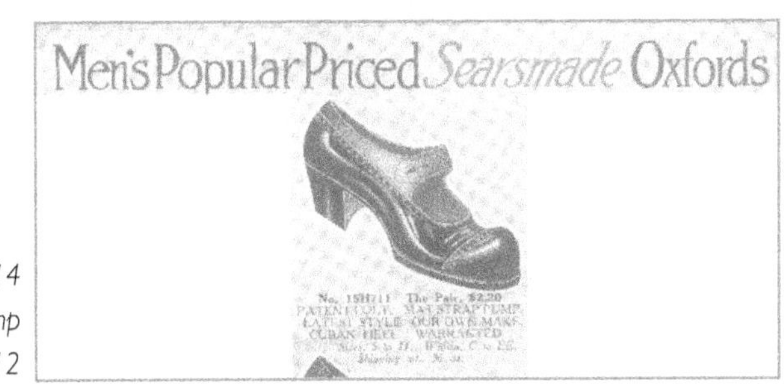

Figure 1-14
Men's strap pump
Oxford, 1912

While neither Sears nor Montgomery Ward carried ads for men's strap shoes after 1912, the style became even more popular for women and children, judging by the number of advertisements and images found in the photographic record. This was especially true for the twin-strap Mary Jane types in 1913, which will be discussed in chapter 3. A few references were found for "men's strap shoes" in several newspapers, but there were no illustrations to show what they looked like. The only picture found of a men's strap shoe from the 1920s was contained in the trade journal *Boot and Shoe Recorder*, May 7, 1921, issue (Figure 1-15). The shoe was made by the Coes and Stoddard Co. of Boston, and the ad copy read: "'Here It Is!! A men's strap' patent leather shoe." The company hoped to market it to male college students. An article that appeared in the April 23, 1921, issue of this journal reported that men, at least in the Akron, Ohio, area, were looking for unusual-type shoes, referred to as "novelties." The merchant reported that "even such styles as those of by-gone days with

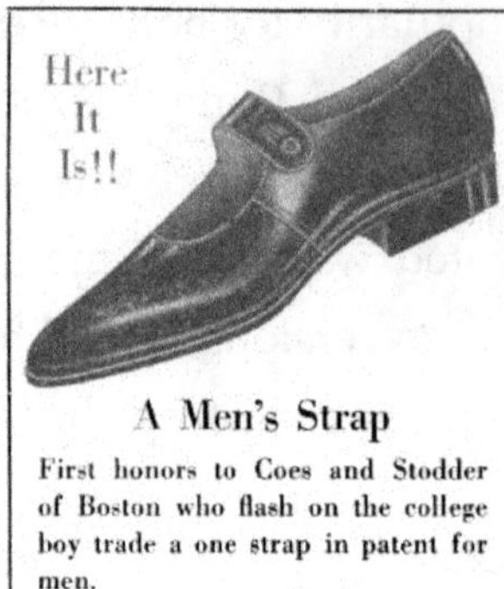

Figure 1-15
Men's strap shoe
1921

leather straps and buckles" were in demand with younger men more likely to be interested in buying novelty shoe styles.[39] Older men, on the other hand, were less likely to buy any shoes until they actually needed them and, therefore, had less interest in novelty shoe styles. This idea may still be as true today as then, but the trend may be changing, as will be seen later in this book.

Chapter 1 Notes

1. O'Keeffe, *Shoes*, 23.

2. Thompson, "Mary Janes," 6. Quote from Wilson, *A History of Shoe Fashion* (1968).

3. Ward, John, *Roman Era in Britain* (London: Metheun Publishing, 1911), 243.

4. Wilson, Eunice, *A History of Shoe Fashions* (New York: Theatre Arts Books, 1968), 64.

5. "Mid Manhattan Picture Collections-Shoes-1599 or earlier 1858–1875," Image No. 825422, New York Public Library (Translated from French by Helene Desruisseaux, 2006), digitalcollections.nypl.org/items/510d47e1-3273-a3d9-e040-e00a18064a99.

6. Carlson, I. M., "Ankle Latched Shoe," *Footwear of the Middle Ages* (Historical Shoe Design, 2005), www.personal.utulsa.edu/~marc-carlson/shoe/SHOES/SHOE24.HTM.

7. Thompson, "Mary Janes," 7.

8. *Boot and Shoe Recorder* (November 19, 1921), 86.

9. Norris, Herbert, *Costume and Fashion* (Minneola, NY: Dover Publications, 1977), 273.

10. Norris, Costume and Fashion, 760.

11. Davidson, H., quoted in "Sex and Sin: The Magic of Red Shoes," Riello and McNeil, *Shoes*, 273.

12. Ibid.

13. Ibid.

14. Weidner, D. "Skeleton Suits," Historical Boys' Clothing (June 2, 2002), www.histclo.com/style/suit/skel/skel.html.

15. ———, "Alfred Fuller (England 1836)," Historical Boys' Clothing (October 10, 2006), histclo.com/B10/op. (Available online through subscription only.)

16. ———, "English Boys' Clothes During the 1820s through the 1850s: The Barretts and Brownings," Historical Boys' Clothing (June 26, 2005), www.histclo.com/country/eng/co-eng-18501.html.

17. ———, "Pen Barrett Browning: Arrival and Parents," Historical Boys' Clothing (September 8, 1998), www.histclo.com/country/eng/coeng18501ebbpen1.html.

18. Bissonnette, A., curator, Kent State University Museum, "Centuries of Childhood," *Alumni Gallery* (September 27, 2000–September 30, 2001).

19. "Fact Sheet: Louisiana Purchase Exposition [1904 World's Fair]," St. Louis Convention and Visitor Commission, n.d., 16, web.archive.org/web/20050315145450/http://www.explorestlouis.com/factSheets/fact_worldsFair.asp?PageType=4 (accessed June 10, 2007).

20. Rexford, N., "The Perils of Choice," Riello and McNeil, *Shoes*, 157.

21. Rexford, "The Perils of Choice," 158.

22. O'Keeffe, *Shoes*, 296.

23. Montgomery Ward catalog, no. 85 (1916), 762.

24. Weidner, D., "Kilts and Kilt Suits," Historical Boys' Clothing (September 20, 2012), histclo.com/style/skirted/Kilt.

25. "Highland Suit," Museum of Childhood, 1995, museumofchildhood.org.uk/collections/clothing/highland-suit.

26. Walton, E., "Commonly Held Misconceptions about Historic Costume," Clothesline: The Online Journal of Costume and Dress (2009), clothesline.com/victorian-myths.

27. Weidner, D., "Dresses: Modern Boys' Views," Historical Boys' Clothing (October 2, 1999). (Available online through subscription only.)

28. ———, "Kilts in America: Kilt Suits," Historical Boys' Clothing (December 22, 2008), histclo.com/style/kilt/kiltusks. (Available online through subscription only.)

29. ———, "Percy's Clothing: 4 Years," Historical Boys' Clothing (June 2, 2005), www.histclo.com/country/eng/pe/1880/per/pc4.html.

30. ———, "Fauntleroy Suits," Historical Boys' Clothing (August 18, 2003). (Available online through subscription only.)

31. Ibid.

32. Jarrott, S., "The Second Bustle," Maggie May's Costume History Page, n.d.

33. Taylor, M., "Photo Detective: A Royal Look for Boys," Family Tree Magazine.com (August 20, 2008).

34. "Three Best Books for Children," *New York Times* (December 8, 1895), 27, col. 6.

35. Ladies Home Journal, June 1907.

36. Paoletti, J. B., "Little Lord Fauntleroy and His Dad: The Transformation of Masculine Dress in America, 1880–1906," *Hope and Glory*, vol. 5, issue 1 (Summer 1991), 18–25.

37. Porter, D., *Howard Hughes: Hell's Angel* (2005), 10–11.

38. Weidner, D., "Sailor Suits: Decline," Historical Boys' Clothing (December 21, 2007). (Available online through subscription only.)

39. "Men Eager for Novelties," *Boot and Shoe Recorder* (April 23, 1921), 83.

INTRODUCTION OF THE NAME "MARY JANE"

The major factor that may have influenced men's and older boys' decision whether to wear strap shoes, at least in the US, was the change in name in the early 1900s. Men's strap shoes that were called "Adventure" or "Social Lion" in catalogs might have appealed to men and boys in 1911. However, strap shoes appear to have fallen out of favor in North America with men when advertisers began to call them "Mary Janes" and "baby dolls." How did this name change occur and under what circumstances?

A search was made to identify trademarks or copyrights involving the term "Mary Jane shoes" dating back to the early 1900s. Correspondence was also exchanged with shoe manufacturers to uncover information on the origin of the name. Unfortunately, no records could be found on the origin of the term, and there does not appear to have been any actual trademarks or copyrights either involving the name "Mary Jane shoes."

Buster Brown and Mary Jane Comics

References were found on the internet that "Mary Jane shoes" were named after the cartoon character Mary Jane who appeared in the Buster Brown comics. Mary Jane is referred to as Buster

Brown's sister or playmate, depending on which source is used. The Buster Brown comic strip first appeared in the *New York Herald* on May 4, 1902, and ran until its creator, Richard Felton Outcault, retired in the early 1920s. Both Buster and Mary Jane wore strap shoes in the comic strip as well as high-tops. Outcault's son, Richard Outcault Jr., was the "original Buster Brown and he had a real-life sister, Mary Jane," who was named after their mother.[1] Buster was portrayed as a "mischievous and prank playing, though well-meaning, youngster" who "quickly captured the fancy and affection of America."[2] Figure 2-1 is an early-1900s image of a Buster Brown impersonator, who wore the characteristic hat, hairstyle, tunic coat with pants, and strap shoes. Countless images exist in the photographic record of boys dressed in this style up to the time of World War I, so the comic strip was influential in affecting clothing styles.

Outcault was not only an artist but also a shrewd businessman who licensed the rights to use his comic characters for advertising various products, such as watches, clothing, dolls, and other items, as well as shoes. Many of these items can be found for sale as collectibles.

Perhaps the most important and long-lasting license sale that Outcault made was granting the right to use his comic characters' names to the St. Louis–based Brown Shoe Company, at the St. Louis World's Fair in 1904. John Bush, a sales executive with the Brown Shoe Company, persuaded his company to purchase the right to use the character names and thereby introduced the first Buster Brown shoes to the public. The company also exploited the name by hiring dwarfs to tour the United States as Buster impersonators from 1904 until 1930. They appeared at various theaters, department stores, and shoe stores to promote the sale of Buster Brown shoes.[3] One of these performances, sponsored

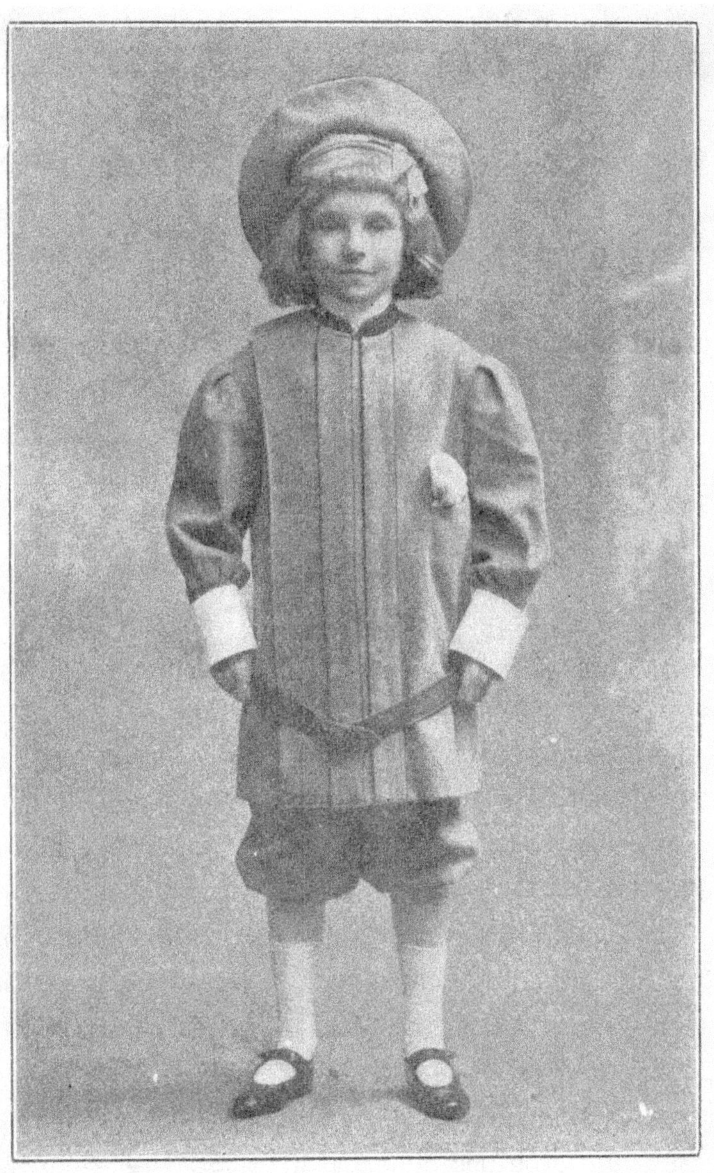

Figure 2-1
Postcard of Buster Brown impersonator, early 1900s

by the Penrose Shoe Company in St. Louis, had as many as 1,600 "kiddies" crowd into the Juniata Theatre to see the "real" Buster Brown and his dog, Tige, in person. These were big events in pre-radio and television days and showed just how popular Buster was. They also unquestionably contributed to the sales of Buster's clothing style, haircut, and strap shoes.[4] This was further encouraged by the one hundredth anniversary of the Louisiana Purchase from Napoleon at the St. Louis fair, where the public was not only introduced to Buster Brown shoes, but also the world's first hot dog and the nation's first ice cream cone.[5] In the early days of the comic strip, Buster Brown was dressed in his characteristic tunic-type suit with large bow tie, knickers pants, short socks, and black strap shoes as shown in Figure 2-1. Unlike the Fauntleroy outfit, Buster's suit became very popular for boys and was appropriately called a "Buster Brown Suit." His hairstyle also became known as a "Buster Brown Haircut." Information could not be found on whether the strap shoes, like the haircut and the suit that Buster wore, might also have been referred to as "Buster Brown shoes" after him, and only later "Mary Jane shoes" after Mary Jane. However, the photographic record and numerous catalog ads do bear out the increased popularity of the strap shoe style among both boys and girls, popularity that continued well into the 1920s and 1930s in North America, and even longer in Europe, Japan, and other parts of the world. A Buster Brown movie that was made in the 1920s featured both Buster and Mary Jane wearing identical strap shoes. At this time young boys' clothing was "just beginning to become a little more masculine than in the past where there was no distinction as to gender."[6]

The Brown Shoe Company came out with a line of sturdy Oxfords and high-top shoes for boys about the time of World War I, reflecting the increased popularity of military styles. Buster began promoting this footwear while Mary Jane continued to wear strap shoes, so, eventually, the shoes became associated with her and were called "Mary Janes." As a result, this "became an American term for strap shoes and a staple in any well-dressed little girl's wardrobe."[7] The only problem with this nice "story" to explain the origin of the name "Mary Jane" is that it cannot be substantiated, and it is not consistent with the facts which were uncovered in research for this book.

Correspondence was exchanged with the Brown Shoe Company, which is still located in St. Louis, and its archivist, Dr. Kris Runberg-Smith, to see if there was information on the origin of the Mary Jane shoe. A representative of the company said that most of the Buster Brown Shoe stores from that era were independently owned and often ran their own advertisements, which may have differed from promotions of the company-owned stores.[8] Shoe ads found online, such as those the company had placed in the *Saturday Evening Post* and the *Ladies Home Journal*, show various strap shoes during this period, as do sites on the internet, but not a single instance could be found where the Brown Shoe Company, or its subsidiaries, actually called strap shoes "Mary Jane shoes." Perhaps, they were aware that by doing so it might reduce sales to boys, who were still wearing them through the 1930s. With respect to trademarks or copyrights to use the name "Mary Jane shoes," the Brown Shoe Company informed us that they couldn't find any evidence that Brown ever trademarked the term. They said, according to their records, they didn't actually use the term until 1913.[9] This was four years before Buster switched to lace-up shoes, as the popular story goes, and two years after the name was used in an ad found for "Mary Jane Pumps" in 1911.

An examination of Buster Brown comic strips between 1904,

the year Outcault sold the right to use the name Buster Brown to the Brown Shoe Company, and 1917, when the US entered World War I, shows that Buster and Mary Jane wore strap shoes as well as high-tops during this period. A comic strip was found in the Library of Congress's Prints and Photographs Division showing Buster exchanging his strap shoes for Oxfords when he joined the Boy Scouts in 1917 (Figure 2-2). Buster's new footwear was probably influenced by military styles, which became popular at the time the US entered the war, and they certainly were worn by Boy Scouts. An ad shows a Buster Brown Shoe that appeared in the *Saturday Evening Post* in 1919 in which Buster is wearing high-top shoes rather than his characteristic strap shoes. But the girl standing next to him in the ad, presumably Mary Jane, is also wearing high-tops in a winter scene, rather than strap shoes, thus showing that she did not wear strap shoes exclusively after Buster stopped wearing them in the comic strips. On this basis it is difficult to conclude that the strap shoes were named after this Mary Jane. Moreover, Outcault writing in 1908 said that Mary Jane was "famous" for her "Mary Jane hair ribbon," "Mary Jane haircut," and even a "Mary Jane table," but he did not mention her being famous for her shoes, which he certainly would have if the term "Mary Jane shoes" was commonly used.[10]

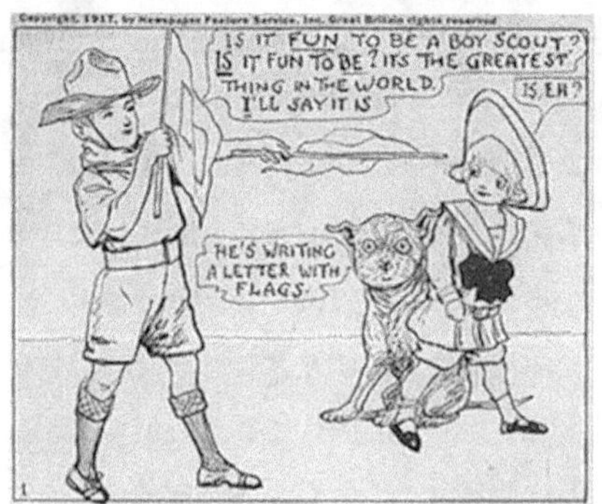

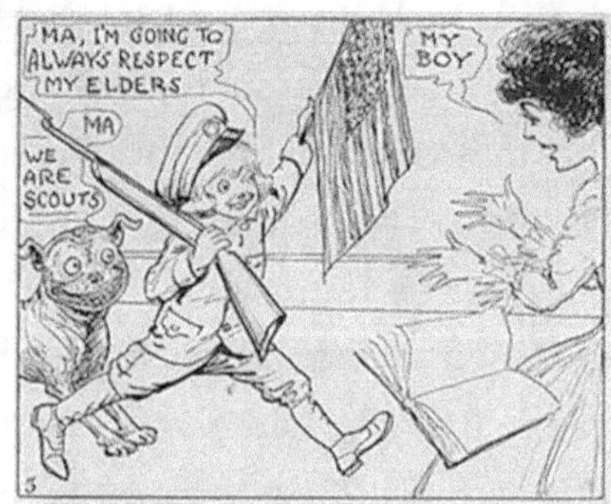

Figure 2-2
Buster joins the Boy Scouts, 1917

A search for clues in pre–World War I newspaper ads revealed the popularity of shoes called "Mary Jane pumps." The earliest one, appearing in the *Colorado Springs Gazette*, Colorado Springs, Colorado, on August 7, 1911, was called a "Big Girl" canvas "Mary Jane pump."[11] The ad does not say that the pumps are a "new" style, so they were probably around even before 1911. In any event, this was two years before the Brown Shoe Company said it first used the term "Mary Jane shoes." There isn't an illustration in the ad to show what the shoe looked like, but there is an illustration of a "Ladies Low Heel Mary Jane Style Sandal" in the 1914 Montgomery Ward catalog having an ankle strap (Figure 2-3). It was made of patent leather with flexible soles, and was a "sensible shoe," according to the ad copy. It was only available in women's sizes (2½ to 8) at a cost of $1.59. The style was not offered in children's sizes, but there was a shoe with the strap over the instep that was called a "baby doll" in the catalog.[12]

Pauline Thomas (2008) of Fashion-era.com says that rising hemlines on skirts together with the tango dance craze about this time may have resulted in the increased popularity of the ankle-strap Mary Jane pump style for women. She states that the addition of the strap ensured that the shoe stayed on the foot during this fast dance, but she has no idea where the name "Mary Jane pump" came from.[13] There were no newspaper ads found before 1911 using the name "Mary Jane shoe," nor was there any information on where the name might have come from in the ads. The first reference to "Mary Jane" footwear that was found in

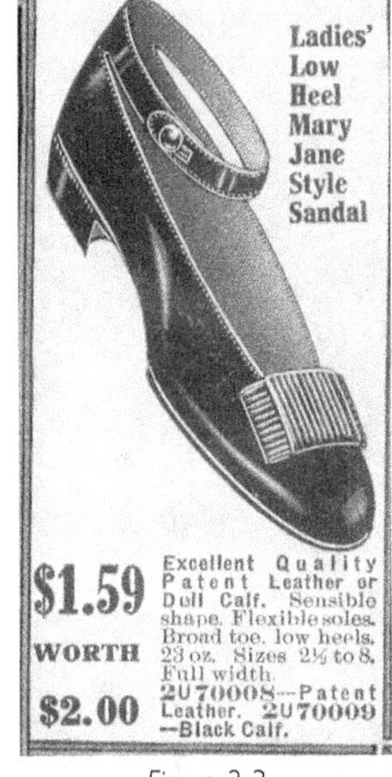

Figure 2-3

Mary Jane–style sandal, 1914

this research was in 1911, but the first use of the name applied to strap shoes may have occurred earlier in 1909 or 1910.

Possible Influence of Mary Jane Candy

Cartoonist Outcault also sold the rights to use his Buster Brown comic characters to the C. M. Miller Company at the 1904 St. Louis World's Fair. While the company had a license to use Outcault's Mary Jane character, the chewy peanut butter candy was actually named "Mary Jane" after the owner's favorite aunt. The candy wrapper had, and still has, a picture of a girl wearing strap shoes.[14] Did this logo play a role in having the public associate strap shoes with the name Mary Jane, especially since the girl is wearing strap shoes on the wrapper shown in Figure 2-4? While the company started making Mary Jane candy in 1914, this was a few years after the term first appeared in newspaper ads, as discussed above. Therefore, it is unlikely that the candy played a role in originating the term "Mary Jane shoes," but it certainly could have played a role in reinforcing the name associated with the shoes, because the candy was very popular and is still made after almost a hundred years.

In any event, the term "Mary Jane shoes" does not appear to have been used very widely until many years later. If it had been commonly used, it is doubtful that so many boys would have been wearing strap shoes, as evidenced in the photographic record in

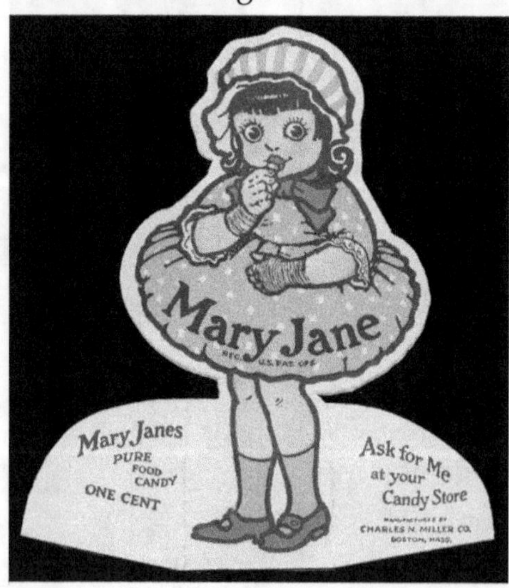

Figure 2-4

Mary Jane candy logo, 1914–Present

the 1910s and 1920s, for fear of being teased for wearing "girls' shoes."

Children's Mary Jane Fashion of the 1920s and 1930s

Figure 2-5 shows an ad that appeared in the 1921 trade journal *Boot and Shoe Recorder*, in which instep and ankle-strap shoes were placed side by side with only one being called a Mary Jane. The shoe on the right side of the ad has the strap fastened around the ankle and was called a "Patent Leather Mary Jane." Except for the lower heel, it closely resembles the women's Mary Jane pump discussed above. The shoe on the left has the strap over the top of the instep and was simply called an instep strap shoe, with no mention of the name "Mary Jane." While the ankle-strap version was called a Mary Jane for at least ten years (1911 to 1921), the name had not been applied yet to the over-the-instep strap shoe. Unfortunately, we may never know for sure whether the Mary Jane that the shoes are named after was Mary Jane Outcault, the candy manufacturer's aunt Mary Jane, or someone else, such as a tango dancer named Mary Jane. On the other hand, one can conclude that the first strap shoes (pumps) bearing the name "Mary Jane"

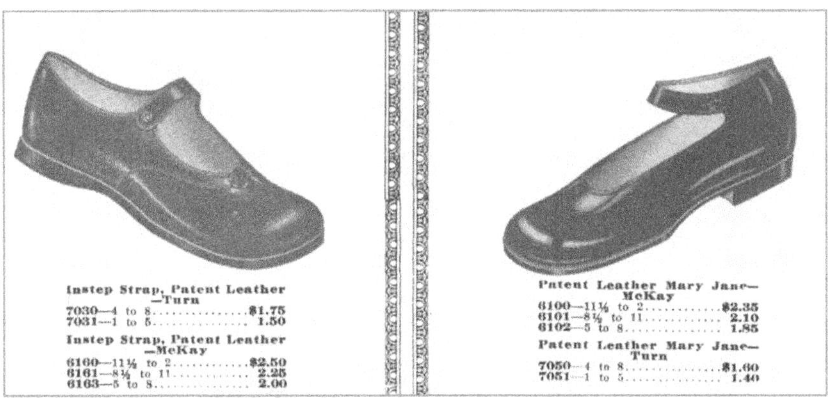

Figure 2-5

Instep and ankle strap shoes, 1921

were adult shoes and not children's shoes. Also, the term was in use before Buster Brown switched to lace-up shoes, according to the evidence found in the actual comics.

While high-top shoes and Oxfords appear to have been the most popular shoe types for children during the 1920s and 1930s, the photographic record shows that many boys and girls wore strap shoes as well during this period, especially for dress-up occasions, such as the formal portrait taken of twins wearing matching strap shoes and white socks in 1922 (Figure 2-6). High-top shoes continued to be worn by men and children, but virtually disappeared as ladies' fashion in the 1920s, even during winter months. High-tops were increasingly seen as being "old-fashioned" or "granny shoes." Strap shoes, on the other hand, became extremely popular for women during the 1920s and 1930s as hemlines rose after World War I, thus making feet more visible and in need of fashion footwear. Men wore them, too, but only for special occasions, such as ballet dancing or by so-called "strong men" as part of their costumes. Jack LaLanne, the health and fitness expert, could often be seen wearing strap shoes during his exercise television program in the 1950s. Men can also be seen wearing strap shoes as part of historical recreation costumes, such as soldiers.

The last time an ad appeared in a Sears catalog offering Mary Jane–type shoes in

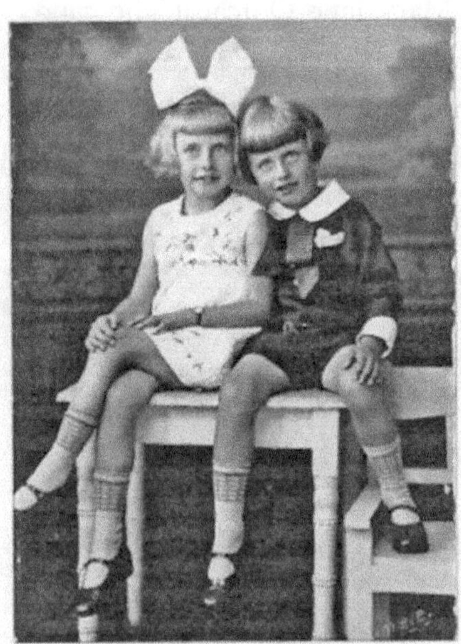

Figure 2-6
Twins wearing strap shoes, 1922

the US specifically for boys (as well as girls) was during the Great Depression in its 1935 Spring/Summer catalog. They were on sale for sixty-nine cents a pair and made of black patent leather with a wingtip design on the toe (Figure 2-7). They were available in girls' and boys' sizes up to children's size 2. They were not called "Mary Janes" in the Sears ad.

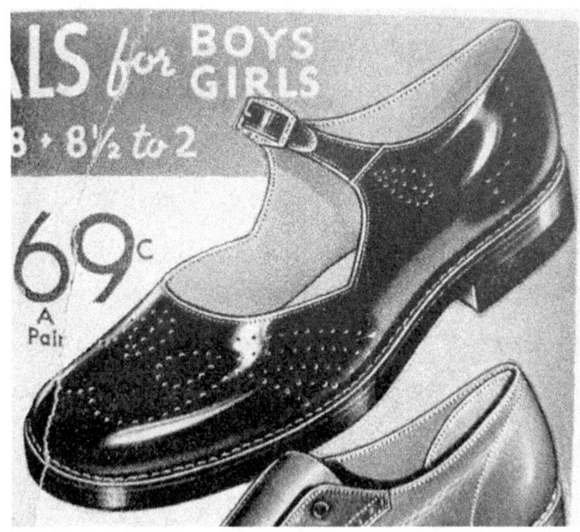

Figure 2-7

Mary Jane shoes for boys and girls, 1935

Strap Shoe Usage around the World

As noted earlier, there were significant geographical differences with respect to wearing Mary Jane–type strap shoes. Generally, they were popular for women and girls in most countries. Without the name "Mary Jane" assigned to strap shoes until very recently, they were worn by men in Europe much later than in North America. European royal families, especially in Britain, tended to favor boys wearing Mary Jane–type shoes, as they had done for centuries. In the UK, the Start-Rite Shoe Company, or its predecessor, has made children's shoes for the royal family for over two hundred years. Their web page still had a white Mary

Jane–type shoe on its infant boys page called "Baby" in 2009. A pink version appeared on the girls page as well, thus making the style unisex as in past years. Princess Diana dressed her sons in strap shoes before they went to school and in T-bar sandals thereafter.

Strap shoes were popular in Italy for boys and girls into the 1950s and 1960s. They were even worn by younger boys who joined the Balilla Fascist youth organization in the 1930s and 1940s (Figure 2-8). While the uniforms were supplied by the Fascist organization, the shoes were usually school shoes and were supplied by the boys' families. They were neatly polished in keeping with military discipline.[15] Boys as young as five years old joined the Balilla ranks and some had not yet learned to tie shoelaces, so strap shoes were a practical solution to avoid having squad chiefs constantly tying thirty pairs of their troops' shoelaces. However, older children generally wore laced shoes.[16]

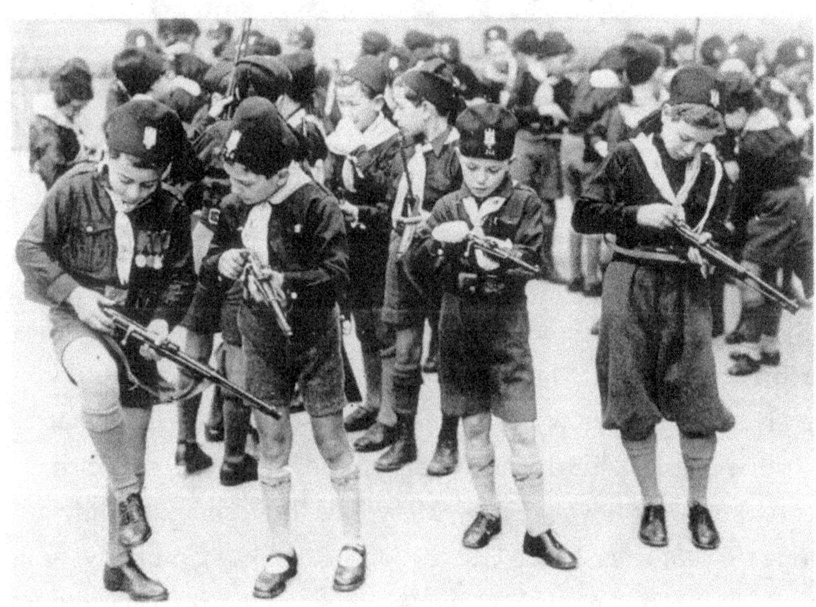

Figure 2-8
Fascist Balilla boy wearing strap shoes, ca. 1930s

Like Prince William and Prince Harry, Bob, a UK resident interviewed for this book (2009), also wore single-bar strap shoes in England when he was two years old, and then T-bar sandals thereafter until he was ten or eleven years old. He states that parents should buy children's shoes based on "gender-neutral and practical styles." He says strap shoes are more suitable for children's growing feet by allowing their feet to breathe because of the large proportion of open area on top of the shoe. Moreover, he says that feet are damaged by improper footwear in childhood; this could "have an impact on extension and flexion of muscles in the legs, the upper limbs, and affect walking and posture." He reports that even in the UK, there has been a trend toward more "gender demarcation in footwear for children right from birth," with manufacturers emphasizing dark, drab colors, such as "ugly brown leather lace-up boots" in the boys' section of stores.

On a positive note, he reports that several shoe manufacturers may be changing this advertising strategy in that T-bar styles are now being considered a unisex style again, rather than just for little girls. Also, red or blue colors are now being considered gender-neutral. He contacted shoe manufacturers in the UK regarding his concerns and inquired if T-bar footwear can be worn by boys. He was told in 2009 that they are "one of their most successful items for little girls as well as little boys." Having worn such footwear himself as a child, Bob had no problem with small boys wearing single-strap shoes for formal occasions, such as weddings, since this is part of a long tradition in the UK.[17]

Strap shoes were also very popular in other European countries, especially France and Germany, where even teenage boys wore them in the days before sneakers became popular. The shoes were often made of canvas, which was much cheaper than leather and, therefore, more affordable during those economically hard times. On the other hand, the photographic record also shows both German and French boys and girls wearing strap shoes who appeared to be very well dressed, indicating that the style transcended socioeconomic differences in those countries.

In 1930, a young German boy and girl were photographed with the boy wearing strap shoes with a short pantsuit while the girl is wearing tie-up Oxfords with a skirt. In the US one might think they were wearing each other's shoes, since they look about the same age. But, in Germany, as in most of Europe, people apparently were not caught up with the girl shoe or boy shoe difference, as in North America that seems to have been encouraged by advertisers and manufacturers to increase shoe sales. The name "Mary Jane" had not been assigned to strap shoes at this time in Europe. Strap shoes were very popular in Germany, where they were called "Riemenschuhe," where *Riemen* means "strap" and *schuhe* is "shoe." In France, they were referred to as "chaussures a bride," with *bride* deriving from the straps in a horse's bridle, and *chaussures* a name for shoes.[18] However, the term "Mary Jane" has now diffused to Europe and may have affected use of the style by men as a result.

Strap shoes continued to be popular for girls throughout the 1900s and carried over into the twenty-first century. One area where boys continued the tradition of wearing strap shoes was for dancing, such as ballet, or in very formal dance classes, as exemplified by the photo of a boy wearing them at a lesson in 1958. Mothers at this time may have wished to emulate royalty with respect to shoe styles, at least in the case of very small boys.

In Canada, a member of the British Commonwealth in the 1950s, small boys wore strap shoes like the boy on the cover of a children's fashion magazine, *The Beehive*, which was published in Toronto. The shoes are identical to those worn by the girl on the

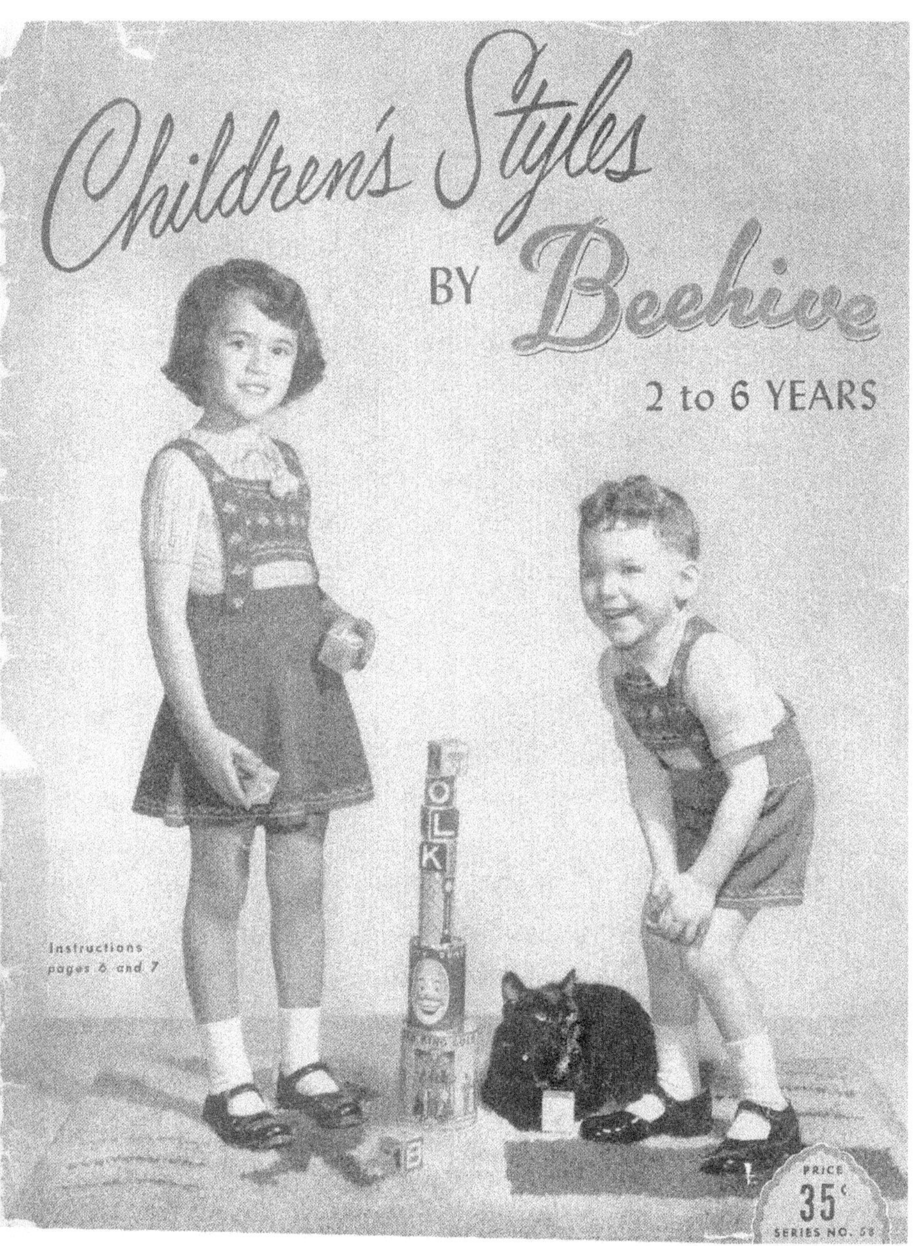

Figure 2-9
Canadian children wearing strap shoes, 1950s

cover of the magazine (Figure 2-9). Jacqueline Kennedy dressed her son John F. Kennedy Jr. (John-John) in strap shoes in the 1960s when visiting Europe, where boys his age were still wearing them. This might have been a case of: "When in Rome, do as the Romans do." Perhaps, Mrs. Kennedy did not want her son to be out of place by wearing typical American Oxford shoes while in Britain, or she may have preferred the look of the strap shoes. On the other hand, Historical Boys' Clothing (1999) reports that John-John was "piling up negative points from his peers because of the sissy styles" his mother made him wear for state occasions when there were sure to be photographers on hand.[19] It is not known if John-John wore single-strap shoes when at home in the US. He was, however, frequently seen wearing double T-strap sandals (barefoot sandals), which are discussed in chapter 5.

During the last two to three decades of the twentieth century, strap shoes remained popular for girls and women, but gradually declined in use on the part of men and boys, with the exception of the children of the British royal family, and the children of those who wished to emulate royalty fashions. Why did this happen? As noted above, the name "Mary Jane" applied to this footwear had a lot to do with the decline in usage on the part of men and boys in the US. This decline may also have resulted from an increased stress on military fashion advertised for boys, such as Boy Scout uniforms. Or it may have been the influence of marketing strategies of shoe manufacturers who preferred two lines of shoes based on gender, one for boys and the other for girls, in order to maximize sales and profits. One of the consequences of this strategy was that it was no longer practical for mothers to use hand-me-down shoes for male and female siblings as in the past, owing to the fact that there were now different-style shoes based on gender. As noted previously, footwear in the early 1900s and before was largely unisex, especially in rural areas, where shoe styles were limited. Cobblers would make the same style shoes for an entire family. But, by the midtwentieth century, boys were refusing to wear strap shoes in the US, because they feared being labeled a "sissy" for wearing their sisters' shoes, even though these shoes, as has been shown, had been worn by warriors and kings, all men. There are many references to the fact that boys do not want to wear "girls'" shoes, especially if they are labeled with a name like Mary Jane. With changing roles of men and women in recent history and the athletic shoe revolution, the question of labeling footwear "male" and "female" needs to be reviewed. There may already be a change in attitudes underway toward strap shoes based on gender, judging by recent trends and the rapid increase in men wearing open- and closed-toe sandals, which of course have straps. The discussion of gender questions with respect to footwear is considered in more detail in chapter 9.

There is no question that Mary Jane shoes continue to have appeal for women and girls of all ages. A trip to just about any local mall will bear out this popularity. However, there may be renewed interest on the part of some men and boys in this style. For example, several male models wore strap shoes while walking down the runway as part of the Dior Homme Spring 2006 menswear fashion collection.[20]

The Dior Spring 2009 collection of menswear also showed male models wearing a two-strap Mary Jane–type shoe as part of their outfits. There is no information available if there is any connection with these fashion shows and several Mary Jane–type shoes for men that have also appeared on the internet.

Shoebuy.com, for example, the self-proclaimed "World's Largest Site for Shoes," listed six men's Mary Janes on its site in January 2009. The men's version is made by Finn Comfort, a company located in

Bavaria, Germany, which offers a classic single-strap style available to men's size 10½. These shoes are also listed on their women's Mary Jane page, so they actually are unisex.

In order to see things in perspective, Shoebuy had a listing of Mary Jane shoes of which 6 were listed for men in 2009, 177 for girls, and 821 for women. This is a total of over 1,000 Mary Janes and shows how popular the style was in 2009, although this total includes high-heel versions that would not be considered the classic Mary Jane style.

Another company on the internet, ShoeDeals4U.com, also advertised several single-strap Dr. Martens shoes listed as "Men's Mary Janes." One of these was called "Dr. Martens Men's Asymmetric Strap MJ" under the category of "Dr. Martens Men's Originals." Several of the Dr. Martens shoes have both men's and women's sizes printed inside the shoe and on the outside of the box, thus making them unisex.

There was also a men's Mary Jane listed as an "Original McMarten," with a tartan design superimposed on patent leather, which sold for $99.99 a pair. These shoes may have been "trial balloons" to see if men would wear strap shoes having the Mary Jane name assigned to them. Correspondence was sent to Shoebuy.com asking if men were really buying these men's Mary Janes. A representative of the company wrote back and said that the listing was an "inventory error."[21] Ten months later the shoes were still listed in both men's and women's sizes, but the name had been changed from "Men's Mary Janes" to "Finn Comfort Men's Adjustable Strap Shoes." This appears to be the first time that single-strap shoes have been advertised for men since the 1920s in the US. In the 2010s strap shoes were still marketed in the UK as "Buckle Brogues," an accessory to men's Scottish kilt outfits. The firm kiltsdirect.com in the UK said in their advertisement that "If those pesky laces still confound you, how about a smart pair of Buckle Kilt Brogues in leather? Perfect for dancing."[22] In 2012 the "Buckle Brogue" had crossed the Atlantic and was offered on the internet in men's sizes up to 15 and widths up to EEEE by the Celtic Trading Post in Sacramento, California. They were available in black or brown at $146.99 a pair, which is about half what they cost in Scotland. They were made in the US, according to the vendor. Black "Buckle Brogues" (also known as "Bar and Buckle" shoes) were also available in Canada from Keltoi Gaelic Clothing in 2019 up to a size UK 14.

One of the most unusual "futuristic" outfits having Mary Jane shoes as an accessory found on the internet was worn by a male model participating in the Fall/Winter 2009 show of avant-garde designer Telfar. The fashion show was held at St. Mark's Church in New York City's East Village. Onderdonk (2009), who attended the show, says it consisted of distinct men's, women's, and unisex styles which had a "relaxed energy mixed with an urban wanderer/industrial vibe." She says that she was "definitely a fan of the muted color palette, the leggings, and Mary Jane shoes on the men."[23] One model wore "deconstructed trousers" that were transformed into a type of skirt, shown in Figure 2-10.

Designer and artist Tijana Pavlov, from Belgrade, Serbia (Yugoslavia), also had a show in 2009 in which the male models wore black or metallic-blue Mary

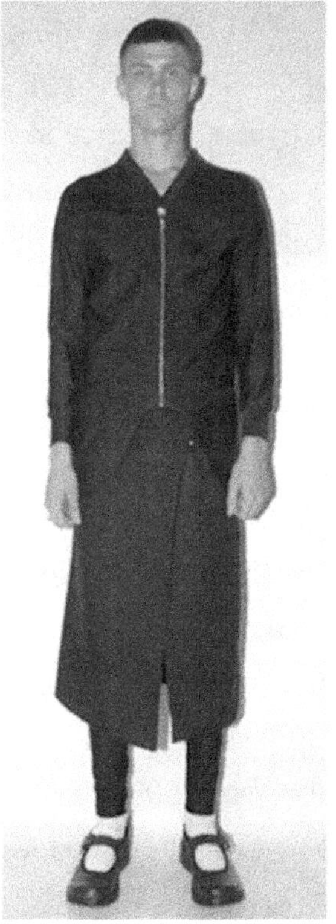

Figure 2-10
Deconstructed trousers and
Mary Jane shoes by Telfar,
2009

Jane–type shoes with futuristic outfits. Could 2009 have been the year of the revival of strap shoes for men? If so, this could be considered a shoe paradigm change of the magnitude similar to the 1700s when avant-garde students at Oxford University took the feminine laced corset shoes and created the Oxford for male mainstream use.

Judging by pictures found on the internet, there might also be a trend toward more boys wearing Mary Jane–type ballet shoes as part of their dancing costumes. Again, geographical differences play a role here in that boys seem to be more inclined to wear such footwear as part of their ballet costumes in Russia and other countries in Europe. Boys there who take up ballet tend to be looked upon as "cool kids" because of all the hard work involved in learning to dance skillfully. In North America people have been conditioned to "believe" that Mary Jane–type shoes are strictly for girls, without exception. As a result, it is not clear whether attitudes on the subject will change much in the short term. To cite an example of such attitudes, Payless.com listed a brown "Boys' Smartfit Rugged Mary Jane" shoe with heavy soles and stitching on the internet in 2009. Payless.com advertised that this shoe is an "updated Mary-Jane casual style" selling for $14.99 a pair, and available in "boys/youth sizes 10½ to 6." Again, was this another "trial balloon" to encourage boys to wear strap shoes in the US, or just a mistake in listing? A check of the Rugged Mary Jane at Payless.com in 2011 showed that the exact shoe that was listed as boys' in 2009 was listed as "Girls' Smartfit Rugged Mary Jane" two years later. Interesting how things change.

Several Payless ShoeSource Inc. stores in the North (Pennsylvania) and the South (Georgia) were visited to inquire about this boys' shoe. All of the female salesclerks at the stores were emphatic about the shoe being a girls' shoe and not for boys.

They said the ad must be wrong. They did say that there was a change in the way children's shoes are arranged at Payless ShoeSource Inc. stores. They are now grouping all boys' and girls' shoes together by sizes, rather than in separate departments by gender. They now are collectively called "kids'" shoes. The shoes considered boys' are grouped at the top of the rack (near the size number), while the girls' shoes are at the bottom area, near the floor. When asked what happens in the middle of the group, the clerks said that the boys' shoes have numbers and they go together as a group. When the numbers run out, then the girls' shoe numbers begin. At least it is now easier for a girl to pick a boys' shoe if she likes one without going to a boys' department. This goes also for boys who might like a style that the company has grouped as girls'.

Mary Janes in Historic Recreations

Strap shoes are appearing more frequently in recent years as part of authentic historic costume recreations, thus calling attention to the fact that Mary Jane shoes were indeed worn by both sexes in times past.

Many companies are making footwear for historic recreation. BattleMerchant.com sells a latchet shoe with strap and buckle that was worn during the "high and late medieval period" between 1200 and 1500. The company says that the shoes are suitable for both men and women, since both sexes wore them in medieval times. They are made of high-quality leather with hand-sewn seams. The price in 2009 was 39.9 euros.[24] As reported previously, such footwear is referred to as "Riemenschuhe" (strap shoe) in Germany rather than "Mary Jane." There also appears to be a change in the way strap shoes were portrayed to children in the early 2000s in North America, possibly demonstrating a more open-minded view of this footwear. For example, the children's television series *Barney & Friends* showed a boy and girl dressed in cavalier-type costumes and wearing identical strap shoes in 2000. The puppet Pinocchio usually wore strap shoes in book illustrations and animated cartoons without anyone raising questions.

Changing Attitudes toward Footwear and Gender

Are children's attitudes toward gender and clothing styles beginning to vary from the more traditional views of their parents? Notwithstanding the fact that instances have been uncovered where strap shoes have been advertised as "Men's Mary Janes" or "Boys' Rugged Mary Janes," there would probably be more interest on the part of boys in the style if advertisers returned to calling them simply strap shoes or bar shoes as in Europe, or else slippers or sandals as they were called in the early 1900s. This could result in both sexes wearing them again in larger numbers.

In Japan, children wear unisex slippers with a single strap called *uwabaki* that are worn both at school and at home.[25]

Finally, we cannot leave this historical review of the classic Mary Jane shoe style without mentioning the return of "royalty" strap shoes to the American TV scene. The Burger King Corporation ran television ads beginning in 2006 showing its mascot, the Burger King, dressed in kingly robes, a crown, and strap shoes. His shoes appear to have been made of patent leather and were a bit shinier than those worn by the original King Henry VIII. Was this part of a movement to once again encourage men and boys to wear strap shoes? Probably not, but it is still an interesting trend to see men using strap shoes again in North America after such a long absence. Marc Bolan of the T. Rex rock band could be seen on the internet wearing Mary Jane shoes. With such TV coverage, mainstream America was bound to notice the footwear.

The Case of Christopher Robin's Strap Shoes

Another interesting geographical difference with respect to strap shoes was the change in footwear worn by Christopher Robin, the character in the popular Winnie the Pooh stories. Christopher was created by author A. A. Milne in the early 1900s and had long worn strap shoes as part of his costume in book illustrations and cartoons in Europe. The character is based on the real son of Milne, who wore strap shoes when a boy, as shown in a photo taken with his teddy bear about 1923.[26]

What is significant is that when Christopher was shown to American audiences in a television series, a decision was made to "exchange" his strap shoes for red sneakers, which presumably were seen as being more appropriate for American viewers in the 1980s. However, there was subsequently a change in the Disney costume policy, which now has the rights to the characters, and Christopher Robin is once again happily wearing his strap shoes and other footwear on both sides of the Atlantic.[27]

Perspective

At the outset of the research for this book it was believed that the single-strap Mary Jane–type shoe was only appropriate for little girls, or women attempting to reclaim an age of "innocence." Surprisingly, the style has been in existence for at least two thousand years and was worn by both men and women, including kings and soldiers, as well as common folk during much of that time. Geographical differences between North America, Europe, and elsewhere were accentuated when the name "Mary Jane" was applied to this footwear, which previously had simply been called sandals or slippers and considered unisex. The term "Mary Jane shoe" was an American invention and occurred in the early 1900s. It had a profound effect on gender usage of the footwear in that the more the term was used, the less men wore the style because of the risk of being seen as unmasculine, or worse yet, being called a "sissy." This change was accentuated by advertisers and manufacturers who conditioned people to be more gender-conscious with respect to clothing and footwear. Information presented in this chapter suggests that gender barriers may be breaking down with men wearing scent, pink articles of clothing, jewelry, and other items once considered taboo for them in the 1900s, a time when women were still considered inferior or second-class citizens as the "weaker sex." As part of this process, we may be witness to men reclaiming footwear styles, including Mary Janes, which have been "lost" to them. In this way they will once again share them with women as unisex footwear as in days past. This may not be as farfetched as it may seem given information presented in this chapter. The question of gender and footwear will be discussed in more detail in the final chapter.

Chapter 2 Notes

1. Schwartz, Steve, "Richard F. Outcault, Jr.," *Tuscania Gallery* (2006), freepages.rootsweb.com/~carmita/history/Regiment/news/213A.html.

2. Nuhn, R., "Buster Brown and Mary Jane," *The Antique Shoppe Newspaper* (February 2, 2005), antiqueshoppefl.com/archives.

3. "Buster Brown," *Wikipedia* (August 20, 2006), en.wikipedia.org/wiki/Buster_Brown.

4. Penrose Shoe Co., *Boot and Shoe Recorder* (November 19, 1921), 92.

5. "Fact Sheet," St. Louis Convention and Visitor Commission, 17.

6. Thompson, M. J., correspondence (June 10, 2011).

7. Weidner, D., "Buster Brown Shoes," Historical Boys' Clothing (April 20, 2007). (Available online through subscription only.)

8. Email correspondence with "Kyle" of the Brown Shoe Co. (June 18, 2007), and with Dr. Kris Runberg-Smith, archivist, Brown Shoe Co. (June 7, 2008).

9. Email correspondence with Dorothy Bell, public relations manager, corporate, Brown Shoe Co. (August 18, 2009).

10. Outcault, R. F., "Mary Jane in Real Life," Stripper's Guide, posted by Allan Holtz (June 6, 2009), strippersguide.blogspot.com/2007_12_02_archive.html.

11. *Colorado Springs Gazette* (Colorado Springs, Colorado, August 7, 1911), Google News Archive (accessed April 13, 2008).

12. Montgomery Ward, Spring/Summer Catalog Supplement, no. 82 (1914), 197.

13. Email correspondence with Pauline Thomas, *Fashion Era* (April 14, 2008), fashion-era.com.

14. New England Confectionary Co. (NECCO), "Mary Jane" (2007), necco.com/candy/mary-jane.aspx.

15. DocAV, Gunboard Forum (May 17, 2009).

16. DMala, Gunboard Forum, (May 20, 2009).

17. Email correspondence with Bob (April 3, 2009).

18. Bill and Norlington2, *Goodie2Shoes* (October 19, 2009).

19. Weidner, D., "The Best Dressed," Historical Boys' Clothing (December 28, 1999). Note: HBC has an extensive collection of images and information on the subject of Mary Jane shoes by country. (Available online through subscription only.)

20. Dior Homme, Spring Menswear Fashion Collection (2006), men.style.com/fashion/collection/S2006. (Also available at www.vogue.com/fashion-shows/spring-2006-menswear/dior-homme/slideshow/collection#51.)

21. Email correspondence with Shoebuy.com (June 9, 2009).

22. Kiltsdirect.com, "Buckle Kilt Brogue (ST-B007)" (September 7, 2009), kiltsdirect.com/accessories.html.

23. Onderdonk, J., "Telfar Fall 2009," Paint It Noir (February 13, 2009), paintitnoir.blogspot.com/2009/02/telfar-fall-2009. (Also available at www.thefashionisto.com/telfar-fall-2009/.)

24. BattleMerchant.com, "Latchet Shoe with Strap and Buckle" (2006), battlemerchant.com/Footwear.

25. Weidner, D., "Japanese School Activities: Music Making–Instrumental Music, Historical Boys' Clothing (October 31, 2006), www.histclo.com/schun/country/jap/act/mus/jsam-inst.html.

26. "Christopher Robin Milne," *Wikipedia* (March 16, 2012), en.wikipedia.org/wiki/Christopher_Robin_Milne.

27. Weidner, D., "Christopher Robin: Disney and American Sensibilities," Historical Boys' Clothing (March 3, 2009), www.histclo.com/lit/uk/cr/cr-dis.html.

MULTI-STRAP MARY JANE SHOES

The history of Mary Jane–type footwear from antiquity to the present is continued in this chapter by focusing on those varieties having more than one strap (bar) across the instep or ankle. Two-bar shoes were actually more popular than the single-strap version during a short period in the early 1900s. Photos and shoe advertisements reveal that there were as many as ten horizontal straps across the foot. Footwear having center vertical straps, commonly called T-strap shoes or sandals today, are discussed in detail in the following chapters, including high-heel Mary Jane shoes.

Multi-strapped styles have ancient origins, which according to Wilcox preceded the Romans, dating back to the Medes, Assyrians, and Persians in the fertile crescent of Mesopotamia. Roman soldiers wore heavy, high-top multi-strap "marching" sandals called "caligae," both open-toe and closed-toe versions. These caligae are the sandals usually associated with Roman footwear because they appear in numerous Hollywood "sword-and-sandal" movies. What most people do not realize is that the Romans also used low-cut sandals or shoes with fewer straps on most other occasions than marching. One such example is the sandal found near Hadrian's Wall in Britain. Research has not revealed whether single-strap footwear evolved from multiple-strap footwear or vice versa, but both forms appear to have coexisted in ancient times.

The distinction between closed-toe sandals and shoes is often unclear because these terms were used interchangeably in early advertisements. It was not until the 1900s that shoe catalogs and newspaper ads referred to any shoe having straps and/or open areas on top as a sandal. On the other hand, even though once called sandals or slippers, in the twenty-first century one- and two-strap shoes are more often called "strap shoes" or, simply, "Mary Janes." Men's two-strap shoes were even called Oxfords in the 1912 Sears, Roebuck and Co. catalog. And there were also instances when people listed two-strap shoes for sale online as Oxfords even though they were fastened by straps. Thus, names for this footwear can be rather arbitrary and confusing.

Closed-toe sandals having three or more straps were usually called "Roman sandals," according to shoe ads dating as far back as the late 1800s. In the 2000s, they usually were referred to as gladiator sandals. For discussion purposes in this study, gladiator footwear is defined as footwear with multiple straps plus a center T-strap.

What was the purpose of having multiple straps on footwear as opposed to a single strap? In the case of the Romans, sandals that covered the entire calf provided protection to the legs during battle. But the purpose of having more than one or two straps on lower-cut footwear is not so easily explained, because one or two straps are enough to firmly secure it to the foot. Why would individuals wear footwear with many straps to fasten? It may have been for reasons of fashion, status, or cost. An ad, for example, that was placed by the Bay State Slipper Co. of Haverhill, Massachusetts, in the 1921 *Boot and Shoe Recorder* trade journal lists a single-strap Mary Jane shoe on sale for $1.65. The company also sold multi-strap Mary Jane versions with up to eight straps, for which they charged an additional five cents per strap to cover the added cost of leather, buckles, and/or buttons.[1] The question then posed is, were sandals with more than a single strap a form of "status" because they cost more than a single-strap sandal? However, the author of this book feels most footwear was worn simply for reasons of convenience, comfort, or appearance rather than for status.

The first ad found in this research for a high-top multi-strap Roman sandal appeared in the 1884 *Chicago Daily Tribune*. This ad states that these Roman sandals were the latest fashion from Paris. The first reference found for a high-top sandal in a mail-order catalog appears in the 1902 Sears, Roebuck and Co. catalog, and this could have played a role in promoting sandals as an alternative to the high-top laced or buttoned footwear in vogue at that time, since they would have been easier and faster to put on and take off, and definitely cooler to wear because of the openings between the straps that provided for foot ventilation.

It took several more years for the multi-strap sandal to catch on as a style for children. But, once started, the wearing of sandals with multiple straps by children continued well into the 1900s because they were seen as providing more support to the foot. Children tended to wear them long after adults had abandoned the style as being old-fashioned. One can see numerous examples of multi-strapped footwear in children's sizes in the Sears catalogs during the 1930s, a time when they were no longer offered to adults. In fact, three-strap Roman sandals continued to be sold by Sears into the mid-1950s. Adults did not wear them again until the turn of the twenty-first century, when they were rediscovered as gladiator sandals.

It was in the 1900s that women's hemlines became shorter, so women became much more conscious of the appearance of their footwear. As a result, women began to abandon high-top shoes even during the colder months of the year in favor of low-cut Oxfords and strap shoes. Initially, women's multi-strapped sandals may have played a role in this transition away from high-top, laced, and buttoned shoes by continuing the high-top "look" found in multi-strap sandals. However, with the fashion trend of the 1920s toward lower-cut footwear, even the multi-strapped sandal itself became old-fashioned and declined in popularity.

To gain perspective, Tables 3-A and 3-B compare strap-shoe popularity with that of high-top boots and shoes and low-cut Oxfords during the period from 1897 through 1932. Strap shoes as a percentage of total footwear was calculated and plotted to show graphically how high-top footwear declined rapidly during the period, while low-cut footwear including Mary Jane styles increased in popularity. Sears, Roebuck and Co. catalogs from the author's collection for the years 1897, 1906, 1912, 1926, and 1932, purchased on the internet and antique stores, were used as the primary source of data. Information from the World War I period could not be accessed in the Sears catalog, so information from a New York–based mail-order catalog, Charles Williams 1918, was used since it was found to be comparable.

Mail Order Catalogs 1897-1932

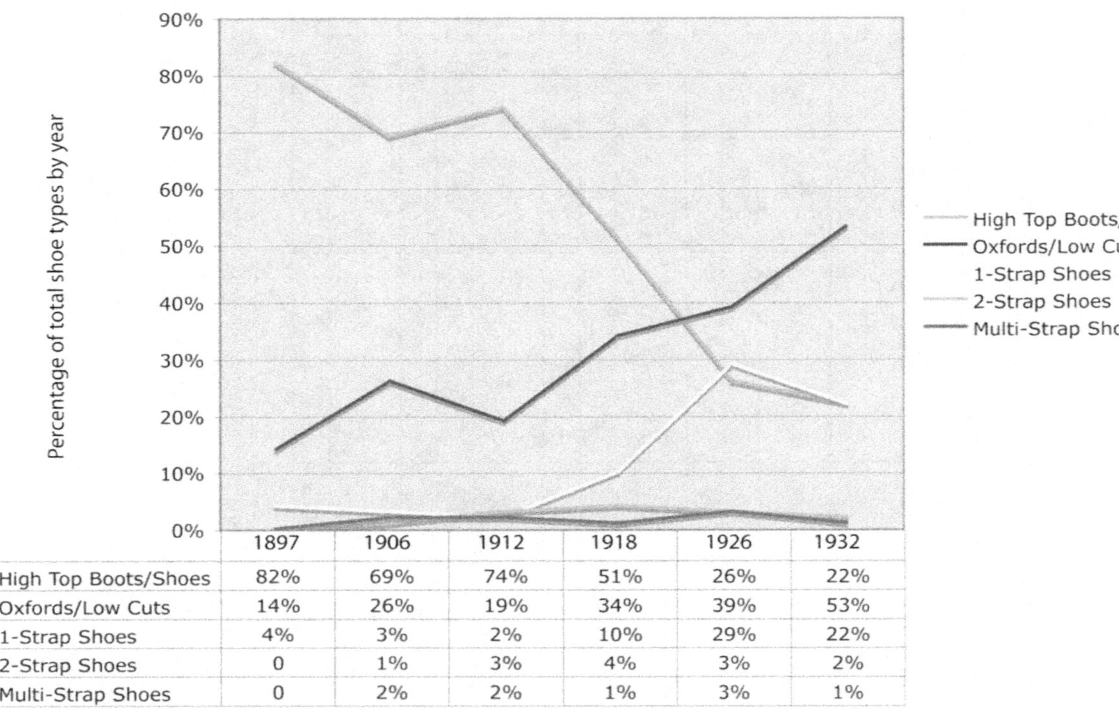

	1897	1906	1912	1918	1926	1932
High Top Boots/Shoes	82%	69%	74%	51%	26%	22%
Oxfords/Low Cuts	14%	26%	19%	34%	39%	53%
1-Strap Shoes	4%	3%	2%	10%	29%	22%
2-Strap Shoes	0	1%	3%	4%	3%	2%
Multi-Strap Shoes	0	2%	2%	1%	3%	1%

Table 3-A

Mail-Order Catalogs	Strap Shoes			High-Tops	Low-Cuts	Total
	1-strap	2-strap	Multi-Strap			
Sears, Roebuck & Co., 1897	7	0	0	160	27	194
Percent of total	4%	0%	0%	82%	14%	100%
Sears, Roebuck & Co., 1906	14	1	8	279	105	407
Percent of total	3%	0%	2%	69%	26%	100%
Sears, Roebuck & Co., 1912	10	12	9	320	82	433
Percent of total	2%	3%	2%	74%	19%	100%
Charles Williams, 1918	40	15	5	212	141	413
Percent of total	10%	4%	1%	51%	34%	100%
Sears, Roebuck & Co., 1926	84	9	8	76	113	290
Percent of total	29%	3%	3%	26%	39%	100%
Sears, Roebuck & Co., 1932	91	6	3	86	212	398
Percent of total	23%	1%	0%	22%	53%	100%

Table 3-B

Comparison of strap shoes to high-top and low-cut footwear, 1897–1932

Source of information for Tables 3-A and 3-B is from the author's original mail-order catalog collection, with the exception of the 1897 Sears, Roebuck and Co. catalog, which is a complete reproduction by Chelsea House in 1969. Percentages are calculated on the basis of the total shoe styles for each year.

The following are some of the results from the analysis:

1. Strap shoes constituted only 4 percent of footwear at the turn of the twentieth century, but increased to a third of all shoes shown in the 1926 Sears catalog.
2. Strap shoes were very popular during the 1930s and 1940s.
3. High-top footwear fell from 82 percent of total boots and shoes in 1897 to 22 percent by 1932.
4. Oxfords and low-cut footwear increased in popularity from 14 percent at the beginning of the period to 53 percent in 1932.
5. Of the seven strap shoes advertised in 1897, only one was available in children's sizes for formal occasions. None were offered in men's sizes during this year.
6. In 1906 Sears advertised over four hundred boots and shoes, three-quarters being high-tops. But in this catalog, there were more strap shoes available than previously, including three single-strap Mary Janes for ladies advertised as dress-occasion shoes. Single-strap shoes were also available in children's sizes that were "suitable for street or dress" wear.
7. According to information in Sears catalogs, the only time that strap shoes were offered for men was in 1911 and 1912 prior to the shoe acquiring the name "Mary Janes" in North America.

With this overview as a guide to provide perspective, the balance of this chapter will present research to trace multi-strapped shoes back in time as was done with the single-strap version in the previous chapters.

Two-Strap Mary Janes from Roman Times to the Present

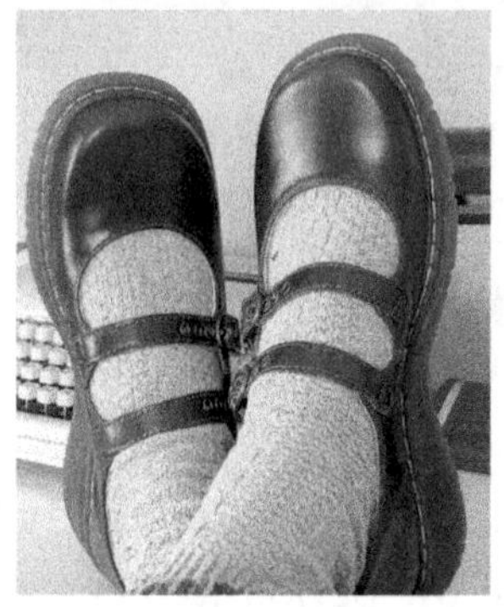

Figure 3-1

Twin strap shoes, 2010

Figure 3-1 shows an example of a two-strap Mary Jane shoe from the 1900s, featuring a blunt, rounded toe and low heels, which are characteristic of traditional Mary Jane shoes. In the 2000s, Dr. Martens offered a similar style, named "Candie," with two straps fastened by buckles. Buttons were also frequently used to fasten the straps, or bars, as they are known in Great Britain and other parts of the world. As with the single-strap Mary Jane, hook-and-loop fasteners are more common in the twenty-first century. Like the single-strapped Mary Jane, the two-strap version also has a long history dating back to Roman times. Figure 3-2 is an illustration of a two-closure Roman shoe that was found at Bar Hill, Dunbartonshire, Scotland, near the Antonine Wall. This twelve-foot-high sod-and-earth wall was built by Emperor Antoninus Pius farther north and parallel to the better-known stone Hadrian's Wall. Both walls extend east and west near the border between Scotland and England. Many shoes have been found well preserved in the wet soil of ditches adjacent to the wall. Wet soil is favorable for preserving leather, which would otherwise have long since rotted away. Since the Romans had no buckles to fasten their sandals, leather latchets or strips of leather were passed through punched holes to secure the shoe to the foot. Ward

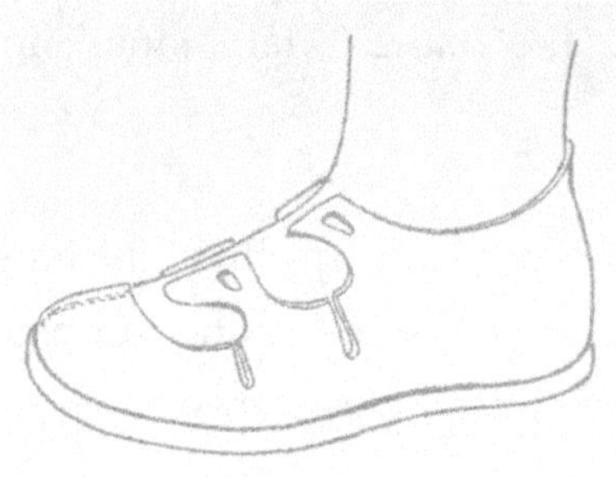

Figure 3-2

Two-strap Roman shoe, 1st century AD

reported in 1911 that these sandals had a "sturdy workaday" look, with the second pair of latchets or straps increasing the grip of the sandal. Besides having straps, several of these sandals also had holes punched into the sides for decorative purposes and to allow air from outside to cool the foot. Ward stated that the cutouts never compromised the integrity and strength of the leather. These sandals also had a piece of stiff leather, or counter, in the back for the purpose of better supporting the heel. Thus, these Roman sandals could allow the wearer to engage in heavy work.[2]

It is a misconception fostered by Hollywood's sword-and-sandal movies that the Romans wore only high-top gladiator sandals with open toes. This style was used, to be sure, as seen on monuments and triumphal arches in Rome, but the Romans also wore closed-toe footwear, especially in the northern provinces of the empire, where open-toe sandals were less practical in ice, snow, and cold weather. Archeological evidence bears this out, as in the case of the shoe found along Hadrian's Wall and which is shown here in Figure 3-3.

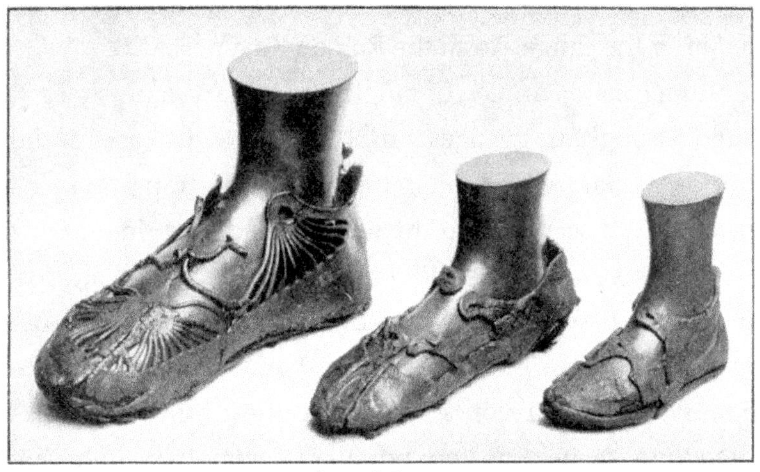

Figure 3-3
Roman shoe, 1st century AD

Curle (1911) reports that such shoes were called "carbatina" and were fastened by leather thong laces passing through loops in the sides of the shoe. He states that such footwear continued to be worn in the Shetland Islands and parts of Eastern Europe until the early 1900s.[3] In the case of the Romans, this type of footwear was generally worn by the civilian population, whereas the Roman legionnaires generally wore the heavy boot-like caligae with open toes and hobnailed soles for marching long distances. Emperor Gaius Caesar wore this same shoe as a child when he accompanied his father, Germanicus, to a Roman outpost. Because Gaius wore a child-sized caligae shoe, the soldiers gave him the name "Little Boots," or "Caligula," the name by which he is known in history. For children in this time period there was no difference between their shoes and those of adults except for size.

As the Romans conquered other lands, they brought their culture and footwear with them. An example reported by Baker in 2007 from archaeological evidence reveals that closed-toe sandals were popular throughout the Middle East during the first century AD. Baker states that the concept of enclosed footwear to better protect the feet, especially in the case of military boots, was modeled after the caligae from the Roman time period.[4]

Numerous examples of single-strap Mary Jane shoes can be found throughout the ages, but this was not the case for the two-strap Mary Jane, even though the additional strap provided a better and more secure fit to the foot. Perhaps the time required to fasten the extra strap, or the cost of adding a second strap during fabrication, may explain why they were not as popular as the single-strap version. In any case, another example of a two-strap shoe in historical records was not found until the Renaissance, when the style became very popular. Norris (1938) in his book on Tudor costumes includes an illustration of a Royal page in 1511 at the "Westminster Tournament wearing a tunic, scarlet hosen and black double strap shoes."[5]

In the seventeenth and eighteenth centuries, neither the single-strap shoe nor the double-strap shoe was popular, with both being replaced by heavy, higher-heel shoes. The double-strap shoe style seems to have disappeared from the fashion scene until rediscovered during the nineteenth century. Figure 3-4 shows a boy wearing double-strap shoes and a tunic suit with long white stockings that were fashionable for the turn of the twentieth century. White stockings generally replaced the black stockings so characteristic of the Victorian 1800s, when dark clothing was the rule.

At the end of the twentieth century, the *Sunday Star-Ledger* of Newark, New Jersey, carried a photo advertising the play *Ragtime: The Musical,* set in 1906 America and based on the novel *Ragtime.* It was performed at the Ford Center for the Performing Arts in New York City.[6] A still shot shows three children wearing clothes typical of the ragtime era a hundred years earlier. The older boy wears high-top shoes while the younger boy is dressed in black two-straps and the girl in the picture wears white two-strap shoes.

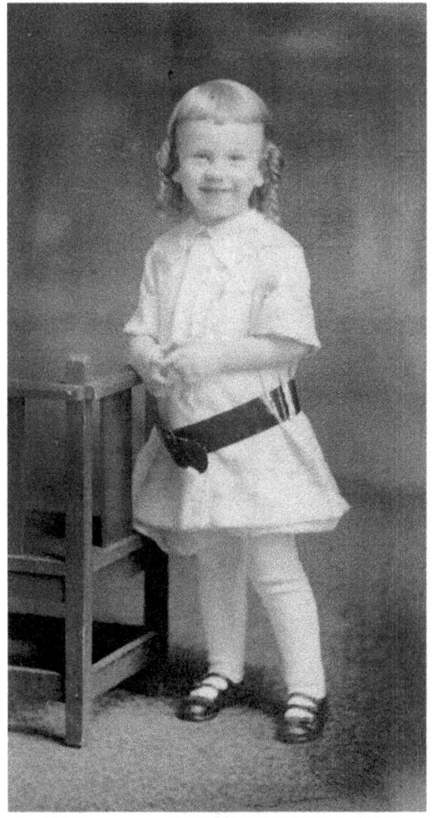

Figure 3-4

Boys' double-strap shoes, ca. 1910

While searching for examples of two-strap Mary Jane–type shoes, a picture was found of a boy wearing a pair together with ringlet curls, a large bow in his hair, and a dress with a petticoat. Kippen, an Australian shoe historian and podiatrist, reports that prior to World War I it was the norm to see little boys in long ringlets and a hair bow.[7] In this time period of the 1800s, boys generally wore dresses and petticoats until the age of five. Weidner states that the boy in the photograph was wearing this outfit as part of a "breeching ceremony," the time when boys exchanged their dresses and petticoats for male attire. The boy's mother had "him delicately lift up the hem of his dress [so] that his lace trimmed petticoat could be seen" (Figure 3-5). In a second photograph, the same child, approximately age five or six, wears the same long, black stockings and twin-bar strap shoes after the breeching. Strap shoes appear to have had no gender connotation because they were worn both before and after breeching.[8]

By contrast, a boy wore the same style double-strap shoes in 1921 but dressed in what would be considered more typical boys' clothing for the early 1900s, consisting of knickers and long socks.

Figure 3-6 shows a shoe ad that appeared in the *Saturday*

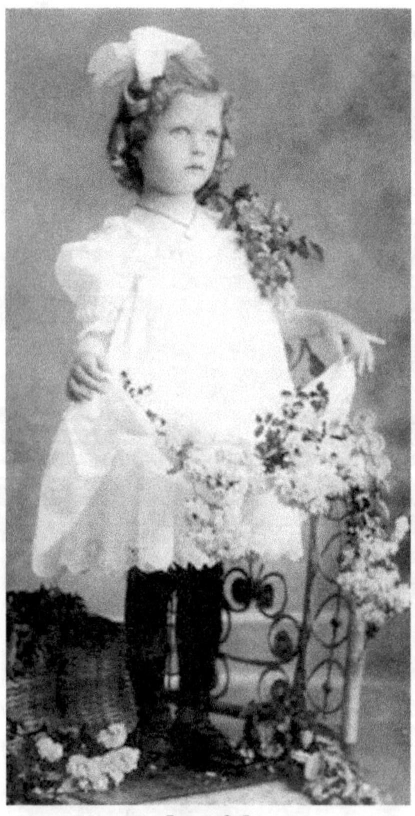

Figure 3-5

Boy with double-strap shoes, ringlets, hair bow, and dress, ca. 1895

Evening Post on March 5, 1922, advertising Buster Brown shoes with twin straps. The shoes were not called "Mary Janes" by the company. Twenty years earlier, R. Hannah & Co. placed an ad in the October 6, 1902, edition of the Wellington, New Zealand, *Evening Post* for "Fashionable Footwear" that states: "Woman's tan 2-bar shoes, very neat" at seven shillings, six pence. This demonstrates how the two-strap style had already become a worldwide phenomenon by the turn of the twentieth century.[9]

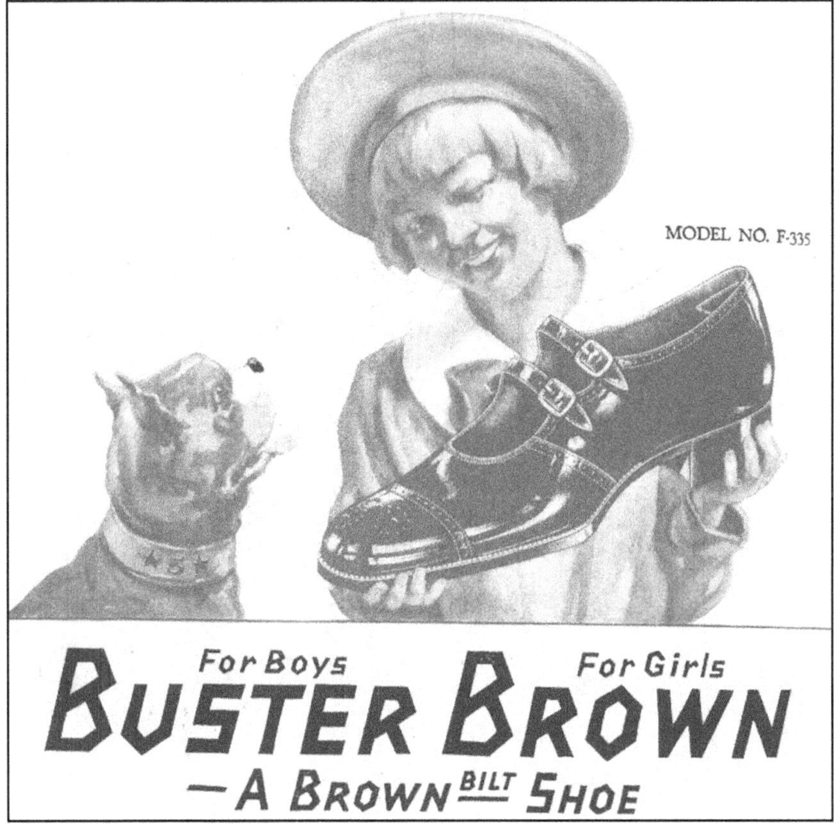

Figure 3-6
Buster Brown two-strap shoe ad, 1922

Double-strap shoes that had once been popular with men during the Renaissance period did not share the same popularity with women and children during the twentieth century. As stated previously, the only ad for a men's two-strap shoe was found in the 1912 Sears, Roebuck and Co. catalog. In 1909 there had been two Sears ads for twin-strap Oxfords for men that had buckles located over the instep. One shoe was called the "Adventure" and the other "Social Lion." While these shoes were not in the true Mary Jane style, they appeared to be a transition to that style that Sears specifically advertised for men in 1912.[10] None of the men's strap shoes were actually called a "Mary Jane." By 1912, double-strap shoes had become so popular for adults and children that their number actually exceeded the number of single-strap shoes for the first time in a Sears catalog. A total of eighteen twin-style shoes were available that year. As discussed in the introduction, there were two single-strap shoes available for men that year as well as a two-strap shoe under the heading "Men's Late Model Oxfords." This shoe was made of patent colt skin with a calf top and military heel. It had a distinctive bump toe to distinguish it from the ladies' version of that same style (Figure 3-7).

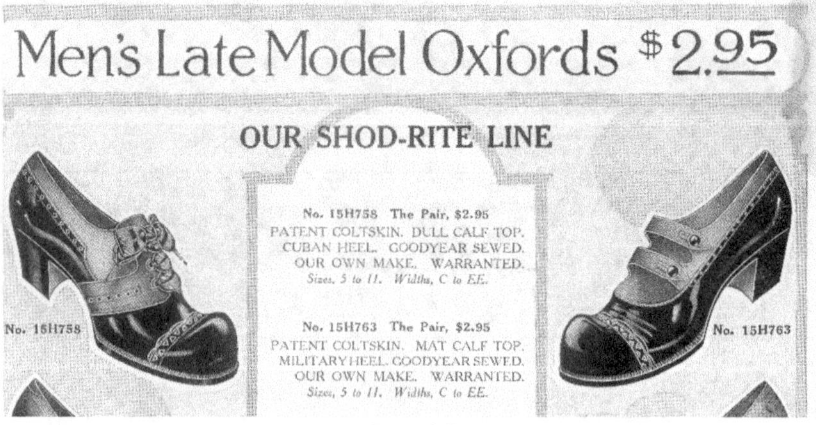

Figure 3-7
Men's two-strap shoe, 1912

The men's two-strap shoe is more rugged in appearance and is referred to as an "Oxford," while the women's version is termed a "popular two-strap slipper," with "light, strong soles" and a "sensible heel and toe." The women's shoes were fancier than the men's version by having small bows on the toes. On the basis of research for this book, 1913 was the first year that the term "Mary Jane" became associated with ankle-strap shoes. Could the term "Mary Jane," applied to two-strap shoes, have resulted in a decision to discontinue advertising this style for men because Sears never listed single- or twin-strapped shoes specifically for men after 1912?

Two-strap Mary Jane–type shoes continued their popularity for women, but even more so for children during the 1920s and 1930s. However, once again the style became eclipsed by the single-strap Mary Jane shoe. Even though in the latter half of the twentieth century a few boys wore two-strap shoes, the style was almost exclusively worn by girls in North America. In Europe, however, a mural was found showing a boy wearing two-strap shoes on a wall in a Berlin museum dated 1952. The same mural also shows another boy and girl wearing single-strap shoes. The clothes they wear appear to be East German Pioneer uniforms. Thus, the two-strap shoe may have been more popular in Communistic East Germany (circa 1950s) than in other parts of the world.

In the 1960s there was a revival of the double-strap style for women, but no evidence was found of this style being available in men's sizes until the twenty-first century, a hundred years after they appeared for men in the 1912 Sears catalog. After the mid-1900s, especially in North America, twin-strap shoes were generally advertised as girls' shoes, and this would have discouraged usage by men and boys. By the mid-1900s buckles had also replaced earlier buttons to fasten the shoes.

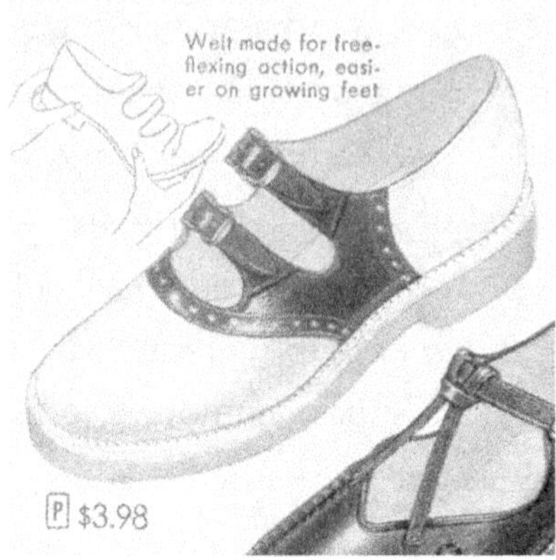

Figure 3-8
Merry double straps, 1953

An interesting variation of the double-strap shoe that appeared in the late 1940s and early 1950s was a hybrid with the saddle shoe which was very popular at that time. The Sears 1953 catalog called it "The Merry Double Straps" (Figure 3-8).[11]

Actually, saddle shoes were created by the Spalding Company in 1906 as the "first athletic shoe." The saddle, sometimes called a "strap saddle," was the darker portion that extended over the instep. This strap was sewn on top of the shoe and acted as a girdle to firmly support the foot during rapid side-to-side motions, as in a game of tennis. Early Sears catalogs sold an item that laced up the front of the foot as a "Hackey Ankle Support," patented May 24, 1887.[12] Possibly this extra support could have been the inspiration for the original saddle-shoe design. Sears first advertised saddle shoes in 1915 within the athletic shoe section of its catalog as tennis shoes and were available only in men's sizes. Saddle shoes, while beyond the scope of this book, are an example of how a shoe originally marketed to men later became adapted for wear by women and children.

A revival of the two-strap style occurred in 2009 when male models appeared on the New York fashion runway as part of the Givenchy Spring Collection. Together with their twin-strap shoes, the models also wore short pants outfits and modified leggings which extended below their pants, reminiscent of pantalettes that were worn in the 1800s.

Other men wore shoes in the collection that had either additional straps extending up the leg to resemble a gladiator sandal, or socks and leggings gathered to resemble the horizontal straps of the high-top sandals worn by other models in the Givenchy show. All of the models in the Givenchy menswear show in 2009 wore socks with their two-strap shoes, which in the US has traditionally been seen as taboo. However, since Mary Jane–type shoes are no longer referred to as sandals, it would now appear acceptable to wear socks with the style. But, according to photographic records, footwear with socks, whether called "sandals" or "slippers," was common. In the twenty-first century, more and more men can be seen wearing socks with closed-toe or sandal/sneaker hybrid shoes rather than the popular open-toe varieties (i.e. flip-flops). And recent archaeological discoveries show that the Romans wore socklike articles with their sandals during colder weather.[13]

Male models wearing strap shoes in Givenchy's 2009 spring collection and Dior's 2006 and 2007 shows may have been just the encouragement such companies as Finn Comfort in Germany needed to introduce two-strap shoes on their men's shoe pages. These strap shoes were called "Jerez," and came in ebony or black. They had two hook-and-loop fastening straps for a modern look and an adjustable fit rather than buckles on the straps. They were fashioned like the Givenchy models' shoes. The Finn Comfort's shoes retailed for $304.95 a pair in December 2008 at Shoebuy.com under the category "Men's Mary Janes." The title was later changed to "Men's Adjustable Strap Shoes" after receiving our correspondence. This same shoe was also available on Shoebuy's women's page, making it a unisex style. ShoeDeals4U.com offered a "Dr. Martens Men's Club Mary Jane" twin strap in 2008 at the same time as the Givenchy Spring 2009 collection mentioned above. As with the Finn Comfort twin straps, these shoes were also found on the Dr. Martens women's page. In fact, many of the

Dr. Martens footwear are unisex because they have both male and female sizes printed on the inside of the shoes and on the outside of the boxes. Thus, while the majority of advertisements for the two-straps Mary Jane has been targeted to women and children during most of the twentieth century, some European companies, like Finn Comfort and Dr. Martens, are once again making the two straps available to men who wish to wear them in the twenty-first century. However, if men choose not to buy them in large numbers, the companies have covered themselves by having twin straps also listed on the women's ad pages. It should be remembered that women are the ones who have bought most of these companies' Mary Jane shoes since the Renaissance time period.

A two-strap shoe reproduction of fifteenth- and sixteenth-century footwear originally worn by German Swiss mercenary soldiers similar to the single-strap version was also marketed in 2010 by Harr Shoes of Ravensburg, Germany, a firm specializing in Renaissance footwear. These shoes were called "Kuhmaulschuh," which means "cow mouth" shoes. They were also known as "bear paw" shoes with slits on the vamp so that the wearer could show off the colorful hose worn with them. They could be ordered from Harr Shoes in various colors and sizes at $69.95 a pair in 2010.

Three-Strap Styles:
From the 1800s to the Present

The only example of three-strap closed-toe shoes found in historical searches of the nineteenth century was an albumen image of a child wearing a pair dating from the 1860s. While the photo of the child is not very clear, the detail of the shoe straps is quite visible. Albumen photography in the mid-1800s was state of the art, using a coating obtained from chicken eggs to give a good resolution to the images. But, over time, the albumen cracked so that photos tended to fade or stain. During much of the twentieth century, as seen in various catalogs and newspaper advertisements, three-strap sandals were commonly called "Roman sandals." The style must have existed somewhere over the millennia, since it appears to be a descendent of the Roman carbatina. The absence of images of three-strap sandals may be because they were not very popular compared to the single- and twin-strap versions. As with other carbatina, this one fastened to the foot by passing strips of leather or ribbons through openings punched in the leather, similar to the one- and two-strap versions. There was no way to determine when and by whom the name "Roman sandal" was assigned to the three-strap sandal because it is often difficult to distinguish between what is a sandal and what is a shoe, especially in the case of closed-toe sandals, so these terms are used interchangeably. If footwear had straps and open areas on top, they were referred to as sandals in catalogs and ads dating from the late 1800s and early 1900s. And, if shoes had three or more straps, they were usually referred to as "Roman sandals" in the ads. For example, an ad containing only words in the *Chicago Daily Tribune* edition of April 6, 1884, states in part: "latest advice from Paris in regard to foot dressing in the mode par excellence is that of wearing Roman Sandals of plain black satin." The *Brisbane Courier*, in Brisbane, Australia, carried an ad on April 6, 1872, that mentions Roman sandals having "thick soles held in place by leather thongs." This was part of an article about the famous Roman slave Spartacus, but there was no illustration of these Roman sandals. The E. B. Orespin Company placed an ad for ladies' black three-bar shoes in the Wellington, New Zealand, *Evening Post*, on March 25, 1895. But six years later the three-strap shoe was called a "Roman sandal" in their ad on December 10, 1901. And, a year later, in November 1902 the *Evening Post* carried an ad placed by R. Hannah & Co. for "Men's Roman sandals." In each case, there were no illustrations, so these sandals could have had two, three, or even more straps. However, if ads can be considered evidence of proof, three-bar shoes were given the name "Roman sandals" in the late nineteenth century.

Assigning names to shoe styles has contributed to some degree of confusion for shoe research because in both Australia and North America, sandals were called "English sandals," but in the UK, they were called "Roman sandals." And "Roman sandals," as discussed above in North America, referred to the three-strap high-top sandal. This question of regional names with respect to sandals will be discussed in more detail in chapter 4.

Initially, it was assumed that closed-toe sandals in the form of single- and double-strap Mary Janes evolved from high-top sandals because of familiarity with the Hollywood high-top sandals portrayed in movies as being typical Roman footwear. Now, the author is not sure. This is because both high- and low-cut sandals coexisted during Roman times to serve different purposes. And, during Victorian and Edwardian times, multi-strap footwear became popular by adding more open areas between the straps to facilitate cooling the foot while still maintaining a high-top look, which was the prevailing shoe style. In any event, a hundred years later at the turn of the twenty-first century, fashion designers and shoe manufacturers rediscovered the Roman sandal. In the Sears 1897 catalog, there were no multi-strap shoes advertised. But in Sears's 1902 mail-order catalogs (page 920), there appears the first ad for an infant's three-strap Roman sandal. This three-strap Roman sandal continued to be advertised in Sears catalogs for fifty years. Figure 3-9 shows an example of a Sears advertisement from its 1950 catalog showing a three-strap Roman sandal.

In the twenty-first century, a Roman sandal was created by the Stylehive Co., which it called "Chloe." The company states that the shoe was a "three strap flat booty! Styled in ever so lightly textured 'crackle' leather; it has rounded toes and three buckle straps all the way up to the ankle. Very Cool." This shoe was priced at $615.00 a

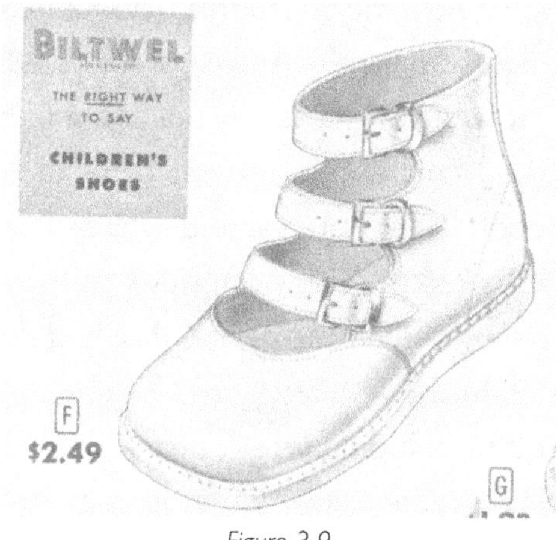

Figure 3-9
Sears Roman sandal, 1950

pair.[14] And, in 2010, a similar three-strap Polyvore Roman sandal was on sale for $560.00 a pair. Polyvore footwear is advertised for "trend-setters and tastemakers" who are generally female and twenty-two years of age.[15] For a revival of this style to take place, the price will have to be more affordable to mainstream buyers. It would appear this already happened, as seen in the Anglomania + Melissa three-strap by Vivienne Westwood in 2009, which was on sale for $36.00 a pair. Likewise, the Japanese firm T.U.K. had a three-strap shoe entitled "La Belle Doll" on its site in 2010 for $39.99 a pair. These shoes had classic two-bar styling with a third ankle strap added at the top.

Styles Having Four or More Straps: Ancient Times to the Present

The earliest multi-strapped, closed-toe footwear found in this research appeared in Wilcox's *The Mode in Footwear*, where it was reported to have been worn by an Assyrian king. This footwear was made of colored leather with encrusted jewels and was a low-cut style with four straps across the instep.

When the four-strap sandal reappeared in the late 1800s, it closely resembled the fashionable high-top shoes of that period. However, fastened by buckles and having an open appearance on the top and sides, it was called a "sandal" rather than a shoe or boot. This footwear must have been much easier to put on and take off than the standard fully enclosed high-button or laced shoes of the time period that had no zippers to ease the operation as do modern versions. By the early 1900s sandals had become quite fashionable. The Sears 1906 catalog carried an ad for a seven-strap ladies' shoe advertised as an "exact duplicate of the sandal worn by the leading prima donna in the past season. It [is] the most beautiful thing we had seen so here it is at one-third the cost of the theatrical boot makers [with] handsomely beaded cross straps [to] be worn in the house, at a party, or for dancing" at $2.13 a pair. This seven-strap shoe was expensive when compared to other shoes of the day that were selling as low as ninety-nine cents a pair for a single-strap "common sense sandal."[16]

Sears, in its 1906 catalog, had an ad for children's multi-strap sandals that states that there was a relationship between age, size, and the number of straps on a sandal in the case of those sandals having more than four straps. For example, a seven-strap, patent-leather sandal was available in the largest children's sizes 2 to 11½, while the six-strap version was found only in sizes 8½ to 11. The smallest shoe sizes for children, 5 to 8, had five straps.[17] Photos were found of boys and girls wearing these sandals with as many as nine straps. But for women it was difficult to determine the number of straps they wore because their feet were usually concealed by long skirts. The Sears 1911 catalog carried an ad for ladies' high-top sandals with nine straps (Figure 3-10).

The only pictures found of men wearing these high-top sandals were of strong men.

Figure 3-11 shows a 1905 photograph of a boy who is about two years old sitting on a chair with his cousin, about four or five years old, standing on the right. The cousin has a bow in his ringlet curls and wears a dress or, quite possibly, a Fauntleroy top with a skirt underneath. He wears a pair of four-strap shoes on his feet. The young cousin has not yet been breeched while the boy in Figure 3-12 has already passed through this "rite of passage." The sandals remained the same both before and after breeching.

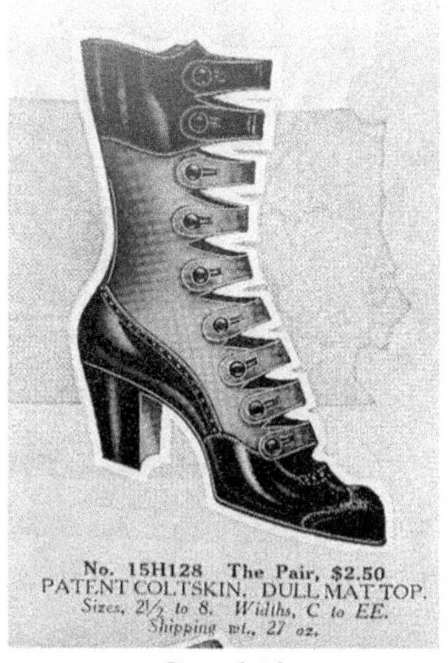

Figure 3-10
Ladies' nine-strap shoe, 1911

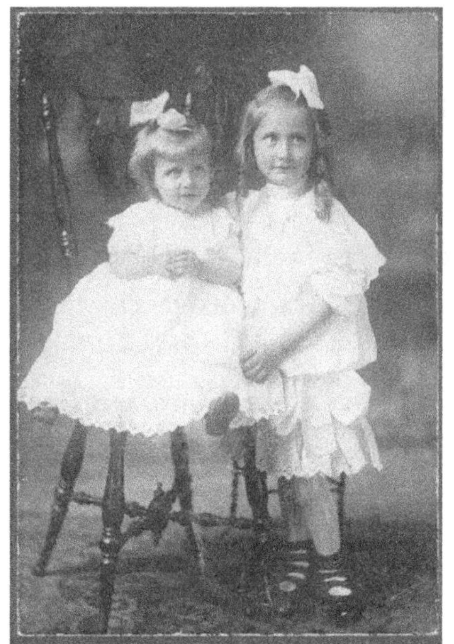

Figure 3-11
Boy wearing four-strap shoes
with dress, 1905

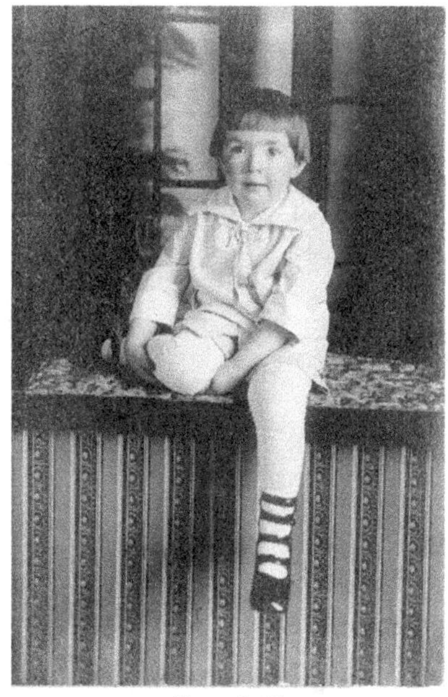

Figure 3-12
Boy with four-strap sandals and more typical
boys' clothes, ca. 1910

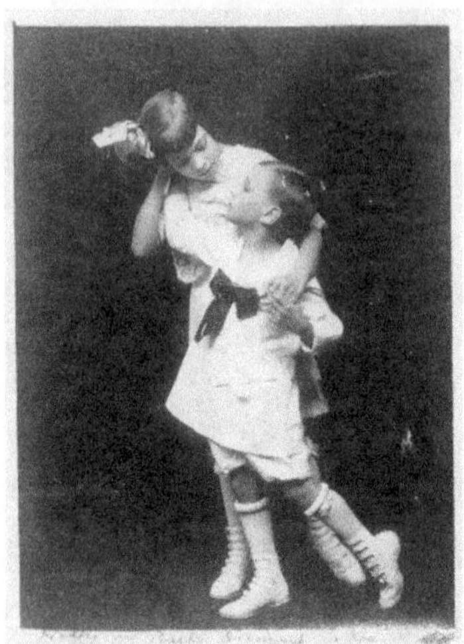

Figure 3-13

Two children dancing the tango wearing six-strap shoes, 1911

Figure 3-13 shows a photo of two children dancing the popular tango at the time of World War I while wearing six-strap sandals. There was probably a limit to the number of straps a person wished to spend time fastening, aside from the aesthetic or fashion standpoint, especially without a zipper as found on modern boots. There were a total of eleven multi-strap shoes for children and four for ladies in the Sears 1911 catalog. None were available in men's sizes.

While high-top sandals kept the feet cooler, especially during the summer months, as the public adopted lower-cut shoes more and more after World War I, sandals with five or more bars tended to decline in popularity for adults. But these shoes continued to be worn by children for many more years as well as high-top shoes after it was no longer stylish for adults to wear them; eventually, only infants wore them. This is an example of footwear that had been originally worn by adults, and then continued to be worn by children, long after adults began to wear newer shoe styles. By 1939 Sears had four- and five-strap shoes only available in children's sizes after being discontinued in adult sizes. The five-strap version targeted to children was, according to Sears, "Just at the age when buckling these Roman Sandals is a big adventure and lots of fun. Growing ankles get needed support, just as from a regular hi-shoe." This five-strap shoe version was available in either black or white for only $1.19 a pair.[18]

An example of a ten-strap sandal is Jeffrey Campbell's Tiempo sandal that was for sale in 2009 at $158 a pair. This ten-strap sandal resembles the Victorian high-top sandals even though the heels are higher than the style available in the 1890s. Thus, the high-top sandal has gone full circle and is still having appeal after more than a hundred years.

The greatest number of straps found on a child's sandal was found in a photo dating from the 1880s or 1890s showing a boy wearing seven-strap shoes and dressed in a sailor suit. One might think the child is a girl because of the long ringlets, but Weidner (2009), who has studied thousands of images from this period, states that "girls did not wear trousers [at that time]. Thus, no matter how girlish a child in ringlets may look, if the child is wearing trousers, he is a boy."[19]

There appears to be a striking similarity between the boy's multi-strap sandals and those worn by strong men at the end of the nineteenth century. For example, Eugen Sandow (Figure 3-14) was a pioneer bodybuilder in the late 1800s and early 1900s and performed in circus sideshows, fairs, and other public events. During this time period he wore multi-horizontal-strapped sandals without a center supporting T-strap. But, by the turn of the twentieth century, Sandow added the center T-strap, possibly to appear more like a Roman gladiator, or for added support to his footwear. He may have also wished to change the appearance of his sandals because so many women and children had adopted his style, which became a symbol of hero worship at the turn of the twentieth century. Because of this change, it appears Sandow may have played a significant role to popularize the T-strap sandal designs. The double-T-strap sandal became available for adults as well as children in the early 1900s, and this style will be discussed in more detail in the next chapter.

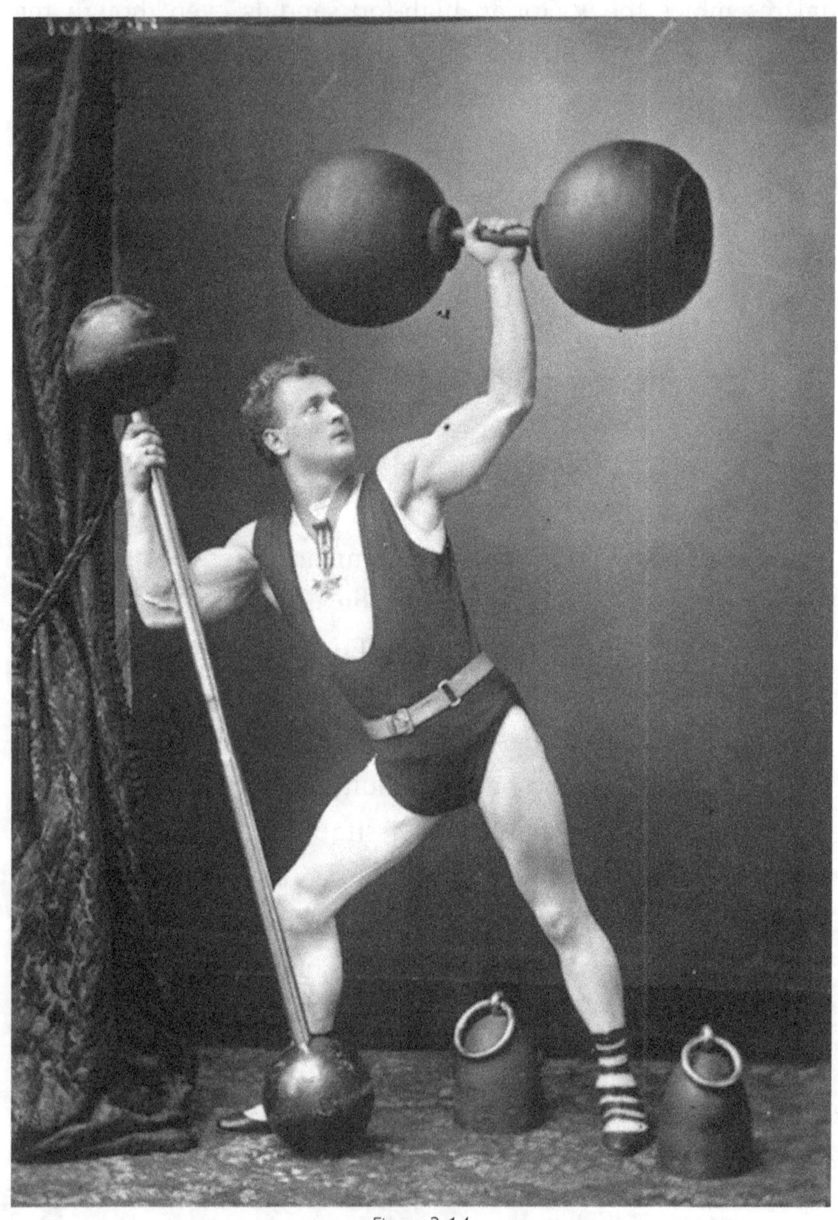

Figure 3-14
Eugene Sandow wearing six-strap sandals, 1889

Chapter 3 Notes

1. Bay State Slipper Co. advertisement, *Boot and Shoe Recorder*, vol. 79 (June 29, 1921), 102.
2. Ward, J., *Roman Era in Britain* (London: Methun Publishing, 1911), 244.
3. Curle, J., *A Roman Frontier Post and Its People* (1911), 150–52.
4. Baker, S. A., "Loosing a Shoe Latchet: Sandals and Footwear in the First Century," *BYU The Journal*, vol. 36, no.3 (1996–97), 196.
5. Norris, H., *Costume and Fashion*, 298–99.
6. Doctorow, E. L., *Ragtime* (New York: Random House, 1975).
7. Kippen, C., "Foot Talk" (December 21, 2005), foottalk.blogspot.com/2005/.
8. Weidner, D., "James Parvin Martin: Before Breeching," Historical Boys' Clothing (September 18, 2001), www.histclo.com/bio/op/m/bop-martinj1.html.
9. "Fashionable Footwear," *Saturday Evening Post*, Wellington, NZ, vol. LXIV, issue 84 (October 6, 1902).
10. Sears, Roebuck and Co. catalog, no. 119 (1909), 338.
11. Sears, Roebuck and Co. catalog, no. 200 (1953), 121.
12. Sears, Roebuck and Co. catalog, no. 111 (1902), 920.
13. Alleyne, R., "Romans wore socks with sandals," *The Telegraph* (April 21, 2010), www.telegraph.co.uk/news/science/science-news/7964516/Romans-wore-socks-with-sandals-new-British-dig-suggests.html.
14. "Chloe Crackle Triple Strap Flats – fashion gladiator," Stylehive (2007), (accessed August 1, 2007), stylehive.com/bookmark/128340.
15. Polyvore.com (accessed February 3, 2010), polyvore.com/cgi/business.
16. Sears, Roebuck and Co. catalog, no. 115 (1906), 925.
17. Ibid., 930.
18. Sears, Roebuck and Co. catalog, no. 176 (1939), 281.
19. Weidner, D., "U.S. Boys' Ringlet Curls: Clothing—Trousers and Pants," Historical Boys' Clothing (January 5, 2009), www.histclo.com/style/head/hair/curl/cou/us/clo/usrc-clob.html.

CHAPTER 4

ONE-STRAP SCHOOL SANDALS

The previous chapters consider single- and multi-strapped Mary Jane–style footwear through history. At some point in the distant past a center vertical T-strap was added to the basic design, extending from the vamp to the horizontal bar(s) that cross the instep or ankle. T-strap footwear has been called "fisherman sandals," "T-strap sandals," or "sand shoes," depending on geographical location. By the 1940s, T-strap sandals became very popular and assumed the name "school sandals" since they were required as part of school uniforms in the UK and elsewhere. Today, they are often advertised on the internet simply as "T-straps" or "Mary Janes." But many people still associate T-straps with Mary Janes because they have straps rather than laces for closure. In the twentieth century, geography appears to have influenced the sales of sandals, with the single-bar T-strap being more popular in Europe. In North America, the two-bar T-strap variety was more popular and called "barefoot sandals" or "English barefoot sandals." The term "English sandal" was not actually used in Britain, where ads used the words "Roman sandals." T-strap sandals with multiple horizontal straps are popularly called "gladiator sandals."

In addition to the number of horizontal straps found on T-strap sandals, cutouts and perforations were other important character-istics. These cutouts through the top, or vamp, of the shoe, originated during the Renaissance period when slits were commonly cut into the popular bear-paw shoes to better show off the colorful hose worn beneath. Footwear with perforations or cutouts on top fall more into the play sandal or school sandal categories, while those with plain toes without cutouts, popular from 1920 to 1950, were used more for dress-up or formal occasions. Both shoe types were advertised extensively in newspapers, magazines, and catalogs.

Purpose of the T-Strap

The author feels that the extra center strap was added to give more strength to the sandal as well as provide better fit and sup-port. Additionally, the vertical "T" provided protection for the foot. According to shoe historian Kippen (2003), the "T" portion of the shoe may actually have originated as a form of tongue, or *lingule*, that provided protection from the rubbing of laces or straps that crossed the instep or ankle. There could have also been an element of social status involved because the *lingule*, at least on Roman sandals, was considered "the mark of a free citizen."[1] Baker (2007), who studied Roman sandals extensively, character-izes footwear with a flat leather tongue or center strap as a "com-posite sandal."[2] And Egyptian sandals, which were open-toe style, also had a center T-strap feature that held them onto the foot by passing the T-strap between the large and second toe, as is found on modern-day flip-flops.

History of T-Strap Footwear

The earliest example of a closed-toe sandal having a center T-strap found in this research is an illustration in Wilcox's 1948 book, *The Mode of Footwear*, which has a number of straps crossing the instep and dates from the Median-Persian period 2,500 years ago. Thus, the T-strap in both closed- and open-toe styling have coexisted for three thousand years. But research could not determine whether the closed-toe T-strap sandals evolved as a modification of the Mary Jane, or vice versa, but they have not changed much in over a thousand years. An early example of a recognizable T-strap sandal dates from the ninth century and is of French origin.

Six hundred years later, during the fifteenth century, the French were still wearing T-strap footwear, although the toe portion was much longer, in keeping with the other footwear being worn during the medieval period in Europe (Figure 4-1).

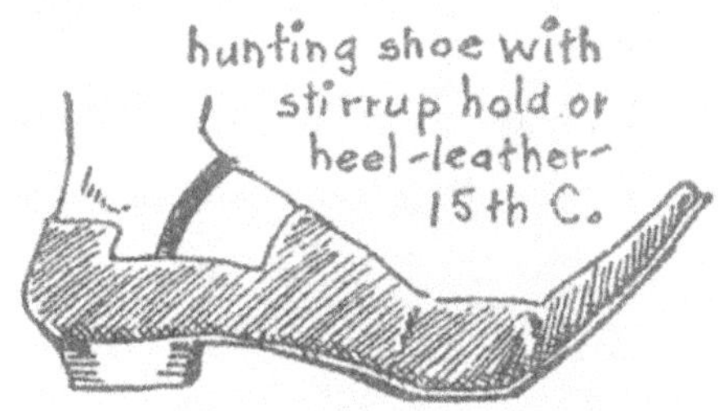

Figure 4-1
French T-strap, ca. 1400

Strap shoes were very fashionable during the 1600s and were worn by men, women, and children of all economic levels. An example of this is found in a portion of the painting *The Merry Company at Table*, painted by Dirck Hals in the 1620s. At that time many of the shoes had an ornamental bow or flower, called a shoe "rose," on the top where it joined the cross-strap. Some roses or rosettes were the price of an entire suit of clothes, making them very expensive. Shoe roses at this time were not popular with women, however, because they interfered with their long petticoats.[3]

Examples of T-strap footwear popular in the 1650s can be seen at the Bata Shoe Museum in Toronto, Canada. This four-story, award-winning museum has ten thousand shoes in its collection on a rotation basis, and, from an historical perspective, it is considered to have the best and most comprehensive shoe collection in the world.

Adult versions of the T-strap closed-toe sandal are often referred to as "fisherman sandals," possibly to make them more acceptable to male wearers rather than terms like "school sandals" or "Mary Jane shoes." The straps on fisherman sandals were originally fastened by leather latchets, and later by buttons or buckles. In recent years, hook-and-loop strips have become popular for closure.

The origin of fisherman sandals is unknown, but it is presumed that the individual for whom they were named lived somewhere along the Mediterranean Sea, where sandals were more suited to a warm climate. While worn by many adults, the T-strap sandal, like the basic Mary Jane, has more often been associated with school-age children, especially boys and girls attending English prep schools, but this may be changing with the advent of the mandal. From the outset of this research, it was assumed the origin of T-strap sandals was in the United Kingdom because of the term "English sandal," but this was proved to be incorrect.

The earliest catalog reference to a single-bar T-strap sandal was found in the Heath-Megargel Company catalog of Rochester, New York, which listed a basic T-strap in its fall styles 1907 catalog (Figure 4-2).[4] As with the original two-strap version, the sides are open and go completely down to the soles, while in later versions the side walls are elevated to keep out dirt and sand yet still maintain the overall appearance of a sandal.

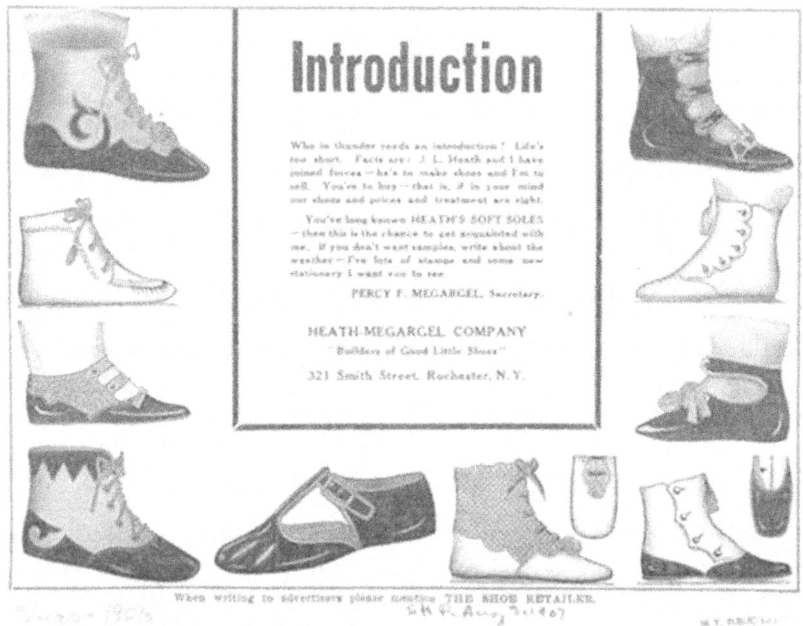

Figure 4-2
Early North American T-strap sandal, 1907

An illustration from the *Ladies Home Journal* in the same year, 1907, also shows a boy wearing T-strap sandals (Figure 4-3). According to the *Journal* article, the boy "is in for a good time and looks the thorough little man with his bloomer trousers underneath the one-piece suit."[5] In looking at this illustration, one might think the boy is dressed like a girl. But with the loose belt style, short "bloomer"-type pants underneath the sailor tunic, and short-style hair, there is no question it was a boy in the early 1900s. Also, girls at the turn of the twentieth century wore their hair in a

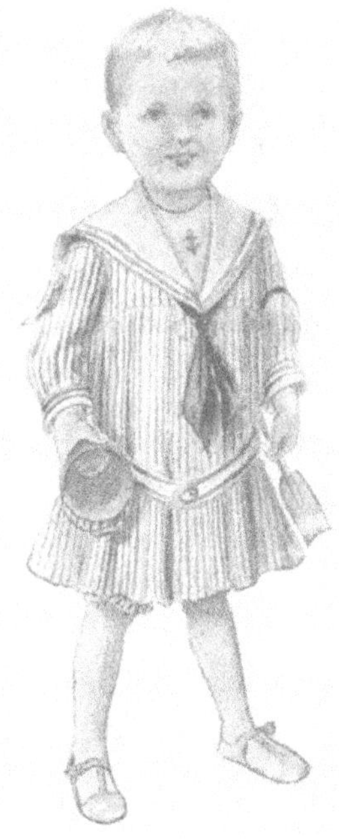

Figure 4-3
*Boy wearing T-strap
sandals, 1907*

longer style and would not have had a belt hanging down in front. Girls generally wore long dresses, as did their mothers, so as not to expose their legs, for modesty. Some say that children were dressed as miniature adults in their clothing.

The Aster Shoe Company has been making T-strap sandals since 1913 in France, called the "Aster Dingo," which in 2020 is still one of their best sellers. Clarks Shoe Company, Somerset, England, has long been associated with T-strap sandals, which it began making in 1937.

In 1972, Clarks discontinued one of its most popular T-straps called "Joyance sandals" after thirty-five years. But, in the early 1970s, T-strap sandals were still popular in children's footwear in the UK, as shown by an ad placed in the *South London Press* on April 20, 1971, by the James Webster Company, which had fully six examples of Clarks children's sandals. The headline read: "Going to be a Sandal Summer with Clarks."[6]

Clarks also made T-strap sandals in adult sizes early on, but by the end of its production of the popular Joyance style, they were only made up to a child's size 5. Subsequently, the company made T-straps with wider center straps for boys who in the 1970s began to identify the older Joyance style as being a girls' sandal. The company continued to make the narrow "T" versions for girls and younger boys, which were usually worn with short or long white socks. Eventually, the center straps became so wide that they began to look like tongues in regular closed-in shoes with less open area on top. As styles were reinvented, tongues again became narrower to allow the footwear better ventilation and to appear more like a sandal. Clarks Company has been making shoes since 1825 and operates the Clarks Shoe Museum near its manufacturing plant in Street (Somerset, England) and is open to the public.

While there are many examples of individuals wearing T-strap footwear in photographic records dating back to the early 1900s, few photos were found in this research showing any adult or child wearing them in the 1800s. On the other hand, there are many examples of individuals wearing single-strap Mary Jane shoes in the 1800s, as reported in previous chapters. This difference could be explained by the fact that T-strap sandals were not worn in formal pictures taken during

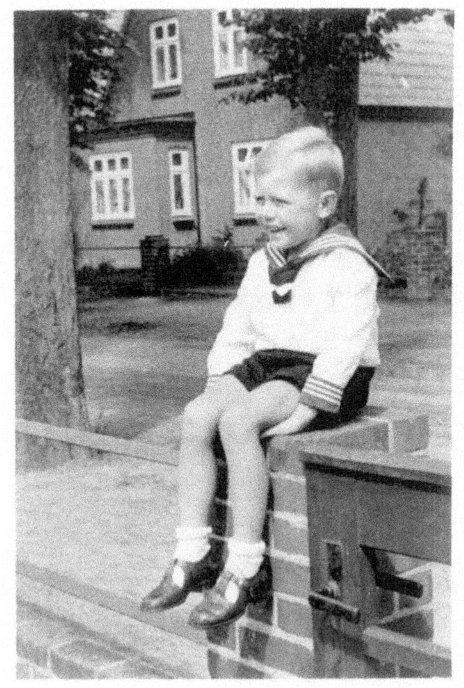

Figure 4-4

German boy wearing T-strap sandals, Early 1900s

Victorian times. Most formal portraits of this time period show people wearing high-top shoes, and to a lesser extent single- or multiple-strap shoes, rather than T-strap sandals. Figure 4-4 shows a German boy wearing a pair in the early 1900s with a popular sailor suit.

Where Did T-Strap Sandals Originate?

Footwear with central T-straps has existed for several thousand years in Egypt, Persia, and elsewhere in the ancient world. Most of these had open toes, often referred to today as "Jesus sandals." The modern single-strap school sandal is likely to be Roman in origin, judging by the evidence discussed in chapters 1 through 3. A closer examination of the Roman shoe found at the

Chesters Roman Fort and Museum, between England and Scotland adjacent to Hadrian's Wall, shows that it has a partial "T" extending from the vamp to the lower horizontal strap. One can make the argument or assumption that modern T-strap sandals were derived from this Roman carbatina-type shoe, and could indeed be called "English sandals," because this one was found in the northernmost part of England. But assigning this name is not so simple.

According to Ward (1911), the carbatina-type footwear was the forerunner of the modern closed-toe strap shoes so common in much of Europe that was brought by the Roman soldiers into the areas they conquered. He reports that the carbatina style had survived through the ages and was in 1911 still in use by Carpathian hill men as well as Italian, Romanian, and Bulgarian peasants.[7] This opened a new direction to follow in the search for the origin of T-straps, since a double-T-strap sandal was found in the 1914 Montgomery Ward catalog that was specifically called a "Bulgarian sandal." In both Romania and Bulgaria, a number of single- and double-T-strap shoes can be seen in museums, as well as worn by people dressed in ethnic costumes as part of folkloric dance groups. At a live folkloric dinner dance show in Sofia, the capital of Bulgaria, in 2006, Bulgarian dancers wore single- and double-T-strap sandals as part of their stage costumes.

Anthropologist Elizabeth Mellish, Ph.D., has researched extensively peasant costumes and footwear in the Balkans and Central Europe. She wore single-bar T-strap sandals to school as a child from the ages of four to eleven. She states that peasants in the Balkans continue to dress in the same traditional style clothing, including the single-bar T-strap sandals, as they have for centuries.[8] Prior to the eighteenth century, single- and double-T-strap sandals were made by the peasants themselves. But in the 1700s local cobblers began to appear in many villages of Europe who were specialized craftsmen who served the footwear needs of the villagers. These cobblers were eventually replaced by "industrial and urban shoemakers" between the eighteenth and twentieth centuries, when footwear became increasingly mass-produced in factories. However, in many rural areas of Romania and Bulgaria, peasants continued to make their own footwear, especially the Macedonian shepherds.[9]

Sandals in Bulgaria that enclosed the entire foot were found to give better protection in inclement weather than more open types. They also featured a shoe tongue with slits that evolved into the T-strap, whereby a cord could be passed through the slit to tie the sandal to the foot. In the early 1900s a second strap was added across the foot and fastened with a buckle.[10] These sandals are referred to as "opinci" in Romania and "tsarvouli" in Bulgaria, with various spellings depending on location and translation from the Cyrillic alphabet used in Bulgaria. The Latin alphabet is used in Romania.

Dr. Mellish (2006) notes that figures of the Dacians, early inhabitants of the Roman province of Dacia, which included much of present-day Romania and Bulgaria, were carved on Trajan's Column in Rome wearing opinci-type sandals.[11] This column is 125 feet high and 13 feet wide and was erected by Emperor Trajan in 113 AD to celebrate the Roman conquest of the Dacians. With the intermingling of customs of ethnic groups in ancient times, it was difficult to ascertain if the Roman carbatina-style sandals were influenced by Dacian footwear, or vice versa. In any event, these tsarvouli and opinci sandals have been worn for generations and are still being made today. Currently, these sandals are produced for tourists or folkloric dance groups to recreate the past.

In 2009, Balkanfolk.com sold traditional tsarvouli two-strap sandals with only the top strap having a buckle, up to European size 46, which is a man's size 12 in North America. The ad stated that the sandals were "the most typical shoes to almost all ethnographical regions in Bulgaria and made of real calf leather and are comfortable for dancing." An additional sole of artificial material is added to the sandal so it won't wear "out too fast." The cost of these sandals in April 2009 ranged from $51.48 to $59.40 US dollars depending on the size.[12]

A photo appearing on the Historical Boys' Clothing website shows Bulgarian students who are part of a choral and dance group marching in a parade in the early 2000s. This group was formed in 1968 and has some three hundred members. The girls wore traditional costumes with Mary Jane single-strap shoes, while the boys wore single-bar T-strap sandals. Besides Bulgarians and Romanians displaying T-strap footwear for special events, Croatia also had male and female folkloric dancers performing in an outdoor theater in Dubrovnik wearing T-strap footwear in 2008. And in one dance both men and women wore identical beige single-bar T-strap sandals.

The Ottoman Turks occupied much of the Balkans, including Romania and Bulgaria, and exerted an influence on clothing. The Turks were expelled during the Balkan Wars of the early 1900s. Interestingly, thin sandals worn by many Bulgarian soldiers may have played a role in the Balkan Wars, as the Bulgarian soldiers could outmarch and outmaneuver the Turks, who wore heavy, cumbersome boots that came almost to their knees. Eventually, the sandals were replaced by boots imported from Germany because they were more durable.

As an added interest regarding military sandals, there was a proposal presented to Abraham Lincoln in 1863 to provide Union soldiers with sandals to ease the pain in their feet caused by sores from marching countless miles. E. Harmon in correspondence with the president proposed to supply two million pairs of "patent military sandals," which he felt would "increase the mobility and consequent efficiency of the army at least 25 percent." Lincoln approved the proposal and sent it to the War Department, where it stayed until resurfacing in 1864. Dr. J. Rutherford Worster was asked by Lincoln to take a pair of the sandals to the front lines at Petersburg so General Grant could try them on. However, Grant wrote back to Lincoln declining the offer because his soldiers were not doing much marching at Petersburg and they were "fit" and had no need of the sandals.[13] Unfortunately, the author could not find an illustration of these military sandals in the correspondence, but it is interesting to speculate on what impact the wearing of sandals by the soldiers would have had on sandal usage in the US, a hundred years before they were rediscovered in the 1960s.

Reasons for the Popularity of T-Strap Sandals

Why did the basic T-strap sandal become so popular during the first half of the twentieth century that it was often the required footwear for school uniforms at many preparatory schools in the UK? Some parents, from an aesthetic point of view, may have liked the overall appearance of their children wearing sandals. Other parents may have felt that because sandals had more area open to the air than either the Oxford or high-top shoe, they were thus healthier for children to wear. Some experts claimed children's feet tended to sweat more than adults. Other authorities felt it was best for children to go barefoot, as foot problems were created by wearing shoes. So "children should be encouraged to play unshod [or] with slippers and sandals [since this is] less harmful than closed-toe shoes."[14] Bob, a UK resident interviewed for this book, says that T-strap sandals were common in the 1960s in the UK: "I wore T-strap sandals until I was ten or eleven because my mother thought they were sensible footwear for young children. Mum thought darker colors were more appropriate for boys' sandals, but my friend's young brother wore white ones." He reported in 2009 that shoe retailers in the UK believed that T-bar sandals were a unisex style, and that red and blue were "considered gender-neutral colours."[15] With regard to color, boys for the most part preferred to wear brown sandals, while girls wore red and blue, as well as brown. Paul, a boy who contributed information to the Historical Boys' Clothing website in 1999, reports that his sandals when he was a boy were "invariably brown" and worn *with* socks. There was absolutely no need to specify the color when his mother took him shoe shopping, as shoe clerks knew exactly what color to bring from the stockroom. He states that "any attempt to make me wear girly colored sandals would have led to an all-out rebellion."[16] An examination of the photographic record reveals that children started wearing sandals to school in the 1920s and 1930s in the UK, but they were not part of a uniform code at that time. By the middle of the twentieth century, as sandal usage continued to increase, they became so common that the term "school sandal" was applied to them and they were worn by both boys and girls of all social classes. During this time period boys usually wore sandals with short pants, for it was commonly believed that very short pants plus sandals promoted discipline. In Scotland, some boys also wore sandals with kilts. One boy said he wore sandals with a kilt to school, and in the summer months for most of his younger life in more casual settings, he wore short socks and sandals with his kilt.[17] Weidner (2005) reports that the double-bar T-strap sandal was popular in Scotland as school footwear as well as the single-bar style.[18] He also notes that by the later 1970s and 1980s sandals began to be replaced by sneakers for boys.

The replacing of T-strap sandals by sneakers appears to have occurred earlier in North America, for by the 1980s sandals were increasingly associated with private schools, which contributed to this footwear being viewed as being only for affluent children. But, once this style became known as a "sports sandal," its popularity increased dramatically to the point that it was worn on the East Coast as mainstream footwear. This is another example of a name affecting the popularity of sandals. Thus, sandals began to compete with sneakers. Weidner reports that similar open-toed sandals were often created by parents who cut out the toe area to allow a child to wear them longer than would ordinarily be possible. However, he said that few boys would have worn such modified sandals unless through utter necessity.[19]

Single-bar T-strap sandals were also popular in other countries of Europe as well as Australia, New Zealand, and South Africa. They were not as popular in North America, where the twin-strap version was favored. While there are many photos of children wearing T-straps in Germany, Weidner says that T-strap sandals for boys were discouraged during the Nazi era because they were either considered too feminine or because they were called "English sandals" and not to be worn with Hitler Youth Organization uniforms. Some small boys did wear them, as shown in Figure 4-4. On the other hand, there were also many pictures found of Mary Jane single-strap shoes worn by German boys during the Nazi era in the 1930s and 1940s, and these apparently were not considered feminine at that time.

While the photographic record shows T-strap sandals were worn primarily by children, these sandals were also seen on adults, but to a lesser extent. A strong man athlete named Paulopitz wore a pair in the 1930s. Most strong men in the late 1800s and early 1900s wore high-top gladiator-type footwear with or without the center T-strap as part of their uniform.

Recent Trends

Traditional closed-toe T-strap sandals declined in popularity among children around the world during the latter decades of the twentieth century, largely because of the trend toward wearing sneakers. However, based on observations, T-strap sandals appear to be increasingly worn in the 2000s.

Companies like Start-rite and Clarks in the UK and Cyrillus in France still produce T-strap sandals in children's sizes. Ann from Cyrillus reported in 2010 that these sandals were still being worn by boys, but for special occasions (i.e. christenings and weddings).[20]

Notwithstanding the wider center straps for boys, the overall design of a T-strap sandal is basically the same for boys and girls. However, some advertisers assign masculine names like "Buster" or "Brigand" to boys' sandals and feminine names such as "Grace" or "Lisbeth" to those targeted for girls.[21] The assignment of such names to guide the consumer as to which style is appropriate for men and women often leads to some confusion. In the US, J-Ray Shoes of Mobile, Alabama, has tried to avoid this confusion by offering T-strap sandals in five colors called "Lamour T-strap" for boys and the same five different-colored sandals on a separate page for girls with the same gender-neutral name. Keds also lists a white T-strap sandal as gender-neutral "Champion." Based on an internet poll, few people actually find such gender-based names useful in selecting footwear.

In the 1960s the popular Clarks Joyance sandal was specifically advertised for boys. The ad shows a boy climbing a tree asking, "Seen any leopards lately?" The ad shows his "special leopard-hunting sandals." By the end of the twentieth century, such sandals would likely be advertised to girls as a type of Mary Jane because of the straps and lack of interest by boys at that time.

In May 2010 a Google search of T-strap sandals revealed that the vast majority of "hits" found were girls' shoes with feminine names applied to each pair to guide purchasers in the direction of the proper gender selection. Girls' styles closely resembled the traditional T-strap sandal but with a narrow center strap and cut-outs on the vamp as made by Clarks, Start-rite, and others over the years. However, there was a new trend toward a marriage of sandals with features of sneakers to incorporate the best of both into a hybrid. These shoes are unisex in style with gender-neutral names like "Mad River" or "Little Harbor," with color being the key indicator of whether the shoe is for a boy or girl. There were a number of T-strap sandals that fell into this hybrid category. Many of these sandals look rugged and have male names like "Bob" and "Patrick" assigned to them. For example, Primigi, a footwear company in Italy, offered a navy canvas/leather boy's T-strap shoe in 2010 named "Drake" that the ad copy said was "perfect for active little boys."

The Start-rite Shoe Company, formerly Southhall established in 1792, continued to manufacture T-strap sandals in the 2010s. This shoe company supplied shoes for children of the royal family for generations. In fact, they received a royal warrant by Queen Elizabeth in 1955.[22] And, to celebrate their two-hundred-year anniversary as a family shoe business, the company published a book entitled *Two Centuries of Shoemaking: Start-rite, 1792–1992*, by journalist Ken Holmes. Few company records exist from the 1800s other than some catalogs and newspaper ads, but Holmes found one catalog that stated the family business "was making sandals and shoes for children during much of the nineteenth century."[23] However, there was no picture of the sandals, so it is not known if they were T-straps or the more common single-bar shoe, also called a "sandal" at the time. Start-rite prided itself on the training given to its shoe-fitting staff. It also maintained a program to test its latest shoe styles at local schools to get feedback from children and parents.[24]

Holmes reports that there was a decline in the wearing of school sandals in the UK because of three major factors:

1. Relaxation in requirements by schools that students wear sandals as part of their school uniforms as opposed to trainers (sneakers)
2. The importation of lower-cost trainers (sneakers) made in developing countries
3. Demands by young people for "stylish shoes to reflect current fashion trends"[25]

Closed-toe T-strap sandals are still available for those who wish to purchase them, but these sandals have most often been worn by small children in recent years. In the 2010s there has been an increase in the number of T-strap closed-toe sandals available in adult sizes manufactured by companies like Dr. Martens, Naturalizer, Propét, and Finn Comfort. The German Finn Comfort company calls their sandal "Tundra," which was originally listed under the category of "Men's Mary Janes." When questioned about this name, the company changed the category to "Men's Adjustable Strap Sandals." Men's T-straps, like the Finn Comfort Tundra, became known as "fisherman sandals" in their ads, while the women's version, which looks the same as the men's, was placed under the heading of "Mary Jane shoes." Buckles for these sandals have given way to hook-and-loop closures for ease in fastening. Sometimes buckles are placed on top of the fastening straps for design purposes, but in this case they are nonfunctional. An ad for a "stylish" 2009 vegan unisex sandal, made in the UK by Ethical Wares, states the shoe was a "return of the closed-toe sandal." It was available in sizes 3 through 12 in the UK, or up to a men's size 13 in the US.[26]

In the 2000s there was a remarkable increase in the number of work shoes on the internet called "safety sandals." Many of these have twin hook-and-loop straps across a center "T." One had a single-strap style with a steel toecap called "Brenta S1 Safety Sandal." It was available from A1 Workwear in the UK.[27] Safety sandals appeared most frequently on northern European web pages. White versions were recommended for men and women employed in pharmaceutical and food-processing occupations. In April 2012 several Chinese and Indian manufacturers advertised the sale of safety sandals in wholesale quantities. This could result in the appearance of the style in cheaper prices in North American outlets and a revival of T-strap sandals for men.

In the past, most shoe styles first appeared as adult footwear, which were later downsized for children. With closed-toe T-straps appearing again for adults in the twenty-first century, following this rule, one could expect the style to become available for children also.

Princess Diana's sons wore T-strap sandals after they stopped wearing single-bar strap shoes when they began to attend school. Also, in recent years, there have been instances when certain celebrities have dressed their children in T-strap shoes. Actress Liz Hurley dressed her son, Damian, in single-bar shoes until he was old enough for school and then T-strap sandals. Damian was photographed at age five wearing his school uniform complete with cap, tie, and sandals in 2007. It is not known if the private school he attended required sandals as part of the uniform code, or whether this was an example of copying the royal princes who also wore them to school. In North America pictures were posted on the internet showing Donald Trump's son Baron wearing white T-strap sandals. His mother, European by birth, had no problem with him wearing T-strap shoes like those worn by royalty in foreign countries. Sandals were common for children when she was growing up. Baron's sandals had a wider center strap, similar to the ones made by Clarks of England. As more men wear sandals, one can assume that children will do so as well. Footwear with dinosaurs may be an exception to this rule, however.

In summary, one can conclude that while closed-toe T-strap footwear dates from antiquity, there were two periods when the style achieved its greatest popularity. This was during the 1600s, when they were worn with fancy shoe roses, and again in the 1900s when sandals became very popular as school footwear for children. Adult versions of the single-bar T-strap also were revived from time to time and are commonly referred to as "fisherman sandals," "safety sandals," "men's adjustable straps," or "Mary Janes" when targeted for women, according to research for this book.

The central strap became wider and wider during the latter half of the twentieth century to appeal to boys, who began to perceive sandals as feminine or juvenile. Thus, while girls continued to wear the style, sandals were eventually worn by very small boys, and then largely for special occasions such as weddings. Two major reasons for the decline in school sandals by the late 1900s were the increasing popularity of sneakers and the relaxing of the requirement that sandals be worn as part of school uniforms. But they continued to be worn by the children of royal families, including Princess Diana's sons, and by those emulating royal styles long after they were no longer fashionable by mainstream wearers. In 2019, Princess Diana's grandson, Prince George, wore navy canvas T-strap shoes for a photo taken on his third birthday. For Queen Elizabeth II's ninetieth birthday portrait, Prince George wore leather strap shoes and his sister, Princess Charlotte, wore T-strap shoes.

The creation of sandal/sneaker hybrids in various colors and fancy decorations is contributing to a revival of T-strap sandals for children in the 2000s, judging by internet ads and sightings in malls and elsewhere. Gender differences are based more on color rather than the design of the sandals. Also, safety sandal work shoes may increase interest in T-straps on the part of both adults and children. But they can still be found in the traditional leather style on internet sites in North America, the UK, and Australia. One of the findings of this research was that the style has been worn for two thousand years in the Balkans, and can still be seen on the feet of children and adults there. As with the Mary Jane style, T-strap sandals were not created as little girl or children's shoes, unless one considers those recent styles with dinosaurs and other decorations of interest to children.

Chapter 4 Notes

1. Kippen, C., "The History of Footwear: Sandals" (Curtin University of Technology Dept. of Podiatry, July 11, 2003), 9, web.archive.org/web/20030701025947/http://podiatry.curtin.edu.au/sandal.html.

2. Baker, S. A., 2007, 197.

3. Brooke, I., *Footwear: A Short History of European and American Shoes* (1972), 55.

4. Heath-Megargel Company, *Catalog of Shoes* (New York Public Library Collection, Fall 1907).

5. Weidner, D., *"Ladies Home Journal*: Good Taste and Bad Taste in Dressing Children in [June] 1907," Historical Boys' Clothing (May 26, 2007), histclo.com/country/us/chron/900/conv/1hj07-01b. (Available online through subscription only.)

6. Weidner, D., "Clarks Sandals: Sandal Summer [197]," Historical Boys' Clothing (April 21, 2009), histclo.com/Fashion/store/mail/cou/eng/chron/1970/71/foot/c71san. (Available online through subscription only.)

7. Ward, J., *Roman Era*, 245.

8. Mellish, E., "European Peasant Footwear," Eliznik (June 2006), eliznik.org.uk/traditions-in-romania/traditional-clothing/footwear/gallery-footwear/.

9. ———, "History of Costume Elements," Eliznik (August 2005), eliznik.org.uk/traditions-in-romania/traditional-clothing/history-of-clothing/.

10. Ibid.

11. Mellish, E., "European Peasant Footwear."

12. Yanakiev, P., "Traditional Bulgarian shoes in 2009," Balkanfolk, balkanfolk.com/shop-product-details.php?category_id=shoestarfvul&product.

13. "E. Harmon to Abraham Lincoln, Monday, January 19, 1863"; Letter from A. Lincoln to General U. S. Grant, June 29, 1864, *American Memory*, The Abraham Lincoln papers at the Library of Congress [Proposal to sell sandals to the Army] (accessed May 22, 2006), memory.loc.gov/cgi-bin/query.

14. "A Case for Bare Feet," Barefooters (September 24, 1999), www.barefooters.org/wp-content/uploads/2015/03/A-Case-for-Bare-Feet.pdf.

15. Email correspondence from Bob (August 24, 2009).

16. Weidner, D., "English School Sandals: Paul," Historical Boys' Clothing (October 25, 1999), histclo.com/Schun/gar/shoe/sandal/su-sandal9601. (Available online through subscription only.)

17. ———, "Open-toe Sandals," Historical Boys' Clothing (September 4, 2009), histclo.com/Style/foot/sandal/sandal-ot. (Available online through subscription only.)

18. ———, "Closed-toe Sandals: Country Trends—Scotland," Historical Boys' Clothing (May 10, 2005), www.histclo.com/style/foot/sandal/type/ct/cou/ctsc-scot.html. (Available online through subscription only.)

19. Ibid.

20. Email correspondence from Ann (July 12, 2010).

21. Weidner, D., "English School Sandals: Paul," Historical Boys' Clothing (November 10, 1999), www.histclo.com/schun/gar/shoe/sandal/su-sandale9601.html.

22. Holmes, K., *Two Centuries of Shoemaking: Start-rite, 1792–1992* (1992), 58.

23. Ibid., 35.

24. Ibid., 57.

25. Ibid., 91–92.

26. "Closed-Toe Sandal," Ethical Wares (2009), ethicalwares.com/142closedtoe-sandal.

27. "Brenta S1P SRC Safety Sandal – Cofra," A1 Workwear (2012).

CHAPTER 5

BAREFOOT SANDALS

The subject of this chapter is the T-strap sandal having two horizontal straps across the instep, frequently referred to as a "barefoot sandal." On the internet the term "barefoot sandals" reveals hundreds of examples of open-toe flip-flop sandals made largely of beads and jewels. But this was not always the case. For most of the twentieth century, the term "barefoot sandal" referred to a two-strap (bar) closed-toe sandal with a low heel, round toe, and center T-strap. Except for the second strap, placed closer to the toe, this style was similar to the classic T-strap sandal. Figure 5-1 shows a typical child's barefoot sandal, so popular during the twentieth century, which can still be found in current shoe styles.

A few years ago, while surfing the internet for Dr. Martens shoes, a two-bar T-strap style was found in *adult* sizes. It had been thought that this footwear was only available in children's sizes. Research showed that Dr. Martens had been marketing these shoes since 1990, but did not call them "barefoot sandals."

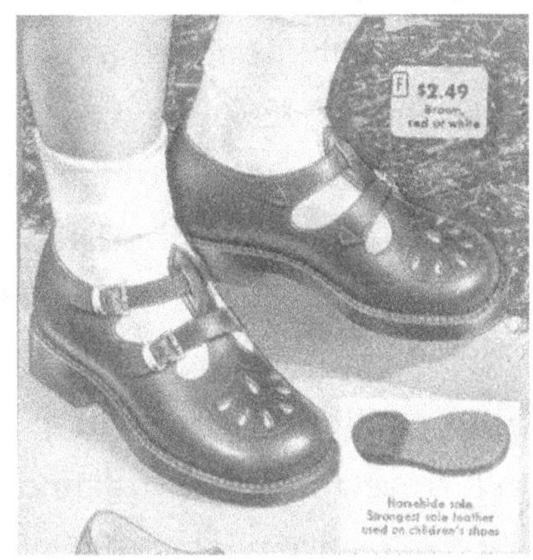

Figure 5-1

Child's barefoot sandal, 1950

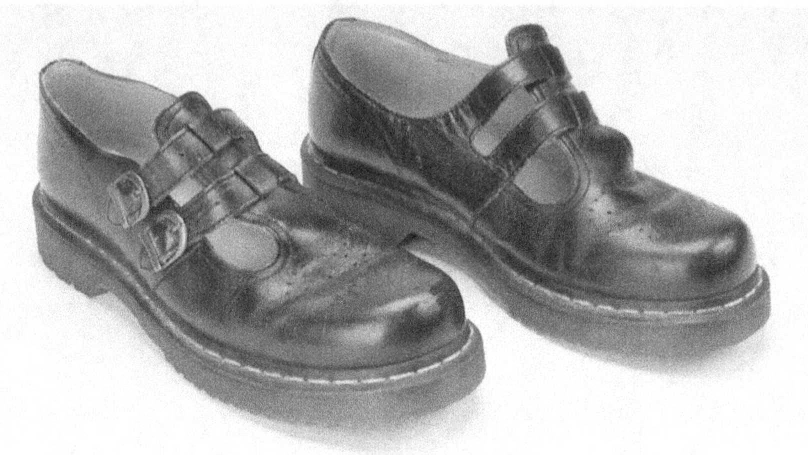

Figure 5-2
Adult Dr. Martens double T-strap shoes, 2009

They were listed as unisex with both men's and women's sizes printed on the box and inside the shoe for their US, UK, and European Union (EU) markets (Figure 5-2). On this basis, it appears difficult to justify the shoe as being solely a style worn by children. This raises the question as to whether the barefoot sandal originated as a child's shoe, and if so, during what time period? On the other hand, was the shoe originally an adult shoe that was subsequently worn by children, as was the case with other styles like the Mary Jane? Furthermore, if barefoot sandals were actually designed as children's shoes, and possibly even as little girls' shoes, why was Dr. Martens selling them as a unisex adult style? Upon further investigation, other advertisers were found that included this Dr. Martens style in the general category of Mary Jane shoes because of the characteristic straps over the instep that resemble the classic one-strap Mary Jane. And to many people, anything with a strap over the instep is a Mary Jane shoe. In the past, the style was almost uniformly called a "barefoot sandal," but since the late 1900s, it is often marketed as an "English sandal" because the original name "barefoot sandal" is used more and more to denote beaded flip-flop sandals. There is no consistency on its name because it is also advertised as an "Oxford," "Mary Jane Oxford," or "double T-strap" in addition to "English sandal." All these various names seemed very confusing, and in need of further discussion.

When Did the Double-T-Strap Design Originate?

Mr. Laventhal, the owner of a local shoe store in Trenton, New Jersey, commented that in the 1970s the barefoot sandal was the "longest continually running" style in his memory, going back almost a hundred years. Now, almost forty years since Mr. Laventhal made this comment, these "double T-straps are still available for those who wish to wear them."

As part of the research for the origin of barefoot sandals and to resolve the question of whether they were made for adults or children, countless hours were spent checking shoe images on the internet, including antique photo auctions, advertisements in old newspapers and magazines, and the microfilm collection at the Rutgers University Library in New Brunswick, New Jersey. Additionally, trips were taken to Europe in search of answers to the origin of the barefoot sandal.

Research showed that the classic barefoot sandal style was popular in the first half of the twentieth century, when it was worn by men, women, and children, and advertised in mail-order catalogs, such as the Montgomery Ward 1923 edition, as being for "the entire family." Literally thousands of photos were examined to establish the point of origin for the barefoot sandal. While most photo images lacked a date when the photo was taken, it was possible to establish a time period through the use of indirect observations of the clothing styles or objects such as cars or toys in the pictures. Information found in fashion magazines, newspapers, and catalogs of the same period was also consulted, and the end result was that it was possible to initially trace these sandals back to the turn of the twentieth century. Most surprising in the research was the fact that barefoot sandals appeared in widely diverse places in the US, Canada, New Zealand, and Australia all at that time period.

Tradition assumes that the barefoot sandal style appeared in only one place and then diffused from its point of origin to other geographic areas. But this is not correct! The style seems to have appeared simultaneously in various parts of the globe. This could have happened as a result of trade journals, international shoe expositions, and fashion shows, which did not limit a shoe style to a single geographic region. An early example of this premise was found in a Glenbow Archives Photographs image of two children wearing barefoot sandals in rural Dorothy, Alberta (near Calgary), Canada, between 1900 and 1903. The children were also wearing Buster Brown outfits, a common clothing style at the turn of the twentieth century, which further corroborates the time period.

Another example was a colorized photograph in the *New York World* magazine October 9, 1904, of the prominent Parker family that shows a boy and a girl wearing brown sandals (Figure 5-3). The boy is wearing a pink modified Buster Brown outfit, which was not perceived as a female color for that time. Retailers in the early twentieth century were kept informed of the latest styles regardless of their geographic location through fashion magazines, newspaper articles, and through shoe trade journals such as the *Boot and Shoe Recorder*, and the *Shoe Retailer*. An early 1900s edition of the *Boot and Shoe Recorder* found at the New York Public Library revealed it to be very sophisticated with respect to sales data, the latest shoe styles, and helpful shoe information for people in the industry. But there were also misleading claims that barefoot

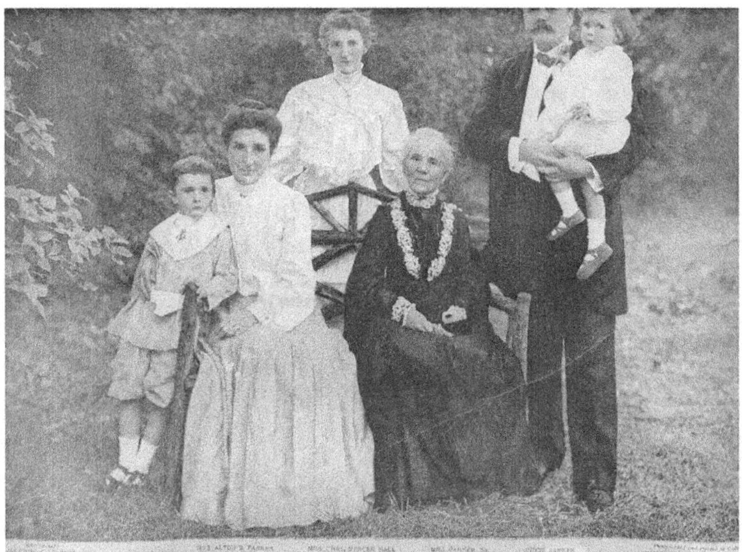

Figure 5-3
The Parker family, 1904

sandals were Victorian or Egyptian, and this made it difficult to trace the origin of the style. Online auctions showed barefoot sandal photos that sellers said dated from the Victorian era. After looking at thousands of images, it was not possible to authenticate two-strap barefoot sandals being worn in the 1800s using the photographic record. The question then appears to be, why did barefoot sandals appear for the first time about 1900 in separate locations? And where did these shoes originate?

It was hypothesized that mail-order catalogs might have been the main reason why barefoot sandals appeared simultaneously in widely separate areas. Perhaps this footwear was worn only in more casual settings, and, not being one's best shoes, were not seen in formal portraits. In fact, the November 1903 Bell, Walt & Co. Philadelphia, Pennsylvania, catalog lists barefoot sandals under the heading of "slippers," as they were considered an informal indoor sandal, not suitable for formal portraits.[1]

Technology may also have played an important role in the appearance of barefoot sandals at the turn of the twentieth century. For example, mass production of less expensive footwear through the introduction of modern machinery, such as stitching machines, enabled more people to afford barefoot sandals. Kippen (2004), a podiatrist and shoe historian, believed it would be "highly unlikely to find an innovative shoe style" in a place like rural North Dakota. Rather, an innovative shoe style would appear first in an urban area and then spread outward to more rural areas. Sandals could have been introduced into North America by immigrant cobblers, who subsequently moved to rural areas to make them for local people. Another idea could be that barefoot sandals were made by North American cobblers who saw immigrants wearing them and copied the style. However, it is more likely that these sandals were mass-produced as part of the industrial expansion of shoe factories occurring in North America, and then mass-marketed through trade journals and fashion magazines. This is because by 1900 traveling cobblers had largely disappeared.

The Rutgers University Alexander Library in New Brunswick, New Jersey, has a complete collection of several newspapers, including the *Newark Evening News*, on microfilm that was very helpful in the search for clues as to the origin of the barefoot sandal. Business ads for barefoot sandals were prolific because of their popularity. The first one found was from June 16, 1905. These early sandals had large cutouts on each side of the shoe that extended to the soles. The price ranged from $0.49 for a child's pair to $1.69 for a man's pair.[2] Figure 5-4 shows an advertisement from A. Alexander, New York.

These sandals being available in men's, women's, children's, and infants' sizes were a welcome alternative to the hot high-top footwear then in vogue. This may be the reason why they were called barefoot sandals in the first place, as they were cooler to wear and much easier to put on and take off than the high-top shoes. A case in point is the boy and girl shown playing harps in Figure 5-5. The boy wears a pair of barefoot sandals that required only buckling or unbuckling the top strap to put them on or take them

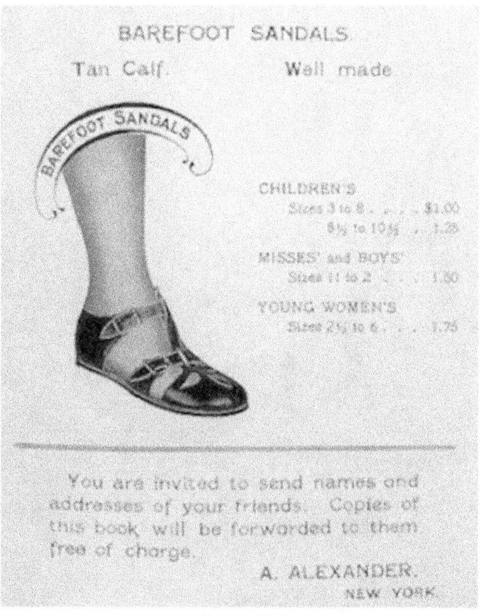

Figure 5-4

Barefoot sandal advertisement, ca. 1905

off. On the other hand, the girl on the right had to lace and unlace fifteen eyelets to perform the same function that the strap accomplished in the barefoot sandal. High-top button shoes could have taken even longer, because one had to use a tool called a "button hook" to fasten and unfasten the buttons. Is it any wonder, then, that these sandals became so popular when they first appeared in North America as alternative footwear, especially in hot summer weather?

Judging by newspaper advertisements, barefoot sandals were also available on the other side of the globe in the early 1900s. An ad dated October 6, 1902, appeared in the Wellington, New Zealand, *Evening Post,* where the sandals were sold by R. Hannah & Co. in a tan color in children's sizes.[3]

The *New York Times* on December 20, 1903, reported that English barefoot sandals were so successful as footwear for boys and girls at the seashore during "the last year or two" that local

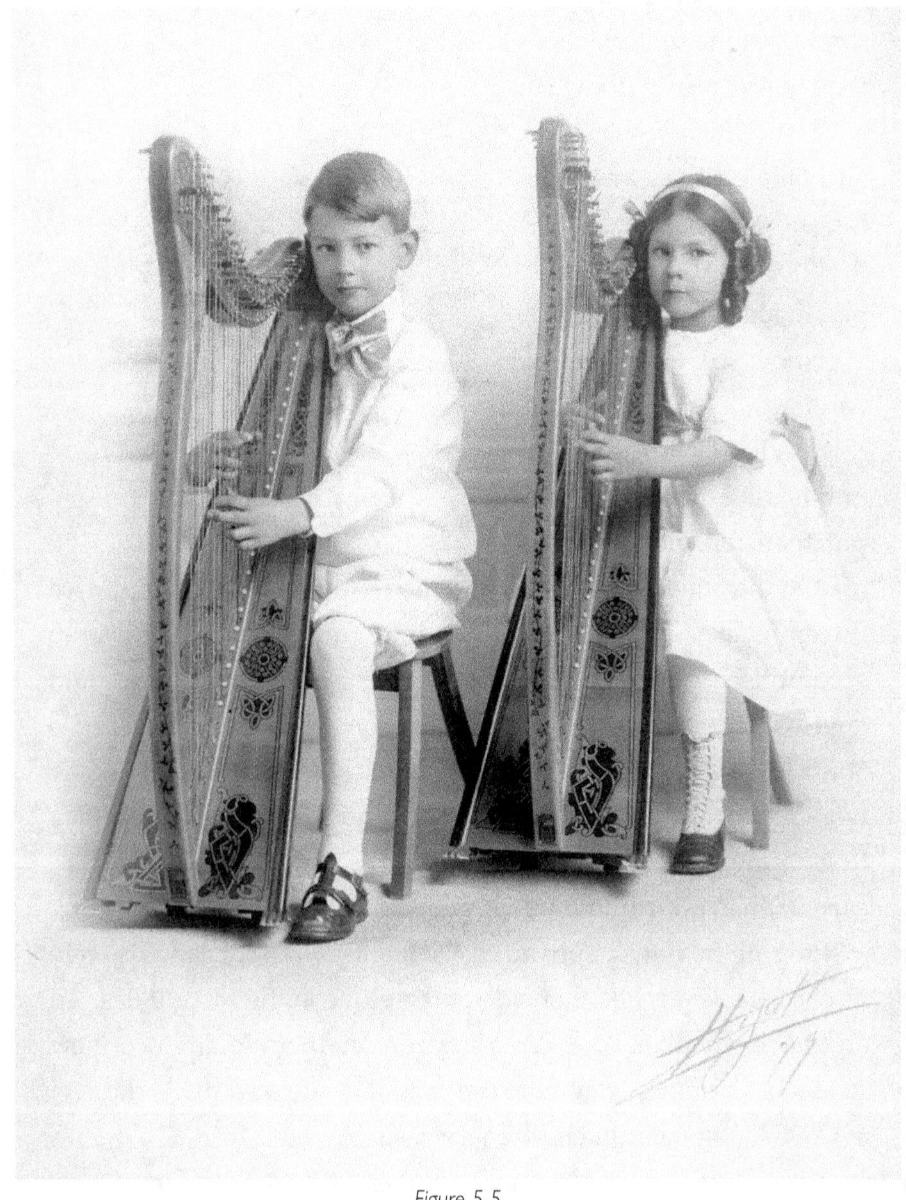

Figure 5-5
Children wearing barefoot sandals and high-top shoes, Early 1900s

supplies ran out. The article also stated that manufacturers would produce a greater supply in the forthcoming 1904 summer season to meet the demand. The sandals were made in the "original," or more open, style, with cutouts going down to the sole. The article went on to state that this design was later modified to provide for a "larger side guard than those commonly worn last year, so as to keep out the sand."[4] The *Daily Sun*, July 1905, in St. John, New Brunswick, Canada, reported a shortage of barefoot sandals which were the "rage of the hour," and that manufacturers "couldn't begin to satisfy the demand . . . for these useful and practical shoes."[5]

The earliest newspaper ad found in this research for a barefoot sandal appeared June 13, 1902, in the *Evening Herald* in Syracuse, New York.[6] All of these ads confirm that the style appeared in the early 1900s in widely separated geographic locations. Unfortunately, these newspaper articles do not shed any light on whether the shoe originated in England or elsewhere.

Barefoot sandals resemble the opinci sandals found in the Ethnic Museum in Bucharest, Romania. According to an attendant at the museum display, opinci sandals were common throughout the Balkans and date from the turn of the twentieth century. They were known by different names depending on the language used. They were, and still are, called "tsarvouli" in Bulgaria.

However, the Romanian sandals were different in that they had a slight upward rise to the pointed toe, reflecting a Turkish or earlier Byzantine influence on this footwear.

In their early history, barefoot sandals were considered unisex, as seen in the May 12, 1907, ad in the Frederick, Maryland, *News* that reported they were available in men's, women's, and children's sizes.[7] The degree of popularity of these sandals is unknown for children versus adults according to information for this time period at the turn of the twentieth century. However, since the sandals were available in adult men's and women's sizes until the 1920s, adults must have worn them, but it was surprising to find no examples of photos in the early 1900s of adults actually wearing them, other than a picture of a young man who undoubtedly took an adult size that was found dating from the 1920s or 1930s (Figure 5-6). The absence of men wearing sandals in photos could be explained by the fact that barefoot sandals had been used almost exclusively indoors as house slippers, and as such were considered too casual for formal portraits. Indeed, the *Syracuse Herald*, June 15, 1906, actually stated in an ad that "men's Barefoot Sandals [are] just right to wear in the house."[8] How many people would like to have formal pictures taken wearing their house slippers? One notable exception to this idea is a picture of Abraham Lincoln taken in the White House wearing his slippers upon removal of his heavy outdoor shoes. Research found no pictures of Abe wearing sandals, although he did approve the proposal to issue sandals to the Union soldiers to cure sore feet as discussed in the previous chapter.

There has always been a difference between outdoor and indoor shoes, which is still seen in different parts of the world. Currently, any gender can wear flip-flops, either indoors or outside, without giving them a second thought, but this was not the case at the turn of the twentieth century when roads were unpaved. According to Brooke (1972), strap shoes were in fact "indoor shoes."[9] She states that for much of the nineteenth century "walking [outdoors] was almost unknown," owing to the condition of roadways and quality of footwear at the time. When a person ventured outdoors, boots were the footwear of choice. And in colder weather one could be called "crazy" for not wearing high-top footwear outside.

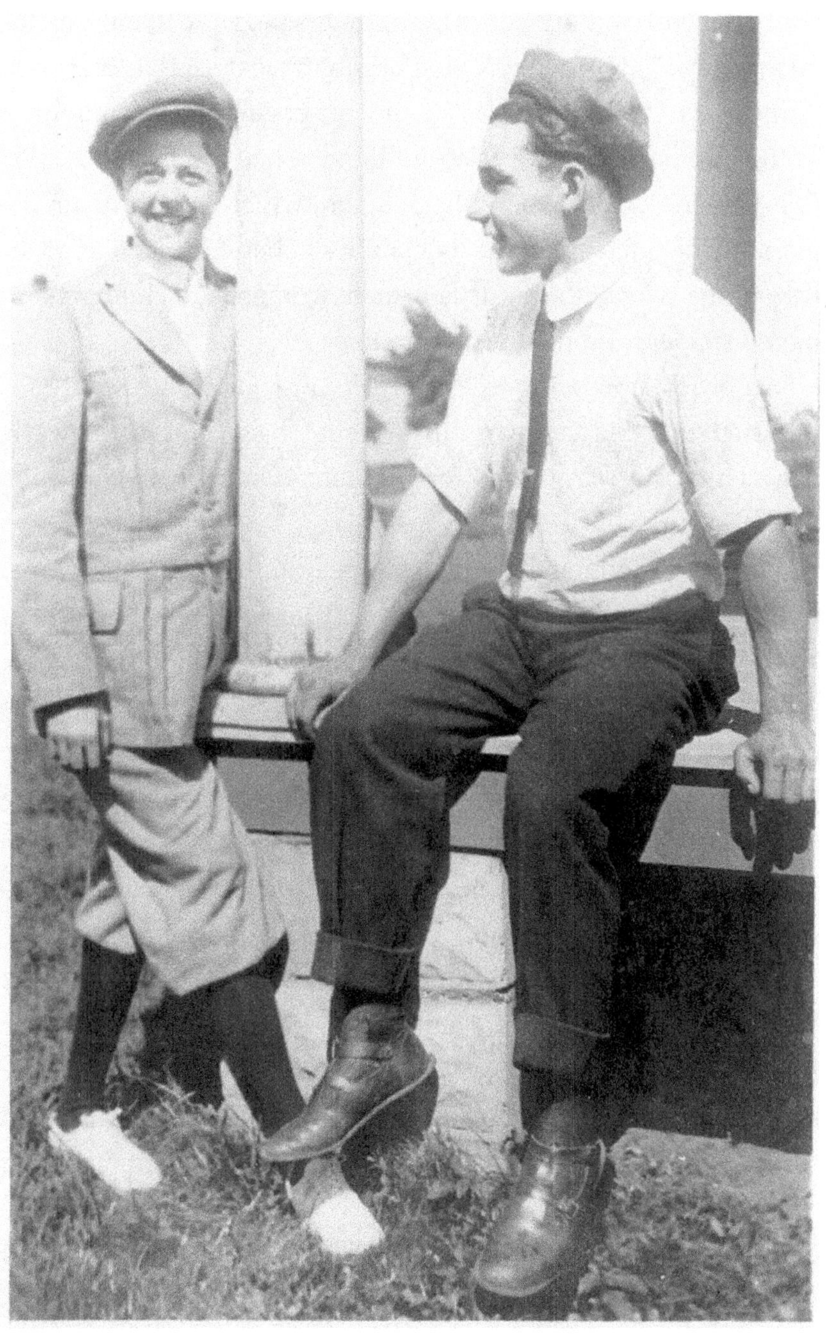

Figure 5-6
Young man wearing barefoot sandals, ca. 1920s–1930s

At the end of the Victorian era, things began to change as the "boot mania" subsided. Women began to wear sandals that were "products of local craftsmen" as people began to take an interest in the outdoors.[10] Mass-produced lighter shoes and sandals soon followed in response to public demand, which could explain the phenomenal increase in the availability of barefoot sandals at the turn of the twentieth century for men, women, and children seen in newspapers and mail-order catalogs.

An article appearing in the *Newark Evening News*, May 1904, reported that Macedonian "insurgents" had come to Newark, New Jersey, to raise funds for the liberation of their homeland from the Turks.[11]

Both male and female soldiers appear in the picture accompanying the article wearing a variation of the double-T-strap sandal and their legs were wrapped and tied in thongs. According to the article, the fundraising campaign began in Newark because of the colony of Macedonian immigrants living in that city. Then the group traveled to other locations around the country to raise more money. Their unique footwear could possibly have contributed to an increased interest in sandal usage in North America as people sought to copy a cooler alternative to their high-top footwear.

As was discussed, footwear of this type was light and credited by some with helping the Bulgarians defeat the Turks in the Balkan Wars of 1910 to 1913. In these wars the Turks wore heavy boots, which prevented them from moving as fast as the Bulgarian soldiers. A moderator and specialist in military uniforms dating from the early 1900s at Gunboards.com maintains that the Bulgarian sandals (tsarvouli) were issued to soldiers because of war shortages at the time, and the Bulgarians were victorious largely because of their high spirits and excellent officer's corps. Bulgarian soldiers also wore these sandals during World War I, but the sandals were eventually replaced with longer-lasting boots supplied by their ally, Germany.[12]

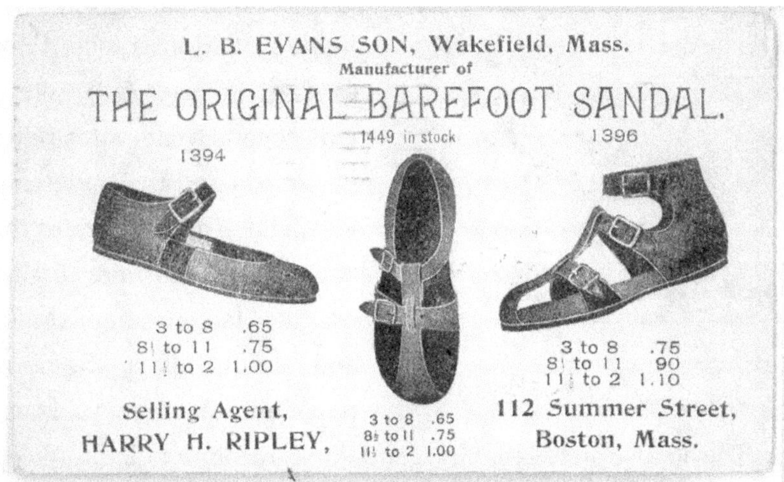

Figure 5-7

The original barefoot sandal, 1903

Research led to an early trade card advertising "Original Barefoot Sandals" printed on a postcard by Harry H. Ripley, selling agent for L. B. Evans & Son Shoe Company of Wakefield, Massachusetts (Figure 5-7). The company claimed on the back of the card to be the "Manufacturer of The Original Barefoot Sandal." The card was postmarked February 20, 1903, and had been issued as a memorial for President McKinley, who was assassinated in 1901. According to the *Scott Specialized Catalogue of United States Stamps*, the card was printed in 1902. Based on these findings, a date can be established for the "original barefoot sandal" at the end of 1902. Although not common, several examples of the "original" sandals were found in the photographic record of the early 1900s. As reported in the *New York Times* in 1903 discussed above, most of the subsequent barefoot sandals produced were of the "closed-in" variety to keep out sand and to better protect the foot.

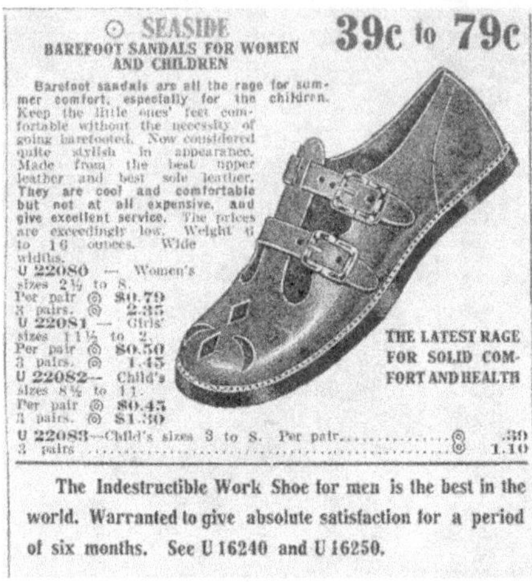

Figure 5-8

Barefoot sandals—the latest rage, 1910

The first advertisement found in a mail-order catalog for a barefoot sandal appeared in the 1910 Montgomery Ward catalog (Figure 5-8), which was several years after newspaper ads and the trade card. The catalog ad copy states that barefoot sandals were "the latest rage for summer comfort and health," just as the newspaper ads had a few years earlier. The ad also stated that the sandal was recommended for keeping the feet comfortable without "the necessity of going barefoot." Montgomery Ward used the following words in their ad about the sandals being "now considered quite stylish in appearance."[13] Further proof of this idea can be verified in a Sears, Roebuck and Co. ad of the same sandal in its 1911 catalog, as well as a Hayward Bros. Shoe Co. ad for the same year in Omaha, Nebraska. In 1913 Montgomery Ward added men's sizes to its ad for barefoot sandals, which sold for one dollar a pair. It stated that the sandal was "used everywhere for summer comfort."[14]

Geographically, the single-bar T-strap sandal discussed in the previous chapter was never as popular in North America in the early 1900s as the two-strap version. Even in Britain, the single-strap sandal was not popular until between the middle-to-late 1920s and early 1930s when it became part of required school uniforms. On the other hand, two-bar T-straps, while occasionally worn in the UK, according to school photos, amounted to approximately 10 percent of the sandals used.[15]

Another example of a barefoot sandal that was available in

adult sizes was found in the Sears, Roebuck and Co. Bargain Center catalog of 1915 (Figure 5-9). The price was $1.29 a pair for "Men's Barefoot Sandals for Hot Weather Comfort."[16] Eight years later in 1923, Montgomery Ward advertised barefoot sandals "For the Entire Family." By that

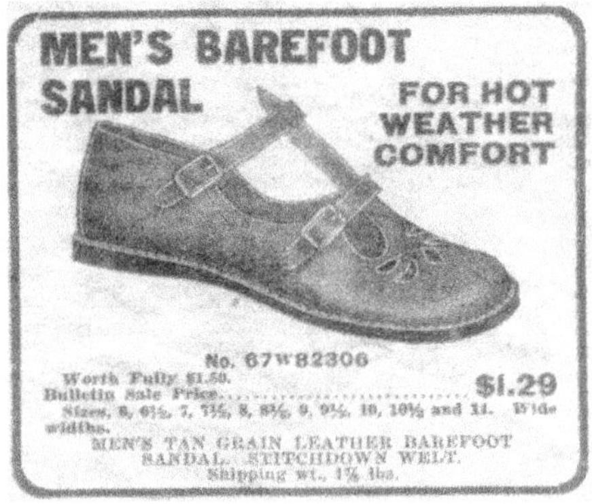

Figure 5-9

Men's barefoot sandal, 1915

time, the price for sandals had increased to $0.98 a pair for children's sizes and $2.19 for men's sizes. While the overall design of the sandal was the same, the cutouts on the top of the vamp were a little different than earlier versions and the soles had heavy visible stitching. As in previous years, the only color available was tan "grain leather." Shipping cost only eight cents "extra" per pair.[17] This was the last time barefoot sandals were found advertised specifically for men in mail-order catalogs. However, they continued to appear in newspaper ads such as "Men's Barefoot Sandals" in the *Gastonia Daily Gazette* (Gastonia, North Carolina), May 3, 1926; and in the *Monessen Daily Independent* (Monessen, Pennsylvania), June 2, 1953, as "Men's Barefoot Sandals [in] Better Grade Sizes 6 to 11."

In the early 1960s, the barefoot sandal appeared in an assortment of colors with pointy toes, rather than the traditional rounded toe. And Sears, Roebuck and Co. advertised the barefoot sandal specifically for boys in its 1953 summer catalog (Figure 5-10). The sandal was included on a page with Oxfords in a category entitled "Just Like His Dad." It was listed as "new" in the ad copy because the sandal had a moc-type toe and crepe sole, features never before seen on barefoot sandals.[18] While this sandal was not

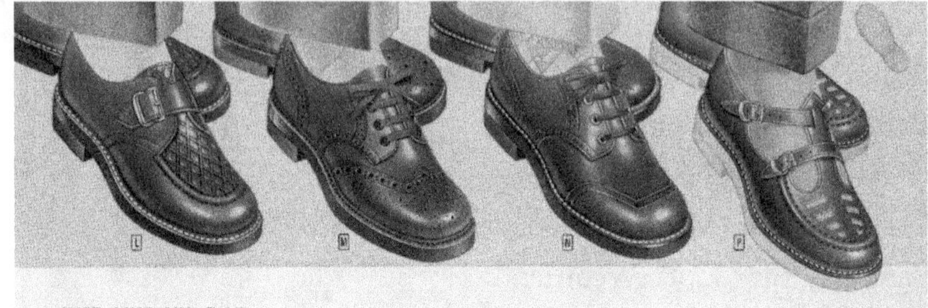

Figure 5-10
"Just like his dad." 1953

included in the men's section of the Sears, Roebuck and Co. catalog, it was the same year that the ad for men's barefoot sandals
appeared in the Monessen, Pennsylvania, newspaper mentioned
previously. One can assume that men were wearing the style in
the early 1950s in some areas of the US, but possibly as an indoor
slipper.

There was a geographic difference regarding closed-toe sandal
usage between Europe and North America. Single-bar T-strap
sandals continued in popularity in Europe during the latter half
of the twentieth century, especially when worn as part of school
uniforms. However, the two-strap barefoot sandal declined in
North America because of the trend for younger and younger
boys to wear them. Older boys stopped wearing them by the 1980s
according to Weidner. Girls, on the other hand, continued to wear
the sandal both in single- and twin-strap variations.[19]

During the latter half of the twentieth century, sandal usage
declined dramatically because of the increased popularity of
sneakers. Figure 5-11 shows two boys taken in the 1950s or 1960s
in which one boy is wearing a pair of sandals with short pants,
and the other boy is sporting the "new" style sneakers and jeans.
It should be recognized that trends come and go, with sandals
once again popular in the twenty-first century worn with short

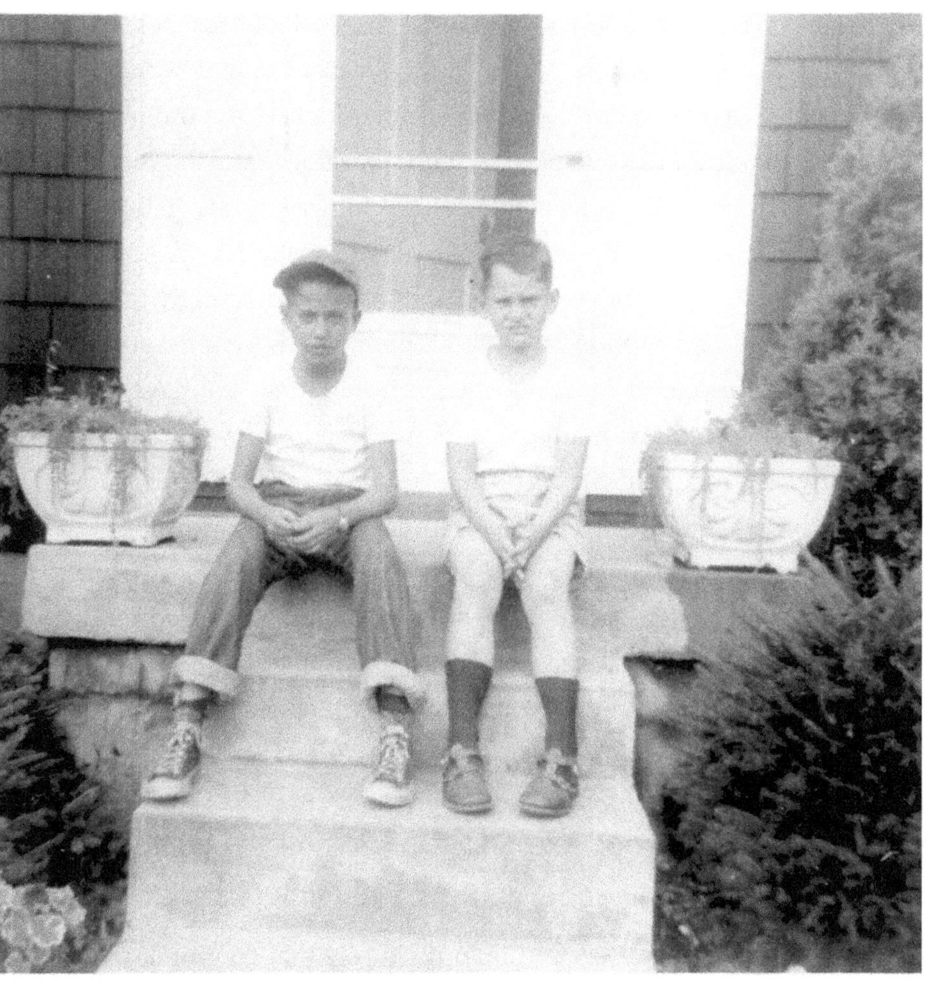

Figure 5-11
Boys wearing sneakers and sandals, ca. 1950–60

pants. As will be discussed later in this book, the best features of sandals and sneakers were merged to produce a sneaker/sandal hybrid.

Weidner stated in 2002 that there was a correlation between social class and barefoot sandal usage in the 1900s for children in North America because "boys from wealthy families were more likely to wear sandals than boys from working-class families." He noted that John F. Kennedy Jr. "wore [barefoot sandals] until 8–9 years of age."[20] Countless images of children wearing barefoot sandals from all walks of life, from all regions of North America, as well as other countries, can be seen on the internet. By the year 2000, there appeared to be regional preferences for shoe styles in the US as reported in communication with shoe sources. In the South, for example, many parents preferred a more "traditional footwear" for their children, like barefoot sandals. And, in the 2000s, these sandals no longer were referred to as "barefoot sandals" but rather have become known as "traditional" or "English sandals" in ads on the internet, often selling up to a hundred dollars a pair in children's sizes. During this same time period, flip-flops and other open-toe sandals sold for much less than the barefoot sandal.

The Search for an Origin by
Contacting Shoe Outlets and Manufacturers

Various shoe outlets and manufacturers that continue to market barefoot sandals in the US were contacted to ascertain the question of the style's origin. Brandon G. Gingerich (2010) of the Badorf Shoe Company Inc. in Lititz, Pennsylvania, reported that his company has been making English sandals as part of the

FootMates line since 1968, and "it is one of our top-selling patterns, a favorite in the southern US markets." Mr. Gingerich continued that while his company certainly knows how to make English sandals, their history was a "bit of a mystery."[21]

In Mobile, Alabama, J-Ray Shoes had FootMates English sandals as well as Amelio English sandals and Willits English sandals for sale in 2011 on both its boys' and girls' web pages. The FootMates English sandals were, according to the ad copy, "beautiful traditional hard-soled shoes for boys or girls, available in white, pink, and navy." The single-bar T-strap sandals were also available for boys and girls, but J-Ray Shoes called them "T-straps," not "English sandals," despite the fact that the shoe with the single strap was so popular with British schoolchildren over the years.[22] None of the respondents, however, knew why the twin-strapped sandals were called "English sandals," other than possibly their close association with school uniforms and the gender-neutral style of the shoe in the UK.

In 2011, Muffy's Enterprises, LLC, in Vernonia, Oregon, also marketed English sandals for adults in sizes 5–12 (women) and 3–10½ (men/boys) in red and navy-blue colors, which they claimed were "just like the [sandals] you remember."[23]

There was a definite geographical pattern with respect to the sale of English sandals in the US, according to representatives at shoe outlets that were contacted. All firms that responded stated that the sandal was currently sold to boys and girls, but mainly in the southeastern states. This distribution of the sandal may be due to the warmer climate in the South better suited to wearing sandals, but also a matter of maintaining family traditions of sandal styles. Becky (2009), a service representative for J-Ray Shoes, said that it is a "southern thing for boys to wear the English sandal." She also stated that the company has "A LOT of boys who wear them with color preferences for white, navy, or brown." While southern boys do *not* wear the pink English sandals that are found on the girls' styles page, she said that boys "DO wear red sandals."[24]

Preston (2008), a Californian vendor who sold English sandals online, confirmed that most of his sales were in the southern states, especially the "Deep South" (Georgia, South Carolina, and North Carolina). Since the English sandal is more of a dress-up sandal than flip-flops or open-toed sandals, little boys wear them to church or formal functions.[25] Dennise (2009), a representative for Littlemonkeytoes.com, also confirmed selling "a lot" more of the traditional English sandals to customers in the Southern states, "but also to customers that have moved from the South elsewhere, who want their boys to wear them and can't find them at any of the local stores [where they now live]." She went on to say the reason is because "of the way we dress the boys down here," such as sandals with "smocking and dressy two-piece outfits," a tradition handed down in "well-bred families."[26] Besides shoe companies and shoe vendors carrying on the tradition of the English sandal, there was also discussion of English sandals on the internet. One mother who bought her daughter a pair at Mobley's shoes in Raleigh, North Carolina, in 2010 stated that many children in the South wear these English sandals and "the great thing is that little boys can wear the white, navy and brown ones. But save the pink for your girls." Another person at the same site commented that her son wore English sandals, but he called the sandals "Christopher Robin shoes" since Christopher was pictured wearing them in addition to his plain Mary Jane strap shoes in children's books.[27]

An advertisement that appeared in the *Boot and Shoe Recorder* trade journal, March 1923, placed by Jones & Thomas Company of Lynn, Massachusetts, calls the barefoot sandal an "Egyptian sandal" and states that it was the "last word in shoe design." They note that the "feminine demand points to [the barefoot sandal] as the preferred form of foot dress for spring" because it had buttons for fastening the straps, rather than the usual buckles.[28] There was no evidence that the Egyptians actually wore these sandals either in ancient times or in the year 1923. Rather, the ad seems to be part of the Egyptian craze that occurred following the discovery of the Egyptian pharaoh Tutankhamun's tomb by Howard Carter in November 1922, one year before the ad appeared.

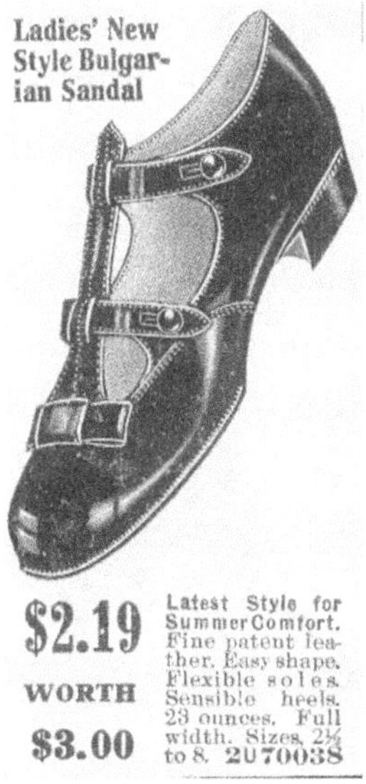

Perhaps one of the biggest "finds" in the research was a dressy patent leather barefoot sandal that appeared in the 1914 Montgomery Ward Spring Supplement catalog that was called a "Ladies' New Style Bulgarian Sandal [the] latest style for summer comfort" (Figure 5-12). As with the Egyptian sandal, the Bulgarian sandal was a dressier design with straps fastened by buttons rather than buckles. It also had a small bow on the vamp and a "sensible heel," according to the ad.[29] This finding

Figure 5-12

Bulgarian sandal, 1914

provides a focus on the Balkans, and Bulgaria in particular, as a possible point of origin for the single and double closed-toe T-strap sandals. Since the Macedonian insurgents were from the Balkans and wearing similar footwear in 1904, this lends credibility to the Balkans as the source of origin for the English sandal.

Mellish (2005), who studies Balkan peasant sandals, reported that the twin strap was actually common and handmade until the twentieth century. She stated the shoe was a "very old style of

footwear" with examples found on various archaeological monuments.[30] One can make the case that these sandals can be traced
back to the closed-toe sandals called "carbatinas," popular during
Roman times. Visits to the Balkans by the author in 2006 and 2008
found these sandals still being worn as part of folkloric Balkan
costumes by singers and dancers in the region. There are also
many pictures of closed-toe sandals on various ethnic and tourist
web pages for that region of Europe.

These tsarvouli sandals resemble the barefoot sandals of North
America, even to the tan color shown in US mail-order catalogs
during the early 1900s. Tsarvouli are still made in Bulgaria using
calfskin in the traditional style at www.balkanfolk.com/shop.php
(Figure 5-13).[31] Eric Methven said in 2009 on his PaleoPlanet website that the sandals were extremely comfortable, and a pair can
be made in less than two hours. He stated that in the past every
peasant farmer could make these sandals for each family member
out of a single piece of leather. The only problem with the shoe

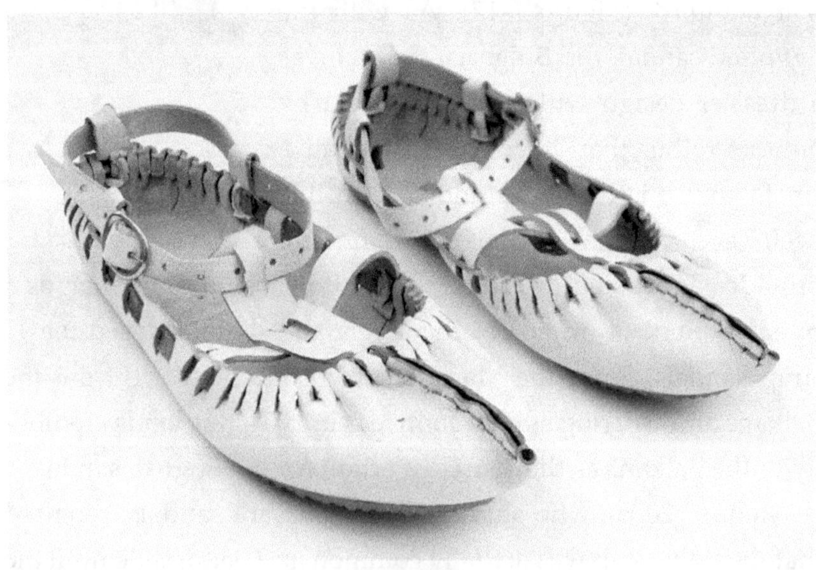

Figure 5-13
Bulgarian tsarvouli, 2019

was that it wore out quickly unless an additional outer sole was added. Methven further stated that folkloric dancers wore mass-produced versions that had rubber soles for longer wear.[32]

On December 16, 1993, the Republic of Bulgaria, as part of its ethnic heritage program, issued a postage stamp set that depicts "Regional Folk Costumes for Men." One of the stamps shows a man wearing double-strap sandals as part of his costume (Figure 5-14).[33] Mellish, who collected these stamps, was able to decipher the Cyrillic inscription, which states that the costume came from the Plovdiv region of Bulgaria.[34]

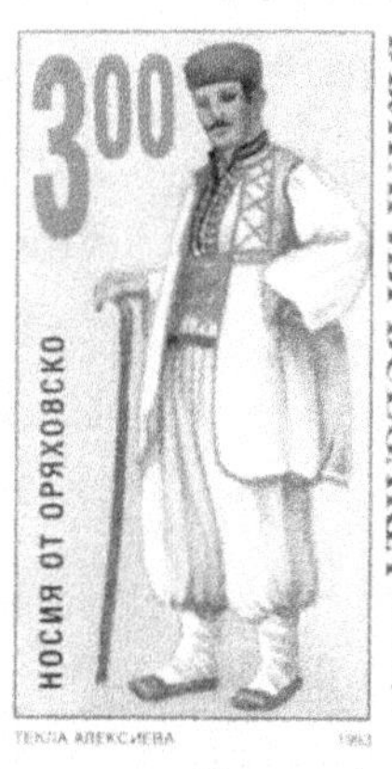
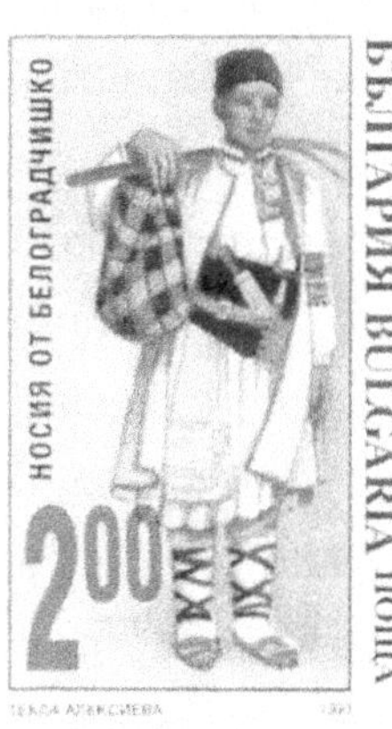
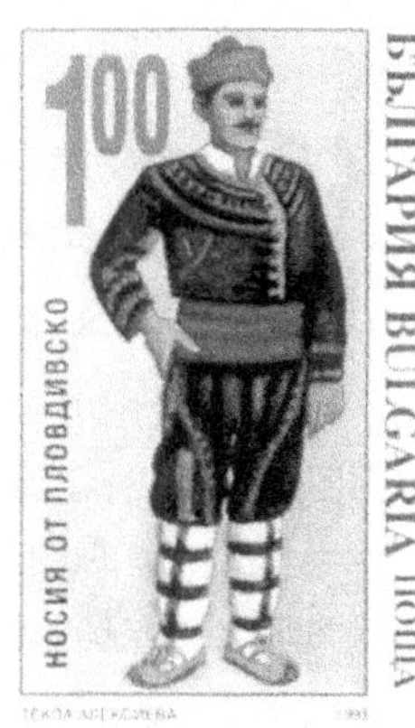
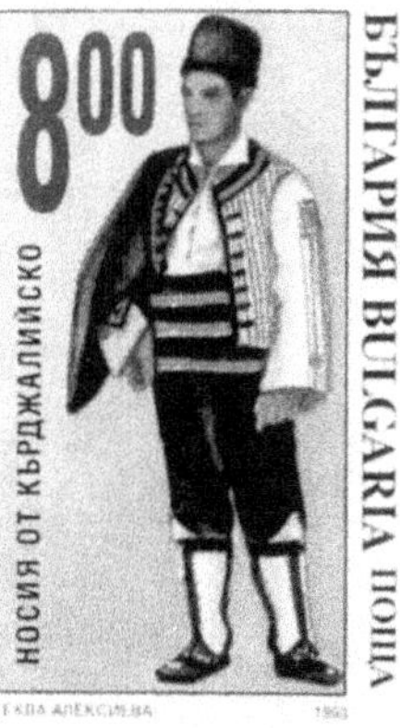
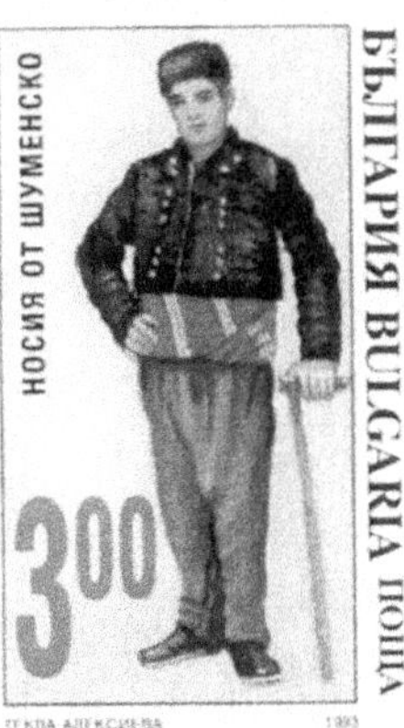
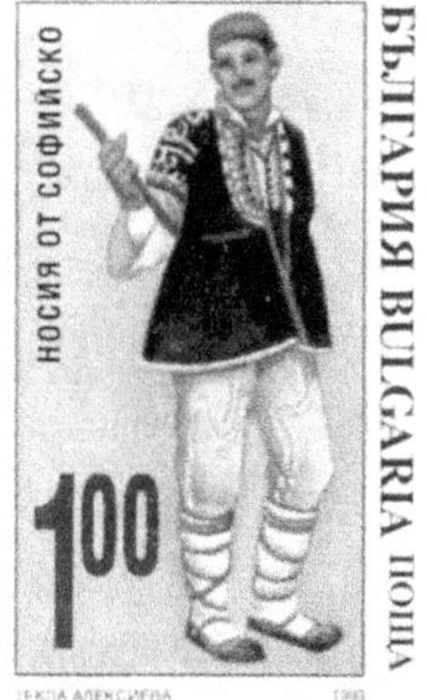

Figure 5-14

Men's fold costume on Bulgarian postage stamp, 1993

There appears to be a very strong case for assuming that the different closed-toe sandals considered in this and previous chapters were descendants of the Roman carbatina footwear like the one found in Britain near Hadrian's Wall. Based on information found at theancientweb.com, following the Dacian Wars in 106 AD, what is now Romania and Bulgaria became the Roman province of Dacia. The "Dacians were recruited into the Roman army and employed in the construction and guarding of Hadrian's Wall in Britannia."[35] It was here that the Roman shoe was found that resembled the Mary Jane and T-strap sandal. However, it was not possible to determine on the basis of existing information whether the Dacians brought the shoe to Britannia, or if the Dacians found the style existing there, and then brought it back to Dacia when they returned home. Even though Dacia only remained a province until 271 AD, the shoe style had been popular with Balkan peasants to the present day and where the author saw examples of the sandals in Romania, Bulgaria, and Croatia.

It was assumed by the author that the tsarvouli/opinci styles were brought to North America by immigrant cobblers from the Balkans or were worn by immigrants with the style, then copied by American cobblers. However, the relatively small number of immigrants from Bulgaria, Romania, and now Macedonia to North America negates this assumption, especially in view of the rapid worldwide dispersal of the barefoot sandal at the turn of the twentieth century. Rather, it is more likely that a shoe designer from a large company saw someone wearing the style and copied the design, possibly in Newark, New Jersey, where there were tanning and shoe manufacturing companies, and where Macedonian immigrants settled. These ideas are all hypotheses that cannot be proven with existing information. Finally, there is the unanswered question of why the shoes were called "English barefoot sandals" in the 1903 *New York Times* article, long before British children wore them as part of their school uniforms.

Another hypothesis for the creation of the barefoot sandal could be that someone had the idea of cutting off the upper portion of a gladiator-type sandal. For example, if one cut the high-top gladiator sandal in half, it could have been the beginning of the barefoot sandal.

Members of the Lucasie family, shown in Figure 5-15, an 1865 Currier and Ives colorized lithograph print, wore both high-top and low-cut sandals. This was long before the barefoot sandal pictures appeared in newspaper ads or mail-order catalogs. The American Museum on Broadway in New York City, where the family appeared, sold photos of the family for fifteen cents each, and this could have been a means by which the public became acquainted with the sandals.[36] This print from the 1860s was the earliest image of barefoot sandal–type footwear found in the research. The maker of these sandals is unknown, but it would have been easy for a cobbler to remove the upper two straps from the high-top version to create the barefoot sandal type for the son. However, it would be forty years before the sandal became available for purchase by the general public, according to the evidence found. These custom-made sandals seen in the Currier and Ives print were also worn by acrobats and circus performers in the nineteenth century and will be discussed in the next chapter as gladiator sandals.

Because the Lucasie family performed in the P. T. Barnum show, many people, including cobblers or shoe designers, saw their footwear and could have duplicated the sandals. This could be the reason how the barefoot sandal style originated in North America, rather than being brought over by immigrants. Also, after leaving Barnum's circus, the Lucasie family performed in other

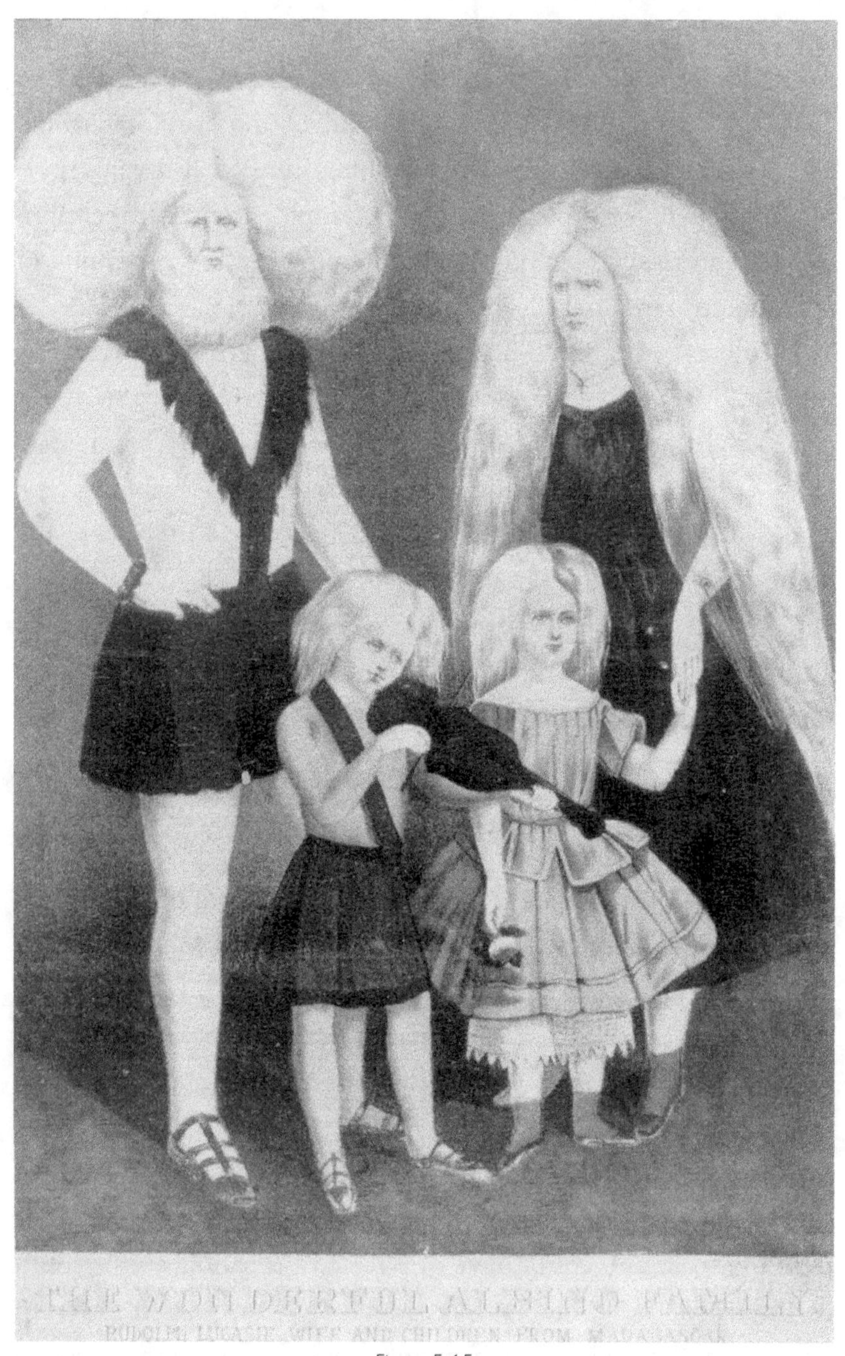

Figure 5-15
Currier and Ives print of the Lucasie family, 1865

parts of the world, including Australia, and people would have seen the sandals there as well.

An inquiry was sent to the Brown Shoe Company, maker of Buster Brown shoes since 1904 in the US, to ascertain if they had any data on barefoot sandals. While they have made the style for many years, unfortunately, no information on sandal design has survived. Also, the Bata Shoe Museum in Toronto, Canada, the Northampton Shoe Museum, and the Clark Museum in England were all contacted, but none had information to share on barefoot or English sandals.

Modern Sneaker/Sandal Hybrids

There continues to be an interest in the barefoot sandal style in the twenty-first century. An enterprising vendor in Texas auctioned the style in 2005. In his write-up, the gentleman called them "Mary Jane Two-Strap Shoes . . . New." In the online auction comments section he stated that:

These classic shoes have been called Mary Jane, strap shoes, T-bars, 2-Buckle T-bars, [and] school shoes, and are still [considered] the standard school shoe in many parts of the world. Here is your chance to go back in time and enjoy the comfort and endless style of these good looking classics.[37]

In Puerto Rico in 2009, the two-buckle T-bar, or school, shoe was evident in photographs of children's school uniforms. In August 2012, Payless.com advertised identical back-to-school barefoot sandals, which they called a women's "Amber Double T-Strap Oxford." It was available in black with white stitching around the sole and up to an adult size 13.

The old saying "What goes around comes around" has definitely been the case with the twin T-strap sandal variation. While it is still manufactured with the traditional look of a barefoot sandal, it was called an "English sandal" in the 2010s and appeared to be making a comeback as judged by the number of new versions. The number of sites on the internet offering the Dr. Martens version of the English sandal or barefoot sandal is large. The style was promoted as "never wearing out." It was usually listed as a Mary Jane because of the presence of straps across the instep. But it was also occasionally listed as a men's twin-strap shoe, or as a unisex style. One of the major updates to the barefoot sandal style was the merging of the classic two-strap design with new features that included easy-fastening hook-and-loop strap fasteners, the addition of a long-wearing non-skid sneaker-type sole, and a padded collar around the top for added comfort. By taking the best features of both the barefoot sandal and sneakers, a sneaker/sandal hybrid was created, as was also the case with other closed-toe footwear discussed in previous chapters.

It should be noted that the center T-strap found on barefoot sandals, as well as single-strap versions, had gotten wider during the latter portion of the twentieth century, resembling a tongue in Roman times. As a result, T-straps began to look more and more like shoes rather than sandals.

The two-bar T-strap sandal has even been transformed into work sandals by northern European companies. These companies have combined the best features of sandals and work shoes to create footwear that are strong and protect the feet, but with enough open cutouts to keep the feet cool. German shoes called "work sandals" (*Arbeitssandale*) or "safety sandals" (*Sicherheitsschuhe*) were created in the 2000s with steel toecaps or fiberglass toecaps to protect the feet in work environments.

The center T-strap, or tongue, has been narrowed to create more open area in the upper sandal for ventilation. An example of a safety sandal, called "Monza," is marketed by the German Esska Co., but is actually made in Italy. The sandal is available in European Union sizes 36–47 (US men's sizes 7–13), and has twin hook-and-loop fastenings for ease of fit.

The internet had some interesting comments about the work/safety sandal. One British reviewer named Seano (2006) said that "the work-sandals looked like sandals I was deeply embarrassed to be sent to school in as a young lad. And, compared to regular work shoes, the [sandals] are very, very light [and] I'd quite like a pair."[38] Grahame (2006), another reviewer, was concerned about the issue of socks being able to be worn with the work sandals.[39] Another comment in 2006 on the internet on the subject of steel-toed sandals read, "There is something rather incongruously cute about a big, burly builder wearing T-bar sandals with a punched pattern on the toe."[40]

The Finnish company Sievi in 2011 marketed a safety sandal in the form of a double T-strap that was available in either black or white colors (Figure 5-16). According to the ad write-up, the white safety sandal version is used by men and women who are employed in the pharmaceutical and food industries for cleanliness purposes.

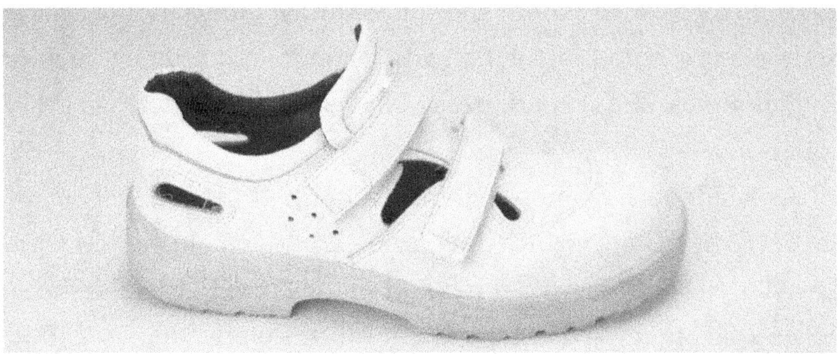

Figure 5-16
Adult safety sandal, 2011

In recent years, closed-toe sneaker/sandal T-straps hybrids have increased in popularity in children's sizes. A boys' blue double-T-strap sneaker sandal made by Minibel Kids, a French company, was offered on the internet by Shoestorediscounts.com and Zappos.com in 2009. The ad copy states that the sandal/shoe is a "wonderful sporty boy's shoe . . . perfect for warmer weather [with a] dual hook and loop strap closures for easy on/off, [as well as a] rugged rubber outsole."[41]

In 2009 a girls' pink double-T-strap sneaker/sandal version called "Arabella" was found on the British internet site Designershoesforkids.co.uk on its girls' web page. The shoe was referred to as a high-quality European shoe made by Alberes with "cut out detail" rather than identified as a sandal. An identical version in bright red was found on the boys' web page and was called Alberes Jumpy.[42] Neither shoe was called a Mary Jane.

From the foregoing historical discussion, it can be concluded that the barefoot sandal style was not created as a little girls' shoe, nor was it called a Mary Jane during most of its history, contrary to what some advertisers have suggested. In fact, of all the footwear discussed thus far, the double T-strap was the most unisex in nature and usage of all the closed-toe sandals. Moreover, while these sandals were advertised in early-1900s mail-order catalogs as being a "new" style "for the entire family," the barefoot sandal style was common in the Balkans for men and women back to Roman times, and it continues to be seen in that region as part of folkloric costumes.

As a sidenote, fashion designer Telfar had his Fall 2009 show in New York City in which both his male and female models wore Dr. Martens twin T-strap shoes and single-strap Mary Jane shoes. Some who attended the show felt the outfits were "futuristic [but] perfect for the twenty-first century."[43]

Likewise, in 2010 Bata Toughees promoted its Durban sandal made in South Africa, rather than China, as being for "boys, girls, and adults. The sandals can be used for school, work, or holiday footwear which adults love to wear."[44] These sandals were advertised for the entire family just like a hundred years ago. Versions of the barefoot sandal in the early twenty-first century were recreated with "new" borrowed sneaker features. The result was a sneaker/sandal hybrid. And, in the case of the double T-strap style (i.e. barefoot sandal and English sandal), "if you can't beat them [sneakers], join them," for the best of both worlds.

Chapter 5 Notes

1. Bell, Walt & Co., (Philadelphia, PA, November 1, 1903).
2. *Newark Evening News* (May 29, 1904), Rutgers University Alexander Library Microfilm Collection (accessed 2008).
3. *Evening Post*, vol. 64 (Wellington, New Zealand, October 1, 1902).
4. "New Styles in Shoes," *New York Times Archives* (December 20, 1903).
5. The *Daily Sun* (St. John, New Brunswick, Canada, July 1, 1903).
6. The *Evening Herald* (Syracuse, NY, June 13, 1902).
7. The *News* (Frederick, MD, May 12, 1907). Number 3 through 8 from news.google.com/archivessearch.
8. The *Evening Herald* (Syracuse, NY, June 15, 1906).
9. Brooke, I., *Footwear: A Short History of European and American Shoes* (1972), 97–100.
10. Ibid.
11. *Newark Evening News* (May 29, 1904).
12. Ltd. Private message re: Bulgarians defeat Turks while wearing *tsarvuli*, Gunboard's Forums, Jelsoft Enterprises (May 3, 2009), forums.gunboards.com/private.php?do=showpm&pmid+426166.
13. Montgomery Ward catalog, no. 79 (1910), 762.
14. ——, (1913), 100.
15. Norlington2, comment (posted August 13, 2009), mary-janeshoes.com/phpbb/viewtopic.php?=5&t=1702&p=7722.
16. Sears, Roebuck and Co. Bargain Counter Bulletin, no. 196 (1915), 14.
17. Montgomery Ward catalog (1923), 213.
18. Sears, Roebuck and Co. catalog (1953), 113.
19. Weidner, D., "Closed-toe Sandals: Styles-Double Bar with Center Strap," Historical Boys' Clothing (April 20, 2002), histclo.hispeed.com/style/foot/sandal/sandal-stsdbc.html. (Available online through subscription only.)
20. Ibid.
21. Gingerich, B. G., email (June 1, 2009, and September 21, 2010).
22. "House of Traditional Children's Shoes," J-Ray Shoes (Mobile, AL, May 5, 2009), www.jrayshoes.com/girls?Shoe%20Styles=Dress.
23. "Modern Fashion," Muffy's Enterprises, LLC (Vernonia, OR, June 6, 2010), muffys.com/modern_fashionl.
24. Becky, J-Ray Shoes, email (May 5 and 12, 2009).
25. Preston, Blogfathers Blog Archive, comment on English sandals (January 21, 2008), theblogfathers.com/2008/01/07.
26. Dennise, email (May 23, 2009), littlemonkeytoes.com.
27. Comments from Henley on the Horn: English Sandals (January 18, 2010), henleyonthehorn.blogspot.com/2010/01/english-sandals.html.

28. Jones and Thomas Co. catalog (Lynn, MA, 1923); page showing Egyptian sandal appearing in *Boot and Shoe Recorder* (March 3, 1923), 67.

29. Montgomery Ward Spring Supplement to Catalog 82 (1914), opposite page 96.

30. Mellish, E., email (December 27, 2005).

31. Yanakiev, P., "Tsarvouli – Traditional Bulgarian Shoes," *Balkan Folk, Ltd.* (April 24, 2009), balkanfolk.com/shop-product-details.php?category_id=shoestsarvul&product.

32. Methven, Eric, "Bulgarian Moccasins," Paleo Planet (March 18, 2009), paleoplanet69529.yuku.com/topic/24380.

33. Bulgarian postage stamp, No. 3806, issued December 16, 1993, *Scott Standard Postage Stamp Catalog* (1998), 790.

34. Mellish, E., email (November 6, 2006).

35. "Ancient Romania," AncientWeb.org (October 7, 2006), theancientweb.com/explore/europe/romania/.

36. "An Album of the First Class," Barnum's American Museum (NY, 1860); posted by John Robinson, *Sideshow World*, "Sideshow Performances from Around the World" (December 27, 2007).

37. "Mary Jane Two-Strap Shoes, Blue, EUR 45, US 12, New," Tenfrogs, eBay auction (McKinney, TX, June 5, 2005).

38. Seano, comment on work sandals, Blue Room Technical Forum (June 20, 2006), blue-room.org.uk/index.php?s=49ec54fd667372b57b11863511fcff47.

39. Grahame, comment on wearing socks with sandals, Blue Room Technical Forum (August 19, 2006), blue-room.org.uk/index.php?s=49ec54fd667372b57b11863511fcff47.

40. Squeak, comment on steel-toed sandals, Halfbakery (November 14, 2006), www.halfbakery.com/idea/Steel-Toed_20Sandals.

41. "Sporty boy's shoe," Minibel Kids Flamingo (May 31, 2009), shoestorediscounts.com/europ.

42. Designer Shoes for Kids, boys' page and girls' page (May 31, 2009), designershoesforkids.co.uk.

43. Telfar Fashion Show (Fall 2009), mycomrade.com/news.

44. "Durban – boys', girls' and adults' smart summer sandal," Toughees Shoe Co. (2010), tougheesshoes.co.uk/index.php?main_page=product_info&cPath=1&products.

MULTI-STRAP CLOSED-TOE GLADIATOR SANDALS

Everyone has some idea what a gladiator sandal is, or do they? By definition these sandals are high-top T-strap sandals with multihorizontal straps that come in either closed or open-toe variations. The open-toe style was predominant in the 2000s. Cartner-Morley, writing in June 2009, stated that this type of footwear had "taken over the [fashion] world," as it has been an "inspiration for women's fashion" since 2001, when Prada put women wearing knife-pleated gladiator skirts and sandals on the "catwalk" and portrayed them as warriors in "modern armour" with their sandals designed to bring out the "fighting spirit." Thus, gladiator sandals have been portrayed as a tougher form of footwear to help cope with today's more stressful life.[1]

Hart (2008) states that the modern gladiator craze is due largely to the pioneering work of Alexander McQueen, a British fashion designer in the 1990s. Gladiator sandals were described as "fierce looking footwear" that connoted a symbol of power in keeping with the ancient gladiator image.[2] Zappos.com advertised its Costume National Nero ankle-strap sandal in 2007 and suggested that the wearer of such footwear could "be dominant in these gladiator-style sandals." At $473.95 a pair, one wonders how many people actually bought a pair in response to the challenge.[3] Cheaper knockoffs have since become available as gladiator fashion footwear has become mainstream so that everyone can now dream of being a gladiator through wearing the shoes.

The rise in popularity of gladiator sandals may have been inspired by the Hollywood sword-and-sandal movies like *Spartacus* (1960), *Revenge of the Gladiators* (1965), and *Gladiator* (2000). In a departure from earlier sword-and-sandal movies, in the movie *Gladiator* (2000), the main character, portrayed by Russell Crowe, as well as other gladiators, wore footwear that resembled the Roman carbatina-style sandal (Figure 6-1). This footwear was boot-like with closed toes and leather laces that passed through loops or holes punched in the sides to better secure them to the foot.

The carbatina bears little resemblance to the modern gladiator-style sandals in vogue in the twenty-first century that are largely open with narrow straps and promoted by Hollywood to be an adaptation of what the Roman gladiators wore.

The multifastened Roman carbatina shown in Figure 6-1 is an actual artifact found in the vicinity of the Antonine Wall in southern Scotland, a short distance north of the better known Hadrian's

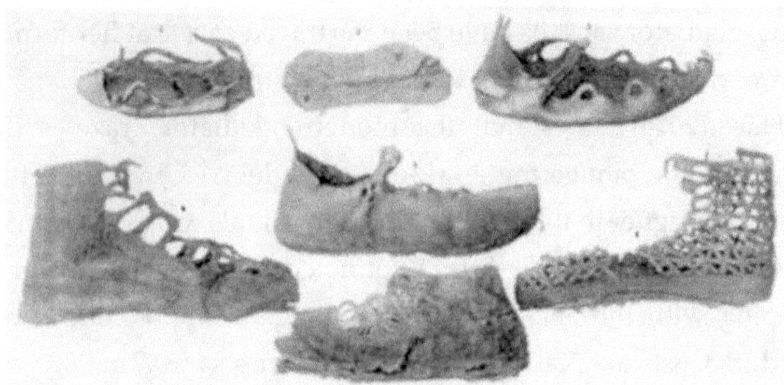

Figure 6-1

High-top Roman carbatina-style sandal, ca. 100 AD

Wall. This basic carbatina style was subsequently modified to have fewer fastenings and more open area to better ventilate the feet and existed in both closed- and open-toe versions. The result of these changes became known as the "caligae," or marching sandal, used by the Roman legionnaires throughout the empire. The open-toe gladiator sandal that laced up the front was the style most commonly seen in Hollywood movies and, therefore, the type most people associate with Roman footwear. However, research found that the closed-toe sandal version like the modern reproduction of a first-century marching sandal, shown in Figure 6-2, may have been even more common, at least in the colder months and northern outposts of the Roman Empire, than the open-toe gladiator sandal, and more appropriate for the Mediterranean Sea provinces.

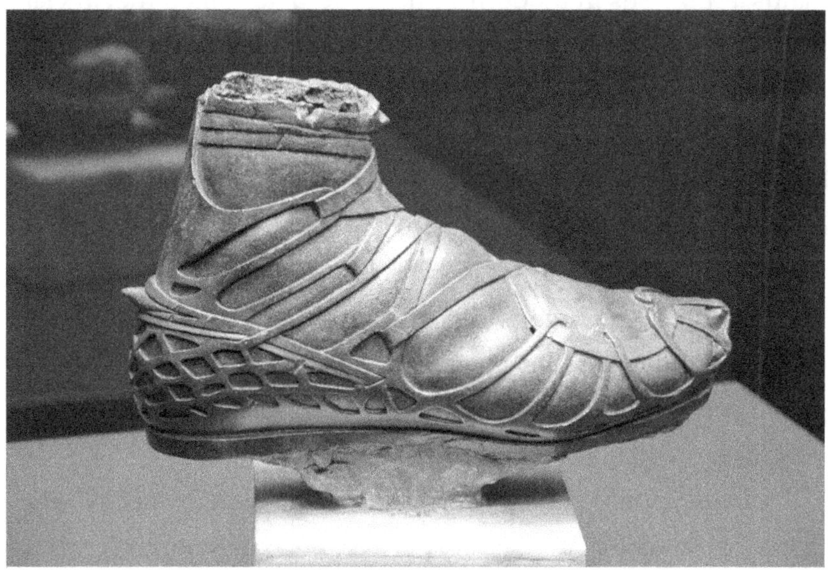

Figure 6-2
Roman caliga *marching sandal, Modern reproduction of 1st century AD*

As discussed previously, it was through the wearing of a pair of caligae (plural form of caliga) sandals with his father in a northern Roman frontier outpost that the Roman emperor Caligula was given his nickname "Little Boots" by the soldiers. Both the open- and closed-toe sandals were constructed of heavy leather and usually had iron hobnails in the soles to improve traction to make them last longer during marches on the rough Roman roads.[4]

As is often the case with many fads and fashion trends, it is necessary to separate fact from fiction. In spite of its popular use, the term "gladiator sandal" may actually be a misnomer. Recent evidence uncovered by teams from the German University of Muenster and the University of Vienna's Austrian Archaeological Institute indicates gladiators were bean-eating vegetarians who fought *barefoot* in the arena.[5] Jones (2007), in the article "What Gladiators Were Really Like," reported that researchers from the Austrian Archaeological Institute in Vienna studied skeletal remains at Ephesus in modern Turkey and determined that ancient gladiators "never fought wearing strappy leather sandals." The institute based its findings on the work of anthropologists Fabian Kanz and Karl Grossschmidt, who studied ancient gladiator bones during the past five years and concluded that high bone density indicates the gladiators did indeed fight barefoot.[6] Correspondence with Josef Eitler at the University of Vienna confirmed that the reason gladiators fought barefoot was because it enabled them to dig their toes into the sand in the arena floor to gain a better footing which would not have been possible if they wore heavy caligae sandals which had less traction.[7]

Normally, only slaves went barefoot in Roman society since footwear was considered a sign of freedom, with sandals removed when entering a house. In this book the high-top closed-toe sandals having a central T-strap will continue to be called "gladiator sandals."

There may be some confusion with respect to the use of the terms "gladiator sandals" and "high-top Mary Jane footwear," which were called "Roman sandals." Both sandals were Roman in origin, or perhaps even earlier. But the major characteristic used in this book to distinguish the two, gladiator sandals and high-top Mary Janes, is that the so-called "Roman sandals" do *not* have a center T-strap, while those which are called "gladiator sandals" do, which is one of its prominent characteristics. This distinction was based on information found in various catalogs and newspaper ads from the late 1800s through the latter part of the twentieth century, where the multi-strap high-top Mary Jane sandals were listed as "Roman." However, other than two ads for custom-made sandals for strong men discussed below, there were no high-top gladiator-style closed-toe sandals (with a center T-strap) for sale to the general public in either catalogs or newspaper ads until the turn of the twenty-first century. However, they did exist based on examples found in the photographic record, where they appear on the feet of athletic and circus performers. The center T-strap may or may not have added strength to the integrity of the sandal, but its purpose was to serve as a visual clue to the superior strength of the performer.

On the other hand, there are numerous sites on the internet selling gladiator sandals to complete the Roman costume look. An example of this is one of the "soldiers" seen "guarding" the Roman Colosseum in 2006 wearing a complete Roman legionnaire outfit except for a pair of fierce-looking gladiator sandals. Rather, the man had on white sneakers as part of his costume. The author observed that tourists paid to take his picture regardless of the footwear.

In the article "Rise of the Gladiator Sandal," Hart (2008) states that gladiator sandals resembled "black/brown bondage footwear." However, he also said shoe designers began to create more ornate and feminine gladiator sandals with metallic or jeweled details that made them suitable for evening wear or beach parties rather than mortal combat as seen in the movies. Magazines, blogs, and TV shows have shown Hollywood celebrities—for example, Mary-Kate Olsen and Vanessa Hudgens—wearing gladiator sandals, which has further popularized the style.[8] With the style being worn by more and more women it has become a mainstream fashion, rather than something unique for celebrities or the rich and famous.

Some people have questioned why men have been largely forgotten when it comes to modern-day gladiator footwear. This concept seems strange because, according to research for this book, the original high-top T-strap sandals were predominantly a male Greek and Roman style. However, there were comments by men on various fashion and accessories blogs that inquired about the suitability of wearing gladiator sandals. One individual stated he was concerned about "look[ing] gay" by wearing them. On the other hand, a married man with two sons replied he had two pairs of gladiator sandals because of the way they looked and felt and he did not "feel gay" at all. Moreover, he stated that men wearing gladiator-style sandals would be "normal footwear" within the next few years.[9] Ulric K. (2009), writing in the blog "A Taste of Tomorrow: Summer Chic-Men's Gladiators," believes gladiators were "catching on as a trend" for men, although there was still a shortage of stores selling them in men's sizes and "men actually wearing them."[10] An example of a gladiator leather sandal with wide straps suitable for men was marketed in the UK by Paul & Joe in 2009 in either black or brown for £174 (British pounds) or $290 in US dollars plus shipping. It resembled a man's fisherman T-strap sandal, although a bit higher at the heel, but still qualified as a gladiator style.[11] The question then becomes will more men wear gladiator sandals in the future given the fact that women dominate the style, even if it evokes an image of the *macho* gladiators of old? At least for now these sandals are not yet encumbered by a name like "Mary Jane gladiators" because of the straps. However, research has shown that many examples of current footwear marketed to women as variations of Mary Janes because they have straps started out as men's shoes in the distant past.

The wearing of high-top Roman-style sandals, as well as sandals in general, largely disappeared in most areas of Europe with the fall of the Roman Empire. This was borne out from a review of footwear examples in comprehensive shoe-style books like Wilson's *A History of Shoe Fashions* and Peacock's *Shoes: The Complete Sourcebook*. An exception was some low-cut carbatina-type sandals that continued to be worn in rural areas of the Balkans and Italy, which evolved into the English and barefoot sandal types discussed in previous chapters. These sandals were also worn by certain religious groups and monks. Low-cut Mary Jane and fisherman T-straps have been worn since the fall of Rome and were referred to as sandals because of the open areas on top of the footwear as opposed to being completely closed in. An examination of paintings done during the various ages, found in books and at museums, showed that no average person wore high-top sandals unless they were attempting to recreate an ancient Greek or Roman scene.

A few examples of the high-top T-strap gladiator sandals were found in the nineteenth-century photographic record. These pictures showed people connected to theatrical or acrobatic shows as judged by their costumes of tights and short skirts, clothing that would have been unthinkable by the masses during Victorian times. Not generally till the twentieth century did sandals reappear in Europe and North America as fashion footwear. The multiple-strap Roman sandal (without the center T-strap) was advertised in catalogs and newspaper ads in the 1890s, but no T-strap features, except for the low-cut double-strap, or barefoot sandal and single-strap school sandal, which mysteriously appeared at the turn of the twentieth century. By the turn of the twenty-first century, the high-top sandal was resurrected from the past to reach an extreme in 2009. This was the year a shoe designer "deconstructed" a pair of Dr. Martens boots by cutting out large sections to create a pair of sandals. However, since these sandal-boots did not have a center T-strap, they could not qualify as a gladiator sandal according to the definition used in this book since a center T-strap was critical. It is interesting that advertisements in the 1800s for Roman sandals had *no* center T-strap, especially since the majority of sandals found on Roman statues and friezes had this feature. Maybe it was cheaper to produce sandals with just horizontal straps, or by the turn of the twentieth century people associated the high-top T-strap sandals with circus performers or strong men, so a stigma existed not to wear them as fashion footwear.

But what could evoke a more masculine image than a gladiator wearing a loincloth and high-top sandals locked in mortal combat or fighting wild animals in the Roman Colosseum? Society has conditioned humans to see gladiator footwear from the numerous Hollywood sword-and-sandal films as unacceptable as women's footwear. Therefore, it was a pleasant surprise that the earliest photo from the nineteenth century showing a person actually wearing gladiator sandals is a woman (Figure 6-3). This photo was, according to an online seller who is a nineteenth-century photography specialist, taken in the 1860s. This individual based his date by the border of the CDV (Carte De Viste) image used by photographers at that time. The photo was taken by Bangs and Hall Photographers in Watertown, Wisconsin. The woman's name was

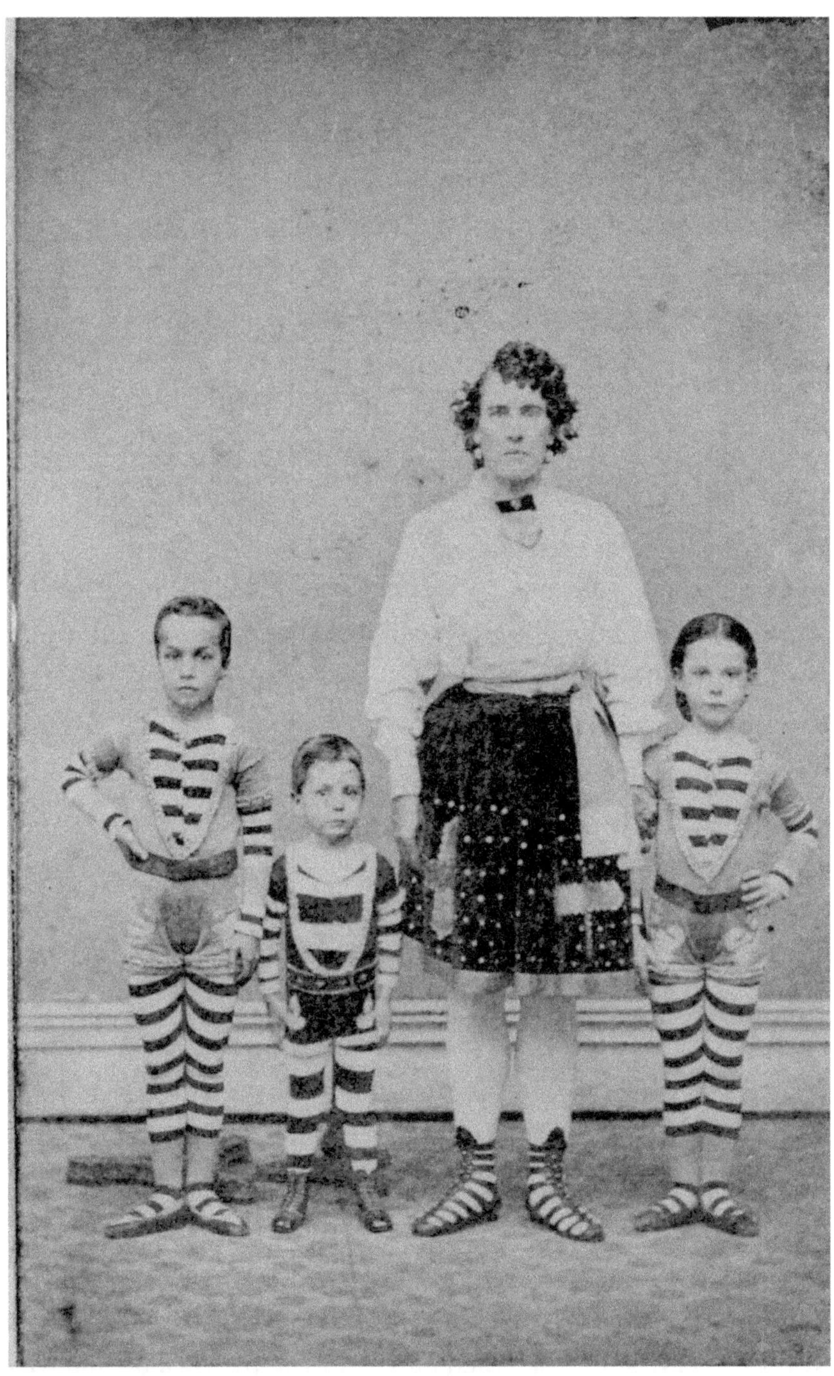

Figure 6-3
Sara Jane and children, ca. 1860s

Sarah Jane, from the handwriting on the back of the photograph, but no other information was given about her or the children next to her. She wore gladiator-type T-strap sandals as part of her costume, and the children, two boys and a girl (based on the parts in their hair), are seen in striped outfits and matching footwear. They are all dressed for some type of performance, possibly as acrobats, who were popular during the time period. The woman's sandals appear very sturdy and were probably handmade for the act. However, it would have been very unusual to see a woman wearing such a short skirt during the mid-1860s, when long-hooped skirts and high-top shoes were the fashion for both women and children.

The second example of a closed-toe gladiator-type sandal found in the photographic record is that worn by Rudolph Lucasie, an albino from Madagascar, who appeared at the P. T. Barnum Museum in New York City. The sandals worn by Lucasie were practically identical to those worn by Sarah Jane. The only difference was that Lucasie had six straps while Sara Jane had seven on her sandals. Lucasie's sandals also appear very sturdy and were probably handmade to go with his costume. Both Lucasie and Sarah Jane have the central T-strap feature, which may have been an attempt to project an image of strength on the part of the person wearing them. But the big unanswered question is, how did this footwear come to be known as "gladiator sandals" rather than the multi-strap "Roman sandals" so popular at this time?

A lot of credit for the popularity of the gladiator sandal type could be given to a man dating from the late nineteenth century. His name was Friedrich-Wilhelm Mueller, born April 2, 1867, in Konigsberg, East Prussia, then part of Germany. As a boy he was sickly but later became known as the "King of Body Builders."

When he was nineteen his father took him to Italy, where he hoped the warmer climate would improve his son's health. While there, Friedrich saw Roman and Greek statues of gladiators, which he studied in detail, even taking measurements with the goal of developing his own body to match the exact proportions of the ancient statues. He also tried to stylize his costume after Roman gladiators, down to the correct footwear. His mentor, Attila, given credit for inventing the barbell, gave him the name "Eugen Sandow," which launched his career in the 1880s and allowed him to perform all over Europe dressed in a leopard-skin costume, pink or salmon-colored tights, and black Roman-style sandals that had six horizontal straps but no center T-strap now associated with gladiator sandals.[12] Sandow probably copied these sandals and the leopard-skin outfit from Attila in the late 1880s. It was not until the 1890s that Sandow added the center T-strap to his six-strap sandals shown in Figure 6-4. It was largely through Sandow's influence that weight lifting was included in the first modern Olympic Games held in Athens, Greece, in 1896.

Sandow's sandals were probably custom-made, as the style could not be found in any catalog or newspaper ads from that time period. In the mid-1900s a strong man named Bill Pearl tried to make his act similar to Sandow's by wearing a hairpiece and mustache, an animal-skin outfit, and "special Roman Sandals like those worn by Sandow [which were] commissioned and made in New York."[13]

Other strong men also became popular in the late 1800s and early 1900s as a result of increased public interest in health and fitness. Images from the period show strong men who followed Sandow by wearing high-top T-strap sandals to look like gladiators. Some examples are the three men shown on the front cover of an early issue of *The Strong Man* magazine in 1911 who competed

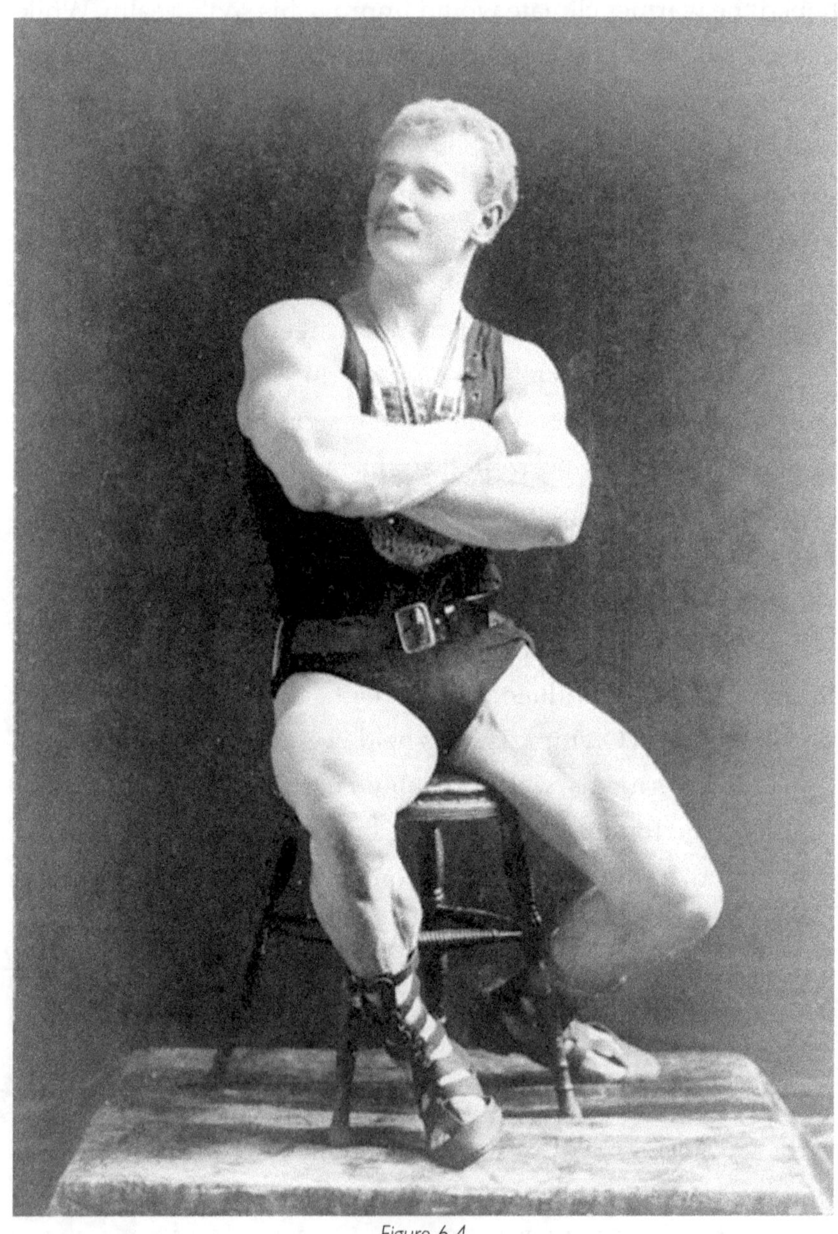

Figure 6-4
Eugene Sandow wearing gladiator sandals, 1897

with Sandow for the title of the "Strong-est Man in the World." Each of the men wore six-strap closed-toe gladiator sandals similar to those worn by Sandow at the time. These men, whose names were Arthur, Kurt, and Hermann Hennig, were also known as the "Saxon Trio." They were German like Sandow and performed weight-lifting stunts throughout Europe in the late 1800s and early 1900s (Figure 6-5).

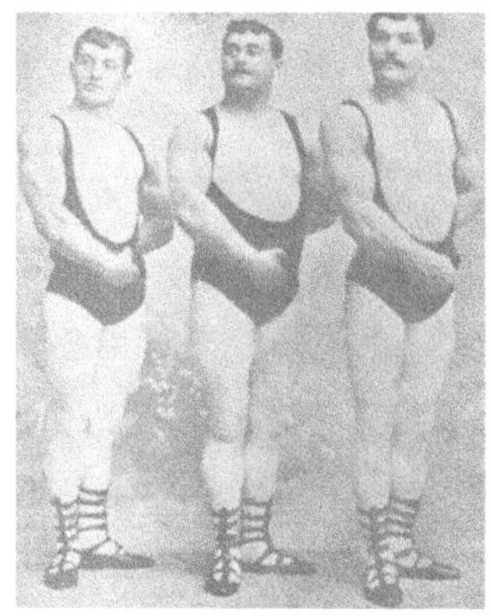

Figure 6-5
The Saxon Trio, 1911

Arthur Saxon also competed with Sandow in the writing of health and fitness books such as *The Development of Physical Power* (1905) and, five years later, *The Text Book of Weightlifting* (1910), in which he discussed the "psychology of lifting weights."[14] One can see each of the Saxon Trio wearing six-strap closed-toe gladiator sandals in Figure 6-5 that are similar to those worn by Sandow at the time.

Another popular strong man in the early 1900s was an Englishman named J. C. Tolson, born in Yorkshire in 1903. He per-formed as either a Roman or Greek warrior dressed in a kilt-like garment with high-top gladiator sandals that had ten horizontal straps. He was known as the "20th Century Gladiator."[15] Figure 6-6 shows Tolson doing a strength-building technique using a chain while prominently wearing his ten-horizontal-strap gladia-tor sandals. He had his own fitness school called the Apollon Institute of Physical Culture during the 1920s in Yorkshire, where he taught weight lifting and bodybuilding. Tolson even had an ad for a "special" sale of strong-man costume items that appeared in his Physical Culture booklet, *Strength Secrets of the Mighty Apollon*, that included "imitation leopard skin trunks for stage wear, posing,

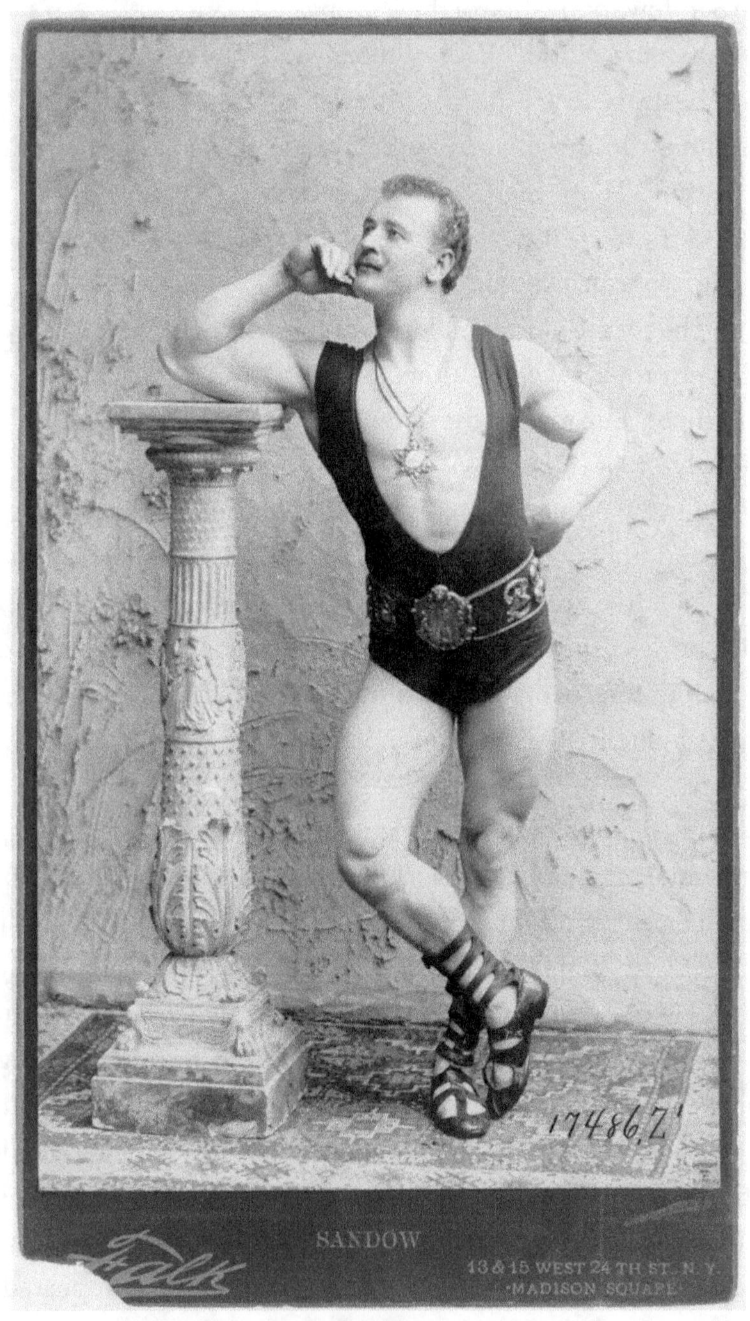

Figure 6-6
"Twentieth-Century Gladiator" with chain and sandals, ca. 1928

etc. of the best quality," and "Gladiator boots [sandals] as worn by myself and pupils, made to measure" for two British pounds a pair, shipping included.[16] The real leopard-skin outfits worn by Sandow and his mentor, Attila, gave way to imitation leopard trunks by the 1920s. On the other hand, high-top Mary Jane–type shoes with multiple straps, like those Sandow and Atilla wore in early pictures dating from the 1880s, continued to be sold into the 1950s to women and children but were referred to as "Roman sandals." And women at the turn of the twentieth century probably would not have worn footwear with the name "gladiator" associated with it, either for themselves or their children. But the term "Roman" became acceptable to them. Thus, in one hundred years of fashion with respect to the gladiator sandal, the use certainly changed as well as acceptance by women for this shoe style.

Another search was made for the origin of the term "English barefoot sandals" that appeared in the *New York Times* 1903 article about the same time these sandals first appeared in North America. There may have been a connection between the appearance of these sandals as a popular fashion and those worn by the strong men at the turn of the twentieth century. According to the Tolson ad, gladiator sandals were indeed custom-made in England. Could this be the reason they were called "English sandals"? More research is needed to determine whether the term "English sandals" first appeared in England, or whether the style originated elsewhere, and under what circumstances.

A theory was suggested that a shoe company or shoe designer may have "cut the top off" of a gladiator sandal in order to create low-cut barefoot sandals that subsequently became the "rage" in North America around the turn of the twentieth century. Interestingly, some of the later strong men who were still wearing sandals in their acts began to wear lower-cut versions of the gladiator sandal themselves. Even Tolson cut the number of straps on his sandals from ten to six or seven during this same time period. And, with fewer straps to fasten, low-cut sandals became easier to put on and take off while still retaining the gladiator look. An example of the lower-cut gladiator sandals worn by strong men can be seen on the two members of a team known as the Brothers Marx, not to be confused with the comedy act the Marx Brothers. The Brothers Marx, John and Aloysius, were strong men born in Luxembourg who became famous for their "gladiatorial statue act" in which they painted their bodies either gold or white, and demonstrated their great hand strength by unbending and breaking horseshoes. The stronger of the two, John Grunn Marx, was known as the "Luxembourg Hercules."[17] A poster (Figure 6-7) found on the internet shows a drawing of the brothers in various weight-lifting poses and features their "Original Gladiatorial Statue Act."

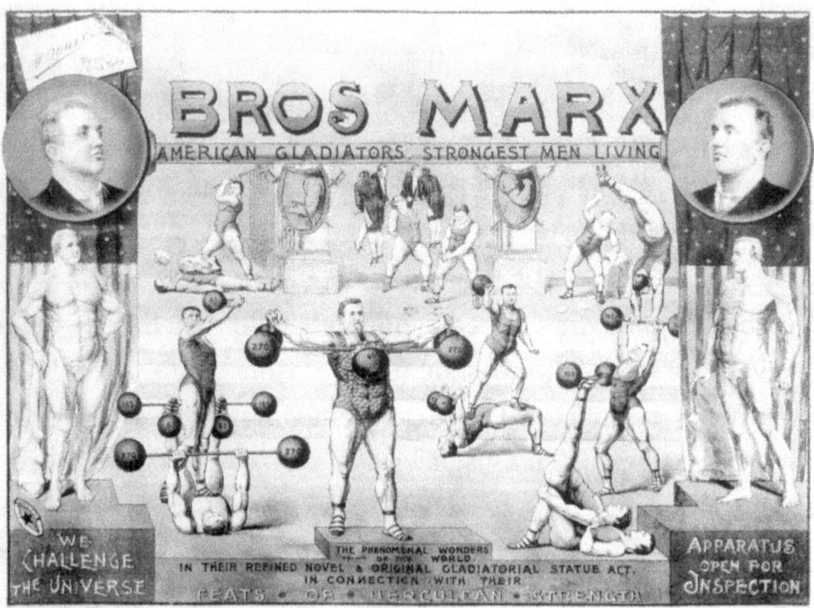

Figure 6-7
The Brothers Marx, Early 1900s

This poster shows them wearing lower-cut gladiator-type sandals, and although undated, appears to be from the early 1900s. While the sandals worn by the brothers are more stylized, they definitely have fewer straps than those worn by other strong men, and more closely resemble the English or barefoot sandal types. John Grunn Marx also wore four-strap sandals shown in other photos. Since strong men performed their acts all over North America in circuses and carnivals and were seen by many people, a strong case can be made that shoe designers may have copied the gladiator style as an alternative to the hot high-top footwear then in vogue, and coined the term "barefoot sandal."

Hero worship may also have played a significant role in encouraging people to wear sandals. For at the turn of the twentieth century, T-strap and multi-strap sandals became common, as seen by the number of newspaper ads and in photographs. Further, an illustration of a boy admiring a strong man was found at the Sandow Museum web page. The caption to the illustration reads, "Gosh Mister, when I grow up, I want to look just like you!" The strong man is wearing high-top gladiator sandals, so one might wonder if the boy is not only admiring the physical appearance of the strong man, but by wearing sandals like the strong man, he would become strong also.[18] It was even possible that Hollywood sword-and-sandal filmmakers as well as costume designers could have received inspiration for the footwear worn by their movie heroes from these modern gladiator strong men rather than from the ancient gladiators, who actually fought barefoot. However, it is unlikely one will ever know for sure what exactly influenced the gladiator design.

While gladiator sandals worn by strong men may have played a role to promote the rebirth of sandals in the early 1900s, these sandals eventually became old-fashioned themselves. And professional strong men became secondary to team sports by the 1920s and 1930s. These sandals also underwent a transformation as times changed to fewer straps and a wider center T-strap to accommodate a more modern lacing system, and the open areas at the sides were gradually "filled in" so that the footwear no longer resembled a sandal. The sandal had thus been transformed into a high-top shoe worn by modern wrestlers, boxers, and others.

As noted at the beginning of the chapter, a rebirth in recent years has occurred of the gladiator-style sandal as fashion footwear. One can see numerous ads geared to women on the internet for this popular footwear, but with much thinner straps than found on the footwear of their ancient ancestors. While most of these gladiator sandals are open-toed, the closed-toe examples were generally found on the more expensive styles. In 2008, MarcJacobs.com advertised a pair of "round toe flat boots with multi-strap detailing." The company called these shoes "gladiator boots" rather than "sandals" with a price tag of $798 a pair.[19] Variations and modifications to closed-toe sandals, including high-heel Mary Janes, will be explored in the next chapter.

Chapter 6 Notes

1. Cartner-Morley, J., "Enter the Arena," *The Guardian* (June 12, 2009), www.theguardian.com/lifeandstyle/2009/jun/12/jess-cartner-morley-gladiator-sandals.

2. Hart, G., "Gladiator Shoe Trend – Summer 2008," excerpt from "Fierce-Looking Women: Footwear to Glamorous Flats," Suite 101.com (April 26, 2008), shoesandaccessories.suite101.com/article.cfm/gladiator.

3. "Costume National 1060002, (Nero) – Ankle Strap Casual Sandals," Zappos.com (2007), zappos.com/n/p/dp/23363077/c/5291.

4. "Caliga," *Wikipedia* (June 2007), en.wikipedia.org/wiki/Caligae.

5. Vargas, J., "Gladiator Truths Counter Movie Myths," Discovery Communications (2007), www.buffalo.edu/content/dam/www/news/imported/pdf/June07/DiscoveryDysonGladiators.pdf.

6. Jones, H., "What Gladiators Were Really Like," *Cosmos Magazine* (June 7, 2007), cosmosmagazine.com/society/what-gladiators-were-really/.

7. Eitler, J., email correspondence, Austrian Archeological Institute (June 23, 2009).

8. Hart, G., "The Rise of the Gladiator Sandal," Suite 101.com (April 8, 2008), suite101.com/bloglearn/the_rise_of_the_gladiator_sandal.

9. "Gladiator Sandals for Men..Gayish or Not?" Yahoo! Answers (2013), answers.yahoo.com/question/index?qid=20080901121031AAXT9ui.

10. Ulric, K., "A Taste of Tomorrow: Summer Chic Men's Gladiators" (June 6, 2009), atasteoftomorrow.blogspot.com/2009/06/summer-chic-mens-gladiators.

11. "Paul & Joe Gladiator Leather Sandals at ASOS" (May 26, 2009), asos.com/Paul-Joe-Gladiator.

12. Chapman, D. L., *Sandow the Magnificent* (1994), 10–12. Accessed on Google Books.

13. Draer, D., "1965-Journey into the Past, Bill Pearl's Sandow Display," excerpted from *West Coast Bodybuilding Scene*, by Dick Tyler (June 2005), www.davedraper.com/pearl-wcbs-excerpt.html.

14. "Arthur Saxon," *Wikipedia* (May 2009), en.wikipedia.org/wiki/Arthur_Saxon.

15. Tolson, M., "J.C. Tolson-Strongman," Tolson Family Genealogy Forum (November 6, 2004), www.oldtimestrongman.com/blog/tag/j-c-tolson/.

16. Fillary, R. and G. Waldron, "Special Strength Secrets by the Mighty Apollon – Part Two," Apollon Institute of Physical Culture (Dewsbury, Yorkshire, UK, n.d.), 32, sandowplus.co.uk/Competition/Apollon/StrengthSecrets/ss02.

17. Wood, J. and Thunderdome Media Inc., "John Grunn Marx," Old-time Strongman Blog (March 10, 2008), www.oldtimestrongman.com/blog/2013/06/14/john-grunn-marx/.

18. Anderson, R. C., "Muscle Champions – 1880 through 1930," Sandow Museum (2001), sandowmuseum.com/musclechampsone.

19. Jacobs, M., "A fabulous gladiator-inspired look" (June 12, 2009), net-a-porter.com/product/18998.

MARY JANE AND CLOSED-TOE SANDAL VARIATIONS

There are literally thousands of closed-toe sandal styles that have evolved from the basic Roman prototypes discussed in earlier chapters of this book. Thus far, two major categories, closed-toe sandals with a center T-strap and sandals lacking a center T-strap, have been discussed. Each of these categories was further broken down by the number of horizontal straps, or bars. In this chapter, other modifications made over the years to the Mary Jane original low-heel and round-toe design are reviewed.

Mary Jane High-Heel Shoes

Over the millennia, most forms of footwear have added high heels, including even modern-day sneakers. However, in Western culture, closed-toe sandals with high heels are relatively recent, which have allowed the wearer to be elevated for stylistic or personal reasons.

The first example of a modification to a basic Mary Jane–stylized shoe was the addition of a slight heel during the medieval period from 1154 to 1399. This shoe with a long, pointed toe was typical in the days of King Richard the Lionheart and Robin Hood.

What is unique is the low wooden heel and single strap that goes over the instep. Wilson (1969) felt it was a type of riding shoe that held the foot securely in the stirrup but noted it may date from the Tudor period when heels were more common.[1] However, Tudor footwear had square toes and no upward point of the sole, a style that could have come to Europe during the Crusades. By the 1500s, the heel on the pointed shoe in Europe was an inch and a half in length for military purposes. This increase in length may have been influenced by the Mongolian horsemen who were en-croaching on Europe from the east.[2]

The wearing of high heels for vanity first occurred in 1533 when Catherine de' Medici of Florence, barely five feet tall, had a pair of "chopines," an extreme form of platform shoes, modified to increase her height by two inches for her wedding to the Duke of Orleans (Figure 7-1).

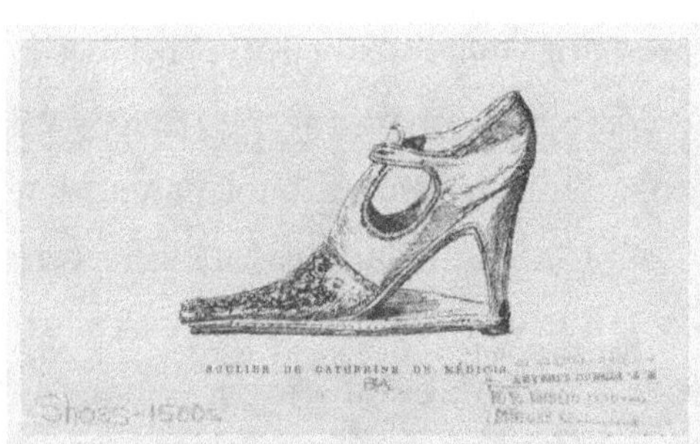

Figure 7-1

Catherine de' Medici high heel, 1533

The chopines had a flat, bendable bottom, which helped pre-vent Catherine from sinking into the dirt or mud as she walked. And, according to legend, Leonardo da Vinci made these shoes for her, but he could not have, as he died in 1519, fourteen years before her wedding. However, she may have seen one of Leonardo's high-heel creations and had a pair produced in Florence to bring to her wedding in Paris. The chopines became an instant hit and were adopted by the French Court.

Today, most people do not realize that in the seventeenth and eighteenth centuries, high heels were worn by both men and women. King Louis XIV, who was five foot three inches, wore shoes with heels five inches high, decorated with miniature battle scenes. Often, he had his heels painted red and allowed only his chosen courtiers to wear red heels as a special favor. These "Louis heels," as they were called, became fashionable for women as well as men.[3]

During Louis's time, a person who wore high heels was known as "well-heeled," which referred to one's connection with wealth and authority. But, with the coming of the French Revolution in the late 1700s, the wearing of high-heel shoes changed radically. A rapid decline occurred in their use as people sought to escape notice and the wrath of French citizens with a possible execution on the guillotine. In fact, Queen Marie Antoinette was executed while wearing two-inch heels in 1793.[4]

Following the Revolution and "throughout most of the first half of the 1800s flats and sandals were the norm for the sexes with the heel resurfacing in the late 1800s . . . among women."[5] Prior to the 1900s, it was hard to assess women's footwear because of the long skirts that covered their feet. However, examples of footwear for this time period can be found in catalogs and magazines. An example is in the December 1867 issue of Frank Leslie's *Lady's Magazine and Gazette of Fashion,* where there were virtually no heels on women's shoes.[6]

By the 1880s higher French heels became more common on strap shoes worn by women. The *Bloomingdale's Illustrated* catalog of 1886 shows an example of a ladies' Dieppe Tie shoe with a high heel. Examples of high-heel closed-toe strap shoes presented in this chapter are done to show the evolution of high-heel Mary Jane footwear. However, the vast majority of people in the latter half of the nineteenth century to World War I wore high-top button or laced boots. These boots, as noted earlier, were used because of the lack of sidewalks and the prevalence of mud. But, at the end of the nineteenth century, one saw a difference between women's and men's footwear. Women's high-top shoes began to have higher heels than similar shoes worn by men. The photographic record for this time period showed that some children's shoes also had elevated heels.[7]

The 1997 Sears, Roebuck and Co. catalog shows closed-toe sandals with higher heels and pointed toes. At the turn of the twentieth century, this style was known as a "needlepoint" shoe and was associated with many foot problems because "the toes were crumpled together so badly that one toe lay upon another," resulting in pain and chronic fatigue. Fortunately, this shoe style was short-lived, for in 1915 a reform occurred in shoe designs where broader-toe footwear again became fashionable.[8] By the 1910s both sexes wore higher heels on their dress shoes (Figures 7-2 and 7-3) with lower heels on their high-top work or everyday shoes.

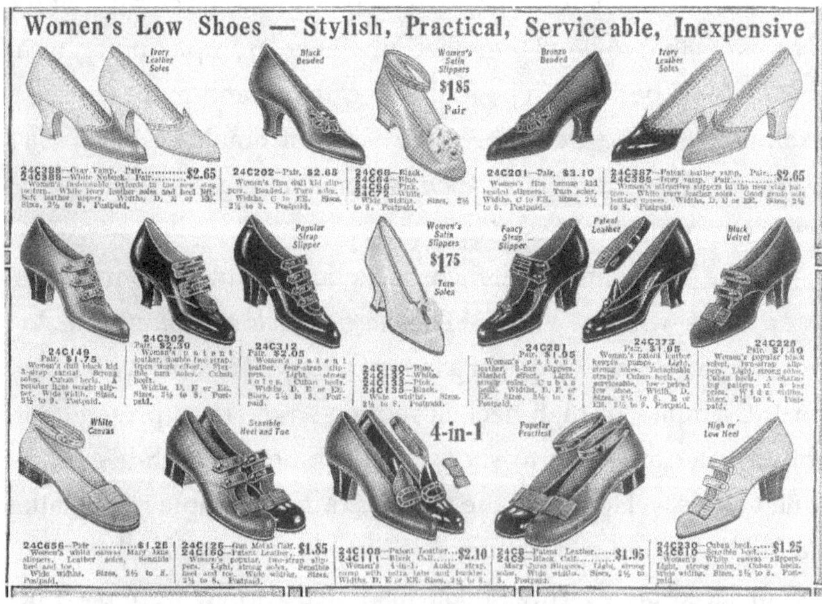

Figure 7-2

Heels on women's shoes, 1916

Men's Popular Priced *Searsmade* Oxfords

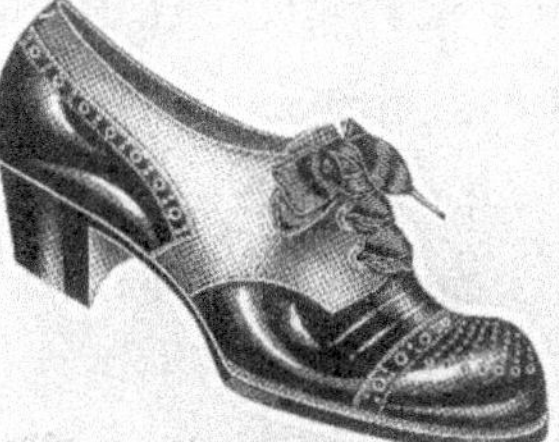

No. 15H746   The Pair, $2.20
PATENT COLT. DULL MAT TOP.
PATENT FOXING. ALL SOLID.
OUR OWN MAKE. WARRANTED.
Sizes, 5 to 11. Widths, D to EE.
Shipping wt., 38 oz.

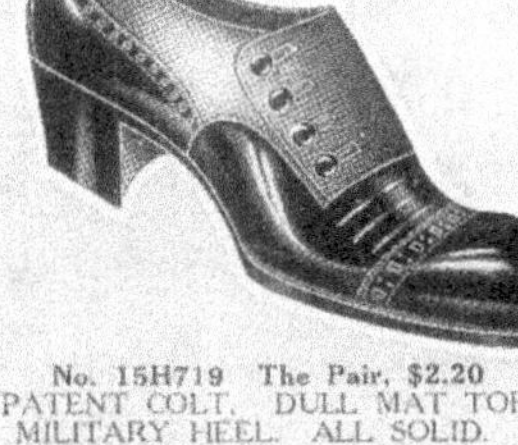

No. 15H719   The Pair, $2.20
PATENT COLT. DULL MAT TOP.
MILITARY HEEL. ALL SOLID.
OUR OWN MAKE. WARRANTED.
Sizes, 5 to 11. Widths, D to EE.
Shipping wt., 37 oz.

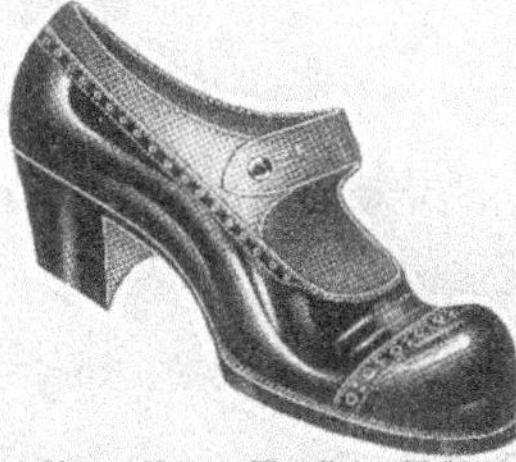

No. 15H711   The Pair, $2.20
PATENT COLT. MAT STRAP PUMP.
LATEST STYLE. OUR OWN MAKE.
CUBAN HEEL. WARRANTED.
Sizes, 5 to 11. Widths, C to EE.
Shipping wt., 36 oz.

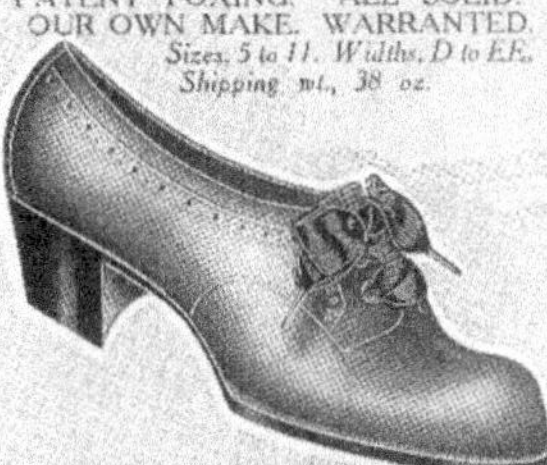

No. 15H718   The Pair, $2.20
GUNMETAL CALF. MAT TOP.
MILITARY HEEL.
OUR OWN MAKE. WARRANTED.
Sizes, 5 to 11. Widths, D to EE.
Shipping wt., 38 oz.

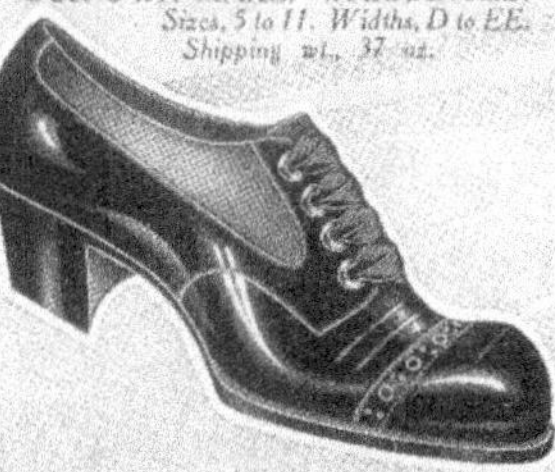

No. 15H731   The Pair, $2.20
PATENT COLT. DULL MAT TOP.
OUR OWN MAKE. SOLID.
WARRANTED.
Sizes, 5 to 11. Widths, D to EE.
Shipping wt., 37 oz.

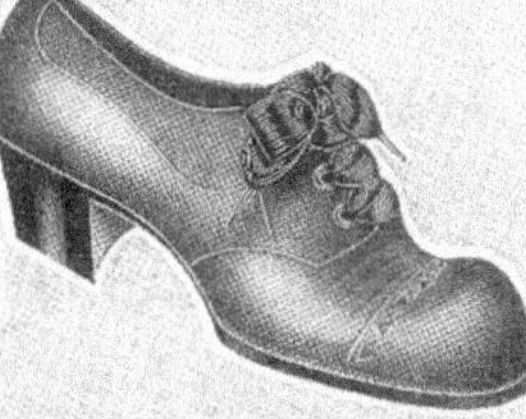

No. 15H771   The Pair, $2.20
GUNMETAL CALF. DULL MAT TOP.
OUR OWN MAKE. ALL SOLID.
WARRANTED.
Sizes, 5 to 11. Widths, D to EE.
Shipping wt., 38 oz.

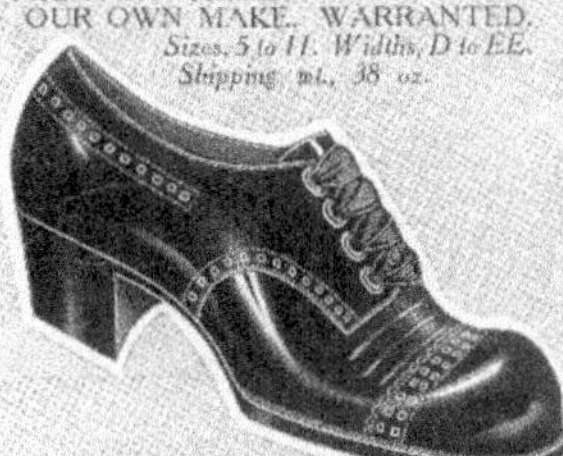

No. 15H962   The Pair, $1.75
ALL PATENT COLT. PERFORATED.
LIGHT SOLE. MILITARY HEEL.
OUR OWN MAKE. WARRANTED.
Sizes, 5 to 11. Wide widths.
Shipping wt., 37 oz.

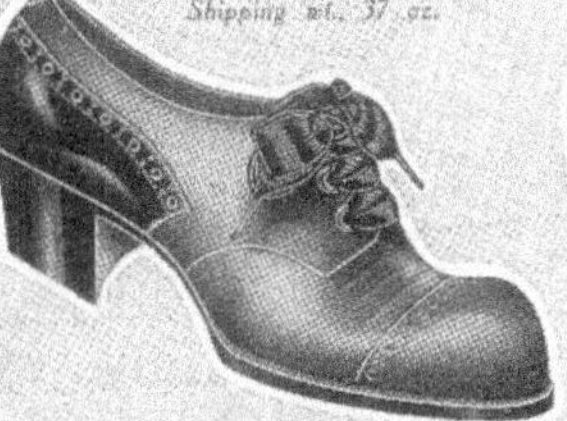

No. 15H952   The Pair, $1.75
GUNMETAL CALF. BLUCHER.
PATENT FOXING. FOOT FITTING.
OUR OWN MAKE. WARRANTED.
Sizes, 5 to 11. Widths, D to EE.
Shipping wt., 37 oz.

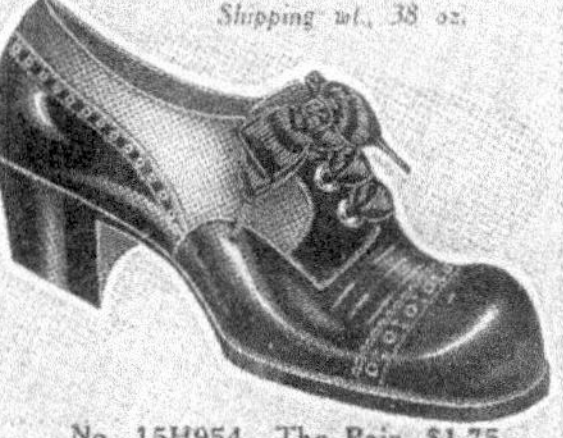

No. 15H954   The Pair, $1.75
PATENT COLT. DULL TOP.
PATENT LACE STAY.
OUR OWN MAKE. WARRANTED.
Sizes, 6 to 12. Widths, D to EE.
Shipping wt., 37 oz.

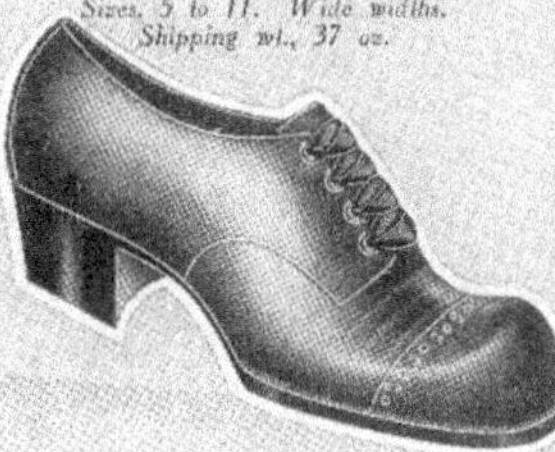

No. 15H979   The Pair, $1.50
MEN'S DONGOLA BLUCHER.
LIGHT SOLE. FOUR EYELETS.
OUR OWN MAKE. WARRANTED.
Sizes, 5 to 11. Wide widths.
Shipping wt., 36 oz.

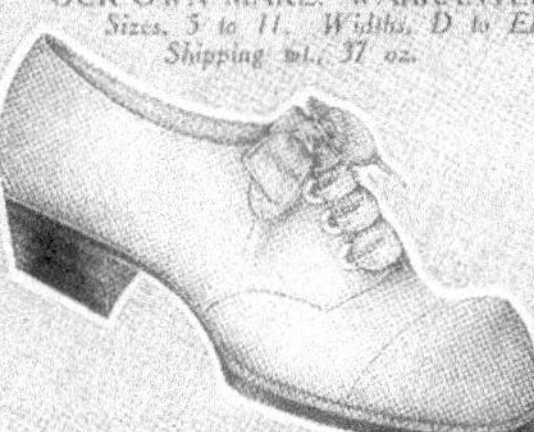

No. 15H957   The Pair, $1.50
MEN'S WHITE SEA ISLAND.
MEDIUM SOLE AND HEEL.
WARRANTED.
Sizes, 5 to 11. Widths, D to EE.
Shipping wt., 30 oz.

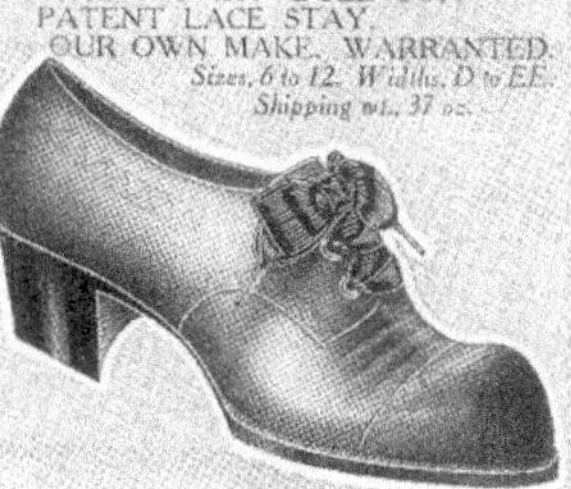

No. 15H955   The Pair, $1.50
GUNMETAL. THREE EYELETS.
MEDIUM SOLE. SERVICEABLE.
OUR OWN MAKE. WARRANTED.
Sizes, 6 to 12. Wide widths.
Shipping wt., 38 oz.

Figure 7-3

Heels on men's shoes, 1912

In the bottom row of Figure 7-2 there are two ankle-strap shoes called "Mary Janes" that were only available in women's sizes. In Figure 7-3 on the first row, far right, is a men's strap Oxford that was rugged looking so as to appeal to men. The ad copy reads that it was a "Mat Strap Pump . . . the latest style" for men. This men's style had a Cuban heel, tapered and of a thick stacked construction, comparable to the height of many women's shoes for that time. During this same time period there were *no* children's shoes called "Mary Janes." If a shoe had a strap across the instep it was simply termed a "strap sandal," "slipper," or a "baby doll." In the early 1900s, there was no gender difference for small children's shoes. Many small boys still wore dresses with strap shoes, as illustrated by an ad in the March 1908 *Ladies Home Journal* for a "little man" two to eight years of age. The ad copy states the dress could also be worn by a girl (Figure 7-4), an example of a unisex dress.

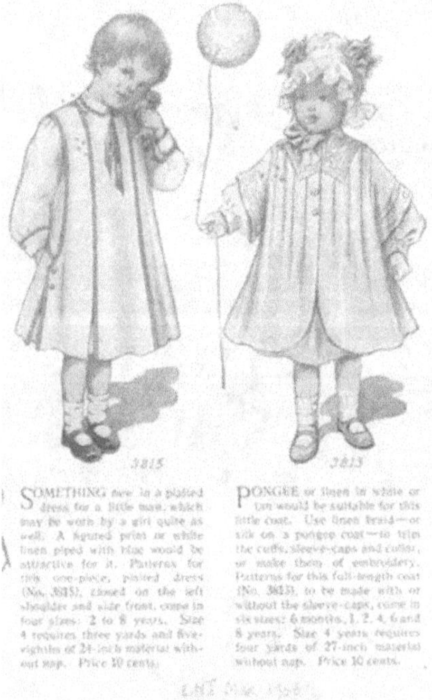

Pageant Archives states that in the 1970s, for a brief time, higher-heeled footwear was available for men because of the influence of John Travolta in the film *Saturday Night Fever* as well as other films. Pageant categorizes a low heel as less than an inch, while mid-heels fall into the range of one to two and a half inches. And any heel over two and a half inches is considered a high heel.[9]

3815

SOMETHING new in a plaited dress for a little man, which may be worn by a girl quite as well. A figured print or white linen piped with blue would be attractive for it. Patterns for this one-piece, plaited dress (No. 3815), closed on the left shoulder and side front, come in four sizes: 2 to 8 years. Size 4 requires three yards and five-eighths of 24-inch material without nap. Price 10 cents.

3813

PONGEE or linen in white or tan would be suitable for this little coat. Use linen braid—or silk on a pongee coat—to trim the cuffs, sleeve-caps and collar, or make them of embroidery. Patterns for this full-length coat (No. 3813), to be made with or without the sleeve-caps, come in six sizes: 6 months, 1, 2, 4, 6 and 8 years. Size 4 years requires four yards of 27-inch material without nap. Price 10 cents.

Figure 7-4

Plaited dress for a "Little Man" 1908

High heels reached new heights in the 1950s with the creation of the stiletto heel, a pointed, narrow heel that resembled a dagger or spike, in Italy. The stiletto heel was created by technology that used a "supporting metal shaft within a heel" rather than the traditional heel of wood or

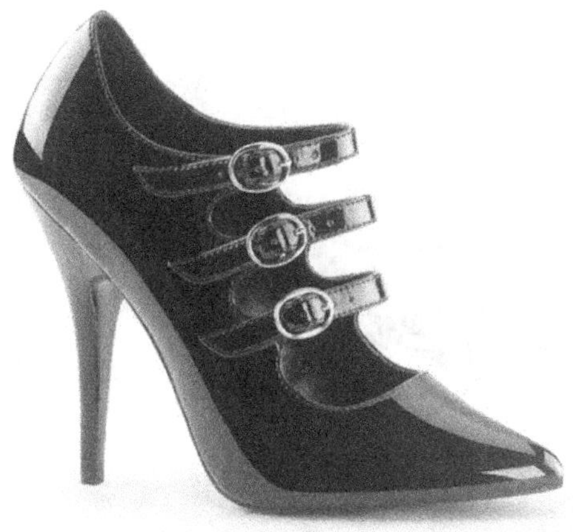

Figure 7-5
Multistrap Mary Jane stiletto-heel shoe, 2008

other materials. According to Hamilton (2006), "not only women, but men wore stilettos" with formal outfits to "gain two or three inches in their actual height and . . . for a better [taller] personality."[10] Figure 7-5 shows a multi-strap Mary Jane–type shoe with a five-inch stiletto heel, which appeared on the Pierre Silber internet site in 2008.

Stilettos have been associated with health problems to female feet and legs as well as headaches, balance problems, and even possible brain injury because of the "compression of [the] nerves and blood vessels."[11] Damage from these heels can also occur to wooden floors. During the 1990s, the style declined in popularity to almost disappear "when professional and college-age women took to wearing shoes with thick, block heels."[12] Yet a revival of very high stiletto shoes has occurred in the twenty-first century in spite of these problems.

Mary Janes also appeared in the form of platform shoes, which have been around since ancient times, but were useful in eighteenth-century Europe for the purpose of avoiding the muck found in urban streets. The soles were made of cork, wood, or synthetic

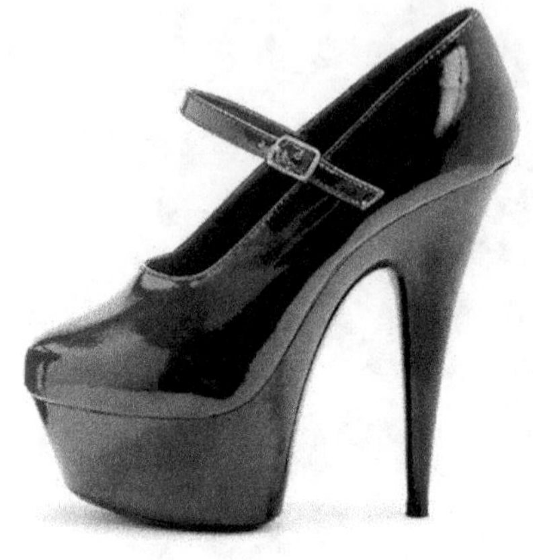

Figure 7-6
Mary Jane platform shoe, 2008

materials, with all types popular in the 1970s and 1980s. UK fashion designer "Vivienne Westwood [was] given credit with reviving high-heeled platform shoes in the early 1990s as high-fashion."[13] Figure 7-6 shows an example of a Mary Jane platform shoe, the Eden, with a four-inch sole and six-inch spiked heel.

Traditionally, spiked heels have been associated with prostitutes, transvestites, or those more interested in the erotic qualities evoked by such footwear. Subcultures whose members wore Gothic and punk clothing also used Mary Jane shoes as part of their fashion statements in the 1990s and 2000s, especially the kinderwhore and Lolita fashion advocates. Figure 7-7 is such an example of a fetish ballet Mary Jane shoe with a seven-and-a-quarter-inch spiked heel that appeared on the Pierre Silber web page in 2008. This shoe can be viewed at the High Heel Shoe Museum in Los Angeles, California.

Pageant Archives reported in 2006 that "while high heels are marketed almost exclusively to women, a small percentage of men have worn, and continue to wear heels for various reasons, including personal preference, medical, gender identity, [or] fetish roles. The number of men wearing heels continues to grow throughout Westernized countries . . .

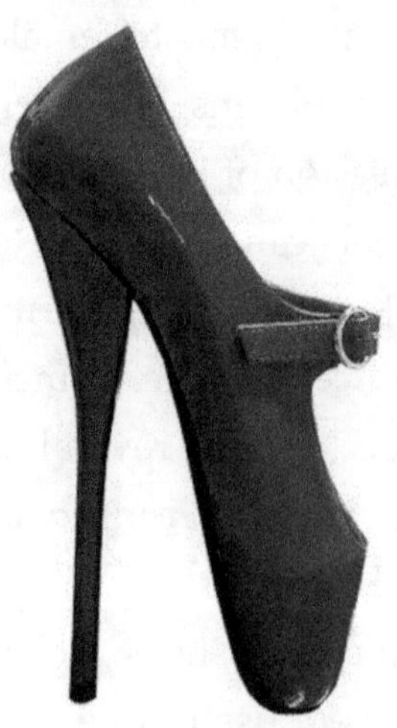

Figure 7-7
*Example of a Mary Jane
fetish stiletto, 2008*

and to a lesser extent Asian countries."[14] Alexander (2005) believes, however, that "while women have for decades plundered the male wardrobe, few men have been happy to embrace feminine sartorial styles."[15]

Rui Leonardes, a shoe designer from the Portuguese Azores Islands, introduced high-heel footwear specifically for men at a 2005 show in London.[16] During a 2006 interview with Filep Motwary, Leonardes questioned "masculine stereotypes" and said, "My heels for men are designed for a man's foot . . . for men have been wearing high heels for centuries."[17]

Crocs Sandals: A Revolutionary Form of Footwear

Some people hate them, others love them, but there is no question that Crocs have become a popular form of footwear since the beginning of the twenty-first century. What are they, and why have they become so popular? Crocs were first introduced at the Fort Lauderdale Boat Show in November 2002. According to their creators, Crocs resemble a crocodile snout and were designed to be the perfect boat shoe because they have skid-resistant soles for slippery decks to help fishermen and boaters maintain their footing. They are made from Croslite, a substance of closed-cell resin material that uses body heat to soften and mold to the foot. By some it has been called "marshmallow fluff," but Croslite is neither a plastic nor rubber.[18] The original style, called "Cayman," has thirteen holes on top with seven around the edge to both allow water to escape and air to enter so as to promote foot ventilation. The strap at the back can be either in the back of the shoe to hold it more securely to the foot, or it can be moved to the front to look more like a clog (Figure 7-8).

The Crocs style first became popular in the central part of the US, and then spread to the East and West Coasts as a result of the

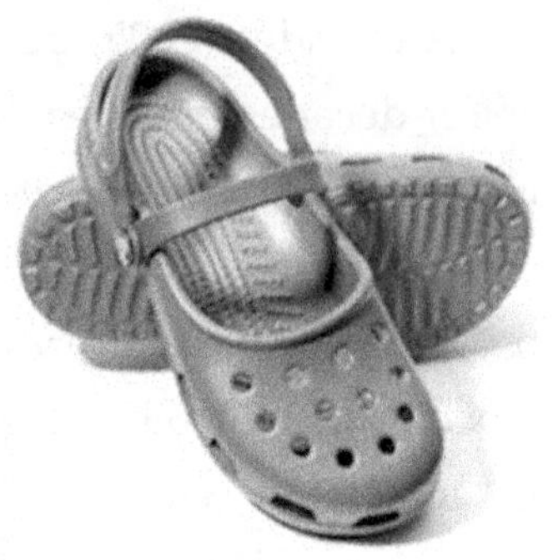

Figure 7-8

Crocs Mary Jane Sandal, 2006

company's extensive marketing campaign with the theme "Ugly can be beautiful."[19] According to O'Rourke (2007), Crocs "represented a kind of rebellion—a vanguard of the comfort movement."[20] Kippen (2008) notes that Crocs came in nineteen colors so "there is a hue to match every mood and outfit."[21]

In spite of negative comments posted by anti-Crocs people on the internet, sales of the shoes dramatically increased as celebrities have worn them since they first appeared in 2002.[22]

Robert Wayne Footwear (2007) reports in the *New York Times* magazine that Crocs wearers range from children to seniors, with sales of the shoes for the first quarter of 2007 three times the same period in 2006, in spite of many knockoffs.[23] A website, CrocFans.com, started by David Chidester in 2007, even posted a photograph of the former US president, George W. Bush, wearing a black pair of Crocs with presidential-seal socks.[24]

In June 2006, Crocs.com modified their original Cayman Crocs style by adding a second strap that passed over the instep as well as a "kitten" orthotic-style heel for a more feminine and dainty appearance. The number of holes on top of the vamp was also reduced to ten and the result became known as a "Crocs Mary Jane Sandal." The original Cayman Crocs style was available in men's, women's, and children's sizes, but the Mary Jane version was found only in female and children's sizes.

There are numerous examples of footwear that have gone from being men's or unisex styles to becoming uniquely a woman's style. The question with Crocs shoes is, will this phenomenon that originally started as a man's boat shoe become strictly a women's style? Will Crocs be marketed solely to women as "Mary Janes" in the future as fewer men wear them because of the implied feminine name "Mary Jane"? To test this hypothesis, the customer service department of Robert Wayne Shoes in Commerce, California, was contacted to learn if this trend was beginning. A representative of the company stated on April 2, 2008, there had been a decrease in sales of the original Cayman Crocs to men "now that the more feminine styles are becoming available."[25] However, the Crocs parent company addressed this concern by relabeling the original Cayman shoe as unisex. The parent company also introduced some new-style Crocs to be more appealing to boys (i.e. Spider-Man, Incredible Hulk, and X-Men) released May 2007.[26] This new version was more slender and sleek than the original boat shoe. According to Joe's Sports, a vendor on eBay in 2008, "These Crocs have [a fun design (that) little boys everywhere will love."[27] These new versions were blue with a red strap with Spider-Man's, Batman's, the Incredible Hulk's, or the X-Men's pictures on the outside of the shoe and center of the rear strap. Unlike the Mary Jane Crocs, there was no strap over the instep.

A Dora the Explorer Crocs version in pink for girls with little charms that could be inserted in the holes of the shoe for individual styling was produced to counter all the boys' superhero Crocs shoes.

In 2009, a men's Mary Jane Coral and a men's Mary Jane Mango Crocs were advertised by Shopwiki.com, which stated they were "classic Mary Jane style fashioned with the comfort and uniqueness of Crocs for $15.00 a pair" with an extra strap over the instep.[28]

In early 2008, Crocs, Inc., released its official Unisex Bistro style, which was advertised on an online auction as:

A new sensation for working people because of [the] increased traction and thicker soles to protect feet in the metatarsal area. The footwear is for the food service industry or health care workers.[29]

Shoe-Glove Mary Jane Sandals

Perhaps the most unusual Mary Jane footwear encountered in this research was contained in a collection of "barefoot alternative" footwear named Vibram FiveFingers. The shoe has individual "compartments" for each toe (Figure 7-9) and could better be called "five toes" since it acts as a "foot glove." This shoe was created by Marco Bramani, a grandson of Vibram founder, Vitale Bramani. He wanted to create a boat shoe that would give the "balance and control of sailing barefoot," but also provide slip resistance and better protection to the foot. This nonslip boat shoe was introduced in the late spring of 2005 to the public.[30] Vibram claimed its shoe allows one to experience the joy of going barefoot without being exposed since the foot is protected by a thin, flexible skin. And a strap across the instep creates a Mary Jane look that holds the foot securely in the shoe. Men's sizes range from EU 41 to EU 47 (US 8–14). Women's sizes are available from EU 36 to EU 42 (US 5–11½) in every style and in five different colors.[31]

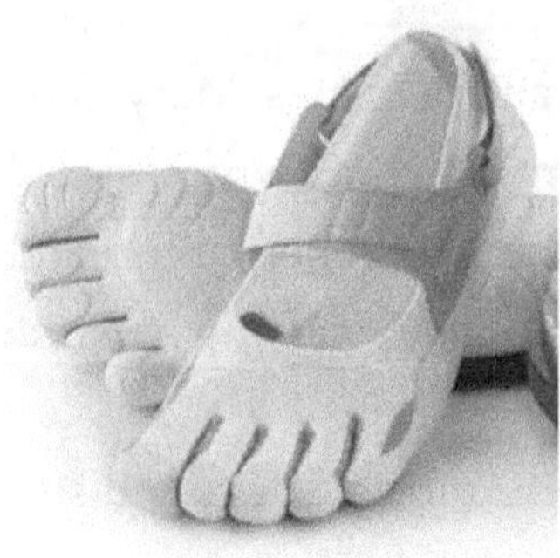

Figure 7-9
FiveFingers Sprint, 2008

FiveFingers footwear has been used by hikers and even marathon runners. Barefoot Ted, a runner, completed the "Los Angeles Marathon XXI in 2006 while wearing Vibram FiveFingers Barefoot Shoes."[32] And in 2010, eighty-nine participants wore FiveFingers footwear in a race in Johnson City, Tennessee. Having a strap over the instep, similar to a Mary Jane shoe, had no effect for those wearing this shoe style, for that was not an issue.[33]

Because of its unique glove-like style, *Time* magazine in its November 12, 2007, issue stated that FiveFingers was one of the "best inventions" that year. The article went on to say that the shoe style was a "barefoot alternative quickly gaining popularity among runners, fitness enthusiasts, martial artists, and others [because] FiveFingers was a reinvention of the sandal."[34]

In May 2009 the author visited the cutting-edge or hip Abbadabba Shoe Store in Little Five Points, Atlanta, Georgia, to see FiveFingers footwear. The store caters to those who want the latest footwear styles or something different. Trying on a pair was comfortable, like wearing a wet suit or walking barefoot. The price was eighty-nine dollars a pair and was sold mainly to people interested in boating, rafting, or kayaking as well as to running and hiking enthusiasts. Football players have worn them for spring training sessions because they can dig their toes into the ground for a better grip, as ancient gladiators did in the arena, even with a strap that gave it a Mary Jane appearance. And a graduate student at Georgia Tech University wearing FiveFingers shoes agrees with Vibram's information that their shoes do help with one's balance by increasing the wearer's foot strength. When this female student started wearing FiveFingers in 2007, she received more "stares" than she did in 2010 because more people started wearing the footwear. Children have given her positive comments while adults are more concerned about the comfort of one's toes in different compartments. She believes FiveFingers styles are unisex, but one may wish to buy the "male or female size version of the shoe that is appropriate for your sex." And her next pair may be the Vibram new style, Performa Jane, appropriate for daily activities, and the Bikila style for running.[35] But they are all sold in either female sizes or in male sizes within the US because there is no uniform size for both genders as in the UK and Europe. The strap over the instep resembles those on other Mary Jane footwear but makes no difference gender-wise for outdoor activities.

While the new FiveFingers Performa Jane was not formally called a "Mary Jane," it strongly resembled one because of the strap across the instep with a "detail button" at the end of the strap. Unlike other styles sold in either men's or women's sizes, the Performa Jane was only available in women's sizes and recommended only for indoor use (i.e. yoga). In 2010 Performa Janes sold for eighty dollars a pair, which was more than the popular Sprint style and made from kangaroo leather.

While the Crocs shoes are still considered by many as unattractive and ugly footwear, they have become popular. So, the FiveFingers shoe-glove footwear could also catch the public's fancy to become a standard style. Moreover, the FiveFingers shoes have created a trend for men to wear a Mary Jane–type shoe.

Sneaker/Sandal Hybrids

One of the most revolutionary changes to sandal design, both open- and closed-toe types, was the marriage of the sandal with the sneaker. Compared to sandals, sneakers, or "athletic footwear," as they are commonly referred to, are a relatively recent phenomenon that date from the Industrial Revolution of the nineteenth century, although Henry VIII three hundred years ago was supposed to have worn a sneaker-like shoe when he played tennis.[36]

Sneaker-type footwear, or plimsoles, as they were first termed in the UK, originated in the 1860s under the name "croquet sandals." The term sneaker was coined by Nelson McKinney in the early 1900s because rubber-soled shoes were quiet or stealthy. But the term sneaker was used in 1873 when street kids wore rubber-soled shoes that allowed them to sneak up on one another.[37] The term "sneaks" was also used for boys' and men's rubber-soled footwear at the turn of the twentieth century in a 1906 ad that appeared in the *Trenton Times* by Dunham's department store in Trenton, New Jersey.[38]

During the 1970s the popularity of running, jogging, and walking as health activities led to advancements in sneaker manufacture, such as the development of synthetic uppers, waffle-style soles, and cushioned midsoles. Athletic shoes and sweatsuits became an American informal uniform. During the New York City transit strike in 1980, many women commuted to work in what became the "standard-issue Reagan-era wardrobe: a suit, a briefcase and [a pair of] sneakers."[39] Gill said in 2008 that advertising transformed the "sports shoe from [an] object of comfort and function [to a] lifestyle commodity" that reflected the tastes, interests, and personality of the wearer."[40]

In the 1970s, athletic shoe companies popularized their products through the endorsements of famous sports figures.[41] But it was Bill Bowerman, a former track coach, who experimented with different athletic shoe designs and ultimately ruined his wife's waffle iron to invent lightweight waffle-tread footwear to better grip surfaces in 1971 that established Nike as a sneaker contender.[42]

Ken Young coined the term "sports sandal," which he patented in 1974 (US Patent No. 3,800,444). This sandal had crisscross lacing and an open-toe area that strongly resembled the ancient Roman open-toe sandal. And Mark Thatcher in 1983 developed a brand of sports sandals under the name "Teva" that became popular for men and women.[43] At the turn of the twenty-first century, an idea developed to combine the basic elements of a sneaker sports shoe with a sandal to create the sneaker/sandal hybrid. This hybrid was characterized as having the strength and support of an athletic shoe but with the openness of a sandal to allow the foot to breathe. It also had the benefit of a toecap that provided toe protection so lacking in open-toe sandals. This sneaker/sandal hybrid was another step in the evolution of "athletic shoes" to open up the top for ventilation without sacrificing support of the shoe.

In 2003, Keen Inc. in Portland, Oregon, was the first company to introduce the original hybrid footwear.[44] Figure 7-10 is an example of the Keen Taos men's sneaker/sandal hybrid suitable for water sports or everyday activities such as eating in restau-

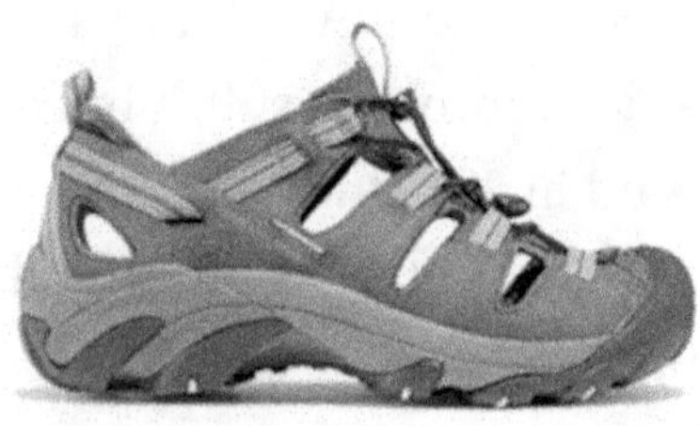

Figure 7-10

Keen hiking sneaker/sandal hybrid, 2006

rants. Similar footwear was also available in women's sizes. The upper part of the sneaker/sandal hybrid was reminiscent of the Roman carbatina sandal except for the addition of sneaker-type heel and sole plus adjustable drawstrings that passed through the straps to hold it in place. Following the sneaker/sandal hybrid prototype, other companies introduced footwear with opened-up sneakers to ventilate the foot without sacrificing strength. This trend continued in the 2010s as wearers discovered the cooling, comfortable advantages of these hybrid sneakers.

Mary Jane variations have been given a facelift with hook-and-loop fasteners in place of buckles and/or buttons to make it easier and faster to put the shoes on and off. Various shoe versions have combined Mary Jane styling with the soles and heels of a sneaker to improve traction. And some of these versions look rugged enough to appeal to wearers of all ages.

A more rugged adaptation of the Mary Jane can be found in the Rift Trainers shoe that derived its name from the Great Rift Valley that crosses the eastern part of Africa from north to south. It was available in both men's and women's versions.

The Rift was inspired by Kenyan runners who run barefoot in their country but who were required to wear shoes when participating in competition running. It was first created in 1995 and was red, black, and green for the colors in the Kenya flag.[45] The uniform characteristic of Rifts was the unique split-toe feature, as was the FiveFingers Mary Jane shoe discussed previously. However, the Rifts had only two toe compartments, one for the big toe and the second for the remaining toes. Having a large, open cutout on the vamp gives Rifts a distinctive Mary Jane appearance, but it was not called a "Mary Jane," presumably to avoid turning away potential male purchasers. Instead, the name given was "trainer," the current term for sneakers in the UK. Rift shoes for men and women look identical in overall design, with the biggest gender difference found in color and patterns, although this is not always clear cut.

As discussed in previous chapters, the "strap" or "bar" shoe was the name given Mary Jane–style footwear until recently in the UK. One wonders if shoe designers gave the Rift Trainers a more rugged appearance so they would be more attractive to men compared to the old-style, classic Mary Jane shoes. In 2012 several online ads stated that these trainers were extremely comfortable and fashionable. One vendor referred to them as unisex sandals for beach or summer wear.[46] One male reviewer brought a pair with him when he moved to the US from the UK and complained that he "was unable to find them for men anywhere in stores" in the US.[47] Nike, Inc., was contacted about the availability of the style in men's sizes, and the company replied that one could get men's sizes from the UK. They said they were not sure why the demand for men's Nike Rifts was greater in the UK than in the US.[48] It was decided to compare the demand for this footwear by examining eBay listings in February 2013 to see any geographical differences between the US and the UK. (See Table 7-A.)

COMPARISON OF US AND UK NIKE RIFT LISTINGS IN 2013 ON eBAY				
GENDER	US NUMBER	US PERCENTAGE	UK NUMBER	UK PERCENTAGE
FEMALE	93	86%	41	34%
MALE	12	11%	33	28%
UNISEX	3	3%	45	38%
TOTALS	108	100%	119	100%

Table 7-A

Source: eBay.com (US) and eBay.co.uk (UK), Nike, Inc., February 9, 2013.

The table shows that in February 2013 there was almost the same number of Rifts footwear on either side of the Atlantic, but the number listed as female was 86 percent of the total in the US, while only 34 percent in the UK. Men's Rifts amounted to 28 percent of the total in the UK while only 11 percent in the US. A total of 38 percent of the vendors believed that the style was unisex in the UK while only 3 percent listed them as unisex in the US. On this basis, one could conclude that it is far more acceptable for men to wear these Mary Jane–type footwear in the UK than in the US. Rifts were also available in children's sizes. They look like the adult versions except they have no separate toe compartments.

Another unique example of a Mary Jane sneaker hybrid was the Roxy GI Jane Camo, with a camo pattern on canvas. It had the traditional buckle rather than hook-and-loop closures and was advertised as a military-chic style with a rugged lug sole.

With so many types of variations of Mary Jane footwear to

choose from, it was difficult to decide which ones to select for discussion purposes. However, it is hoped that a representative sample has been included to illustrate current trends with respect to modifications made to closed-toe sandals and Mary Jane–style shoes over the years. The next chapter on mandals explores recent trends with respect to men who wear closed-toe sandals.

Chapter 7 Notes

1. Wilson, *History of Shoe Fashion*, 80.

2. O'Keeffe, *Shoes*, 73–74.

3. "History of High Heels," Andrew's High Heel Page (2008), web.archive.org/web/20130318082103/http://users.powernet.co.uk/wingett/History1.htm.

4. "Dangerous Elegance: A History of the High-Heeled Shoes," *Random History and Word Origins for the Curious Mind* (2008), www.shoera.com/history-high-heels-dangerous-elegance/.

5. "High Heels," Pageant Archives (2006), tiza.com/pageant-archives-archives/highheels.

6. Leslie, F., *Lady's Magazine and Gazette of Fashion*, vol. XXI, no. 6 (December 1867).

7. Swann, J., *Shoes*, 7.

8. Winkler, S. J., "Take off your shoes and walk," *The History of Foot Trouble* (1961), unshod.org/pfbc/toysaw.htm.

9. Pageant Archives (2006).

10. Hamilton, M., "Those Stylish Stiletto Heels," *Ezine Articles* (August 8, 2006), ezinarticles.com.

11. "High Heel Shoes Damage Your Brain," *Lifestyle* (2010), associatedcocontent.com.

12. "Stiletto heel," *Wikipedia* (February 17, 2013), en.wikipedia.org/wiki/stiletto_heel.

13. "Platform shoes," *Wikipedia* (March 22, 2008), en.wikipedia.org/wiki/Platform_shoe.

14. Pageant Archives (2006).

15. Alexander, H., "Graduate's high heels for men are staggering for models," *Telegraph* (June 10, 2005), telegraph.co.uk.

16. Ibid.

17. Motwary, F., "Un Nouveau Ideal," Interview with Rui Leonardes (June 22, 2006), filepmotwary.blog.com/832437.

18. Crocs Mary Jane Sandals (2007), rei.com/product/748390.

19. Walker, R., "Croc On," *New York Times* magazine (July 15, 2007).

20. O'Rourke, M., "The Croc Epidemic: How Crocs Conquered the World," *Slate* magazine (July 13, 2007), slate.com/news-and-politics/2007/07/how-crocs-conquered-the-world.html.

21. Kippen, C., *Foot Talk* (May 9, 2008), foottalk.blogspot.com.

22. Fans of Croc Shoes, "What are Crocs?" (2008), littlerubbershoes.com/what-are-crocs.

23. "Shop by Brand," Robert Wayne Footwear (Commerce, CA, 2007), robertwayne.com/product2 ext.cfm?d=15369.

24. "Leader of the Free World is a Crocs Fan" (June 13, 2007), crocfans.com.

25. "Shop by Brand," Robert Wayne (2007).

26. Ibid.

27. "Crocs Cayman Spiderman Kids," Joe's Sports (2008), joessports.com/product/index=2833689. (Also available at m.shoes.com/crocs-spiderman-cayman/244344.)

28. "Crocs Men's Mary Jane (Coral and Mango)," Shopwiki (2008). shopwiki.com/detail/d=Crocs_MEN'S_MARY_JANE_CORAL.

29. Unisex Shoes Crocs Bistro (2008), www.crocs.com/p/bistro-clog/10075.html.

30. "Barefoot Racing or Almost Barefoot Racing Gaining Traction in Running War," SNEWS (April 17, 2006), snewsnet.com/cgi-bin/snews.

31. "Vibram FiveFingers," *Wikipedia* (2013), en.wikipedia.org/wiki/Vibram_FiveFingers.

32. "Barefoot Ted's Adventures: Los Angeles Marathon XXI wearing Vibram FiveFingers" (2006), barefootted.blogspot.com/2006/03/los-angeles-marathon-xxi-wearing.html.

33. Owings, J., "The World's First Ever FiveFingers 5k Race," Birthday Shoes (2010), birthdayshoes.com/the-world-s-first-ever-five-fingers-5k-race.

34. "Vibram FiveFingers Named a Best Invention of 2007 by *Time Magazine*," Trailspace.com (November 12, 2007), www.trailspace.com/articles/2007/11/12/vibram-fivefingers-named-a-best-invention-of-2007-by-time-magazine.html.

35. Steele, Jessica, interview (June 2, 2010).

36. "The Sneaker Era," (May 4, 2008), nike.us/sneaker/post/kicks.

37. Bellis, M., "Footwear and Shoes," About.com: Inventors (2008), about.com/library/inventors/blshoe.

38. Shoe ad for Dunham's Department Store in the *Trenton Times* (July 9, 1906).

39. Brown, P. L., "Design Notebook: Once Lowly Sneaker is Pedestrian No More," *New York Times* (May 28, 1992), nytimes.com/health.

40. Gill, A., "Limousines for the feet-the rhetoric of sneakers," *Shoes: A History from Sandals to Sneakers*, Georgio Riello and Peter McNeil, eds. (2008), 377, 382.

41. "Bill Bowerman," *Wikipedia* (2008), en.wikipedia.org/wiki/Bill_Bowerman.

42. Bellis, "Footware."

43. Ibid.

44. "Keen-The Original Hybrid Footwear," Shoe Peddlers (2008), shoepeddlers.com/index.

45. Nike Air Rift Shoes, Squidoo.com (2013), squidoo.com/nike-air-rift. (Squidoo no longer active.)

46. "Nike Rift Sandals Unisex!!!" (2010), cgi.eBay.com/NIKE-AIR-RIFT-UNISEX-160456929570.

47. Jacko, "Nike Air Rift Men's Casual Shoes Reviews" (September 7, 2011), buzzillions.com/reviews/men-nike-air-rift-casual-shoes-reviews. (Buzzillions no longer active.)
48. Correspondence from Jamie, NikeStore (July 29, 2010).

CHAPTER 8

THE MANDAL DEBATE

T his chapter examines trends in male sandal usage and the concept of the term "mandal," or "man sandal," which was used to encourage men to wear this footwear. O'Keeffe (1996), in her book *Shoes*, has noted that many types of footwear first worn by men were subsequently "appropriated" by women.[1] According to research for this book, this has been especially true of Mary Jane and other closed-toe sandal-type shoes. In the latter half of the 1900s, any footwear with straps, with the possible exception of the monk strap, which is not a sandal, was increasingly labeled as "Mary Jane" and, therefore, avoided by men. However, this trend may be reversing with certain strapped footwear as men have rediscovered the benefits of sandals in Europe and North America. About the turn of the twenty-first century, a new term given to men's sandals, "mandal," came into vogue. Under this term men can now enjoy the freedom of wearing strapped footwear both for formal and casual wear that they would never have dreamed of wearing a few years ago.

Mandal Types

There are four basic types of mandals: the thong sandal, the slide sandal, the sport sandal, and the fisherman sandal. The main

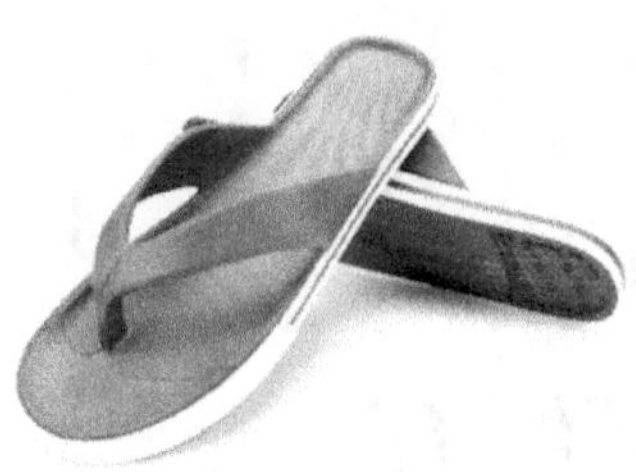

Figure 8-1
Basic thong/flip-flops, 2010

characteristic of the thong sandal, shown in Figure 8-1, is a strap that fits between the big toe and the other four toes which is attached to a flat rubber sole. Pictures show that ancient Egyptians wore these sandals in tomb drawings, such as from King Tut's tomb discovered in the early 1920s.

Slides are flat-soled sandals with bands that go across the instep and are open in the back to allow the feet to more easily slide in and out. These shoes are very popular in different parts of the world, especially in warm-climate countries. In Europe and North America, popularized styles of slides are made by companies like Birkenstock.

Sport sandals can vary from one or more straps across the foot, to the more complex forms where the foot is covered, including the various sneaker/sandal hybrids. Young (2006) maintains that sport sandals are a good way to go for those who own no sandals, because they can "ease into the trend" through this type of mandal.[2]

Fisherman sandals are a dressier type of sandal with one or more thick straps that cross the instep and pass through a center T-strap on top of the foot (Figure 8-2). In a fisherman sandal, the

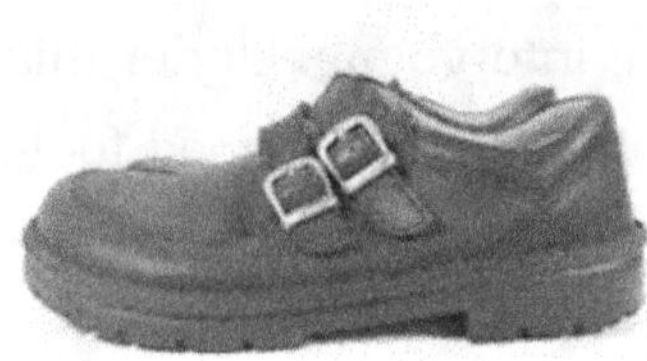

Figure 8-2
Fisherman sandal, 2009

foot is completely covered. The history of this sandal is unknown, but the hypothesis is that they originated in a warm-climate locale. They could also be a form of Roman sandal with the toes enclosed for use in a colder part of the Empire.

Trends Past and Present

Besides the four basic categories of mandals, there are hybrids as well as specialized types. One, the Givenchy closed-toe "Brogue Gladiator Mandal," walked down the runway in 2008. And, as noted in the previous chapter, gladiator styles have appeared more frequently for men in the 2000s, but are still not listed as mandals.

Both men and women have worn sandals since ancient times. But, except for warmer parts of the world and places like the Balkans and Italy, sandal-making became a lost art with the fall of the Roman Empire. A person from Romania who commented on a blog called "Do Men Wear Sandals?" confirmed that men have indeed been wearing sandals in that Balkan country since Roman times.[3]

Recently, in North America, sandals were rediscovered by men as the "comeback kid of footwear" as men have searched for something more comfortable to provide freedom from being trapped in stuffy sneakers or lace-up shoes. In 2006, Chris Larson, the sixty-year-old owner of Larson's Shoe Store in Gloucester, Massachusetts, stated in the *Eagle Tribune* newspaper that sandals are like short pants because "men didn't wear either 50 years ago," but are now wearing them in the twenty-first century.[4] And Joel Habib, a forty-five-year-old resident of Lawrence, Massachusetts, in the same 2006 newspaper article, strongly recommended that men switch to sandals. He said emphatically, "Go for it because of the comfort and breathing room for your feet; you don't know what you're missing."[5] Finally, in the same *Eagle Tribune* 2006 article, Mark-Evans Blackman, chairman of the menswear design department at the Fashion Institute of Technology (FIT) in New York City, was upbeat about the future of sandals, and mandals in particular. He said that the younger generation of men is doing more shopping than their fathers and grandfathers did, and as a result more mandal styles will "pop up."[6] Judging by footwear seen on older men in shopping centers and elsewhere, they are trading in their sneakers and lace-ups for sandals in increasing numbers.

Since the turn of the twenty-first century, sales for men's sandals have skyrocketed. Between June 2003 and May 2004 American men spent $977 million for the purchase of sandals, both open- and closed-toe varieties. From June 2005 to May 2006 they spent a total of $1.25 billion on sandals, an increase of 27 percent over the previous period.[7] According to the NPD Group Inc., a market research company, sales of men's sandals increased another 13.4 percent between 2006 and 2007, or about $1.5 billion per year. While this is only a fraction of the women's sandal market ($6.2 billion), the gap is narrowing.[8] However, there may have been a decrease in sales of shoes and sandals during the recent recession because people may have cut back on footwear purchases and used shoes on hand rather than purchasing new ones. But, as existing footwear becomes worn and economic conditions improve, sales of sandals should again increase.

In 2015, the NPD Group reported that "total sandal sales among independent retailers grew 8 percent to $1.2 billion in the 12 months ending March 2015, following a 9 percent increase in the previous year."

"Sandals have transcended traditional limitations and become season-less, making room for new product and sales opportunities," said Marshal Cohen, chief industry analyst of the NPD Group, Inc. "Clothing and footwear once designated for a specific purpose are now being worn anytime, and anywhere (with and without socks), because consumers are comfortable in them."[9]

With respect to sandals, there are hundreds of women's sandals for sale on the internet, not to mention those for sale in women's retail shoe stores. The shoe styles for women are far more numerous than those for men in popular shoe outlets. On this basis, it is doubtful that men's sandal styles will ever be as numerous as those for women. However, the sale of mandals is definitely increasing, as borne out by the number of sightings of men wearing them at malls, shopping centers, religious services, and even the workplace.

To help answer the question of when did men rediscover sandals, the mail-order catalogs of Sears, Roebuck and Co. and Montgomery Ward were examined because they had the widest distribution at the time and were mailed to the most remote parts of the US. No sandal for men was found until the early 1900s, when the barefoot sandal was marketed to the "entire family" as discussed in chapter 5. This sandal style eventually disappeared in men's sizes, but continued to be popular for boys and girls for most of the twentieth century and was occasionally revived for women, as seen in the mail-order catalogs.

From the early 1900s until the mid-1950s, there was an absence of sandals listed specifically for men in the mail-order catalogs inspected. In 1950, three fisherman sandal types were advertised in the Sears catalog for men and boys, but these were only 2 percent out of a total of 140 men's boots and shoes that year (Figure 8-3).[10] A note of interest is that Ronald Reagan wore a pair of fisherman-type sandals in some scenes of the 1949 film *The Hasty Heart*, costarring Patricia Neal. It is possible that an actor who wore sandals could have made them popular enough for Sears to list them in their 1950 catalog.

Twenty-one years later, in 1971, there were still only four sandals listed in the Sears catalog for men and boys, but they were

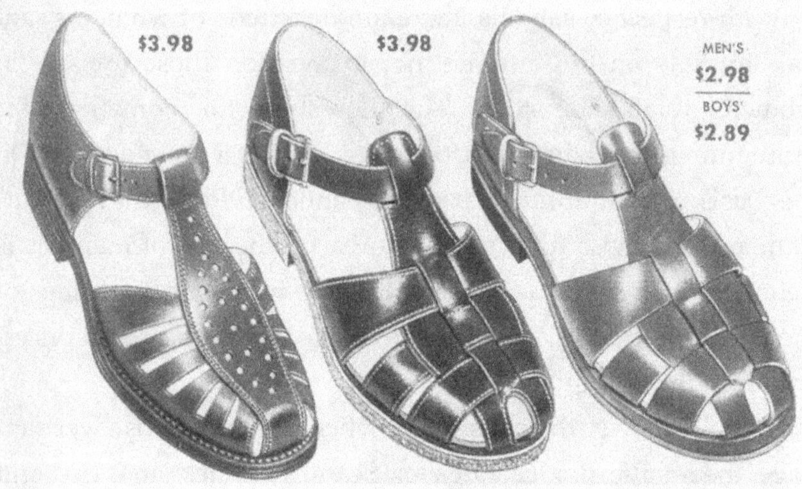

Figure 8-3

Men's and boys' Gold Bond sandals, 1950

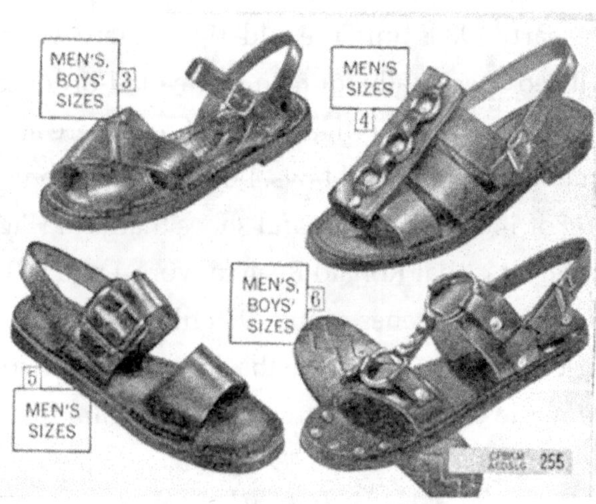

Figure 8-4

Men's and boys' sandals in Sears, Roebuck and Co. catalog, 1971

not the closed-toe fisherman style, rather a two-strap Birkenstock slide-type sandal with open toes and a strap in the back (to hold the foot in place) (Figure 8-4).[11] These sandals were, according to O'Keeffe (1996), "unisex and became the counterculture's back-to-nature, anti-fashion statement."[12]

Besides the Sears catalogs, old newspapers were also checked for men's sandal ads. The *Times Recorder* of Zanesville, Ohio, on May 25, 1928, offered a pair of men's sandals in "moccasin black or tan." And the *Sheboygan Press* in Sheboygan, Wisconsin, on June 6, 1936, ran an ad for men's sandals costing only forty-nine cents a pair. All of these ads were similar to those in the 1971 Sears catalog.

The *Newark Advocate* of Newark, Ohio, carried an ad on July 2, 1937, for "men's ventilated work sandals." Unfortunately, there was no picture of these sandals in the ad, but it is assumed that they were designed to keep feet cool in the workplace. As noted in the discussion on Crocs, the new Bistro style was targeted specifically to working people, especially food service workers. Barefoot sandals, discussed earlier, were sold to men for less than one dollar a pair in the early twentieth century, but were not durable for heavy work and fell out of favor because they could not compete with work boots and shoes.

The Esska Company of Germany in 2009 developed a work sandal concept called safety sandals. The sandals looked similar to the barefoot sandal but had steel toecaps, oil- and slip-resistant soles, and openings on the top so one's foot could breathe. This sandal/work shoe in 2012 became more current with the addition of hook-and-loop-fastened straps rather than the traditional-style buckles.

Sandals may not have been very popular for men in the 1930s and 1940s, but they were still available for those who desired them. In fact, ethnic groups from southern Europe who had worn sandals in the old country provided a market for them in the New World. The sandal was rediscovered as women's fashion footwear in the 1930s and 1940s, as judged by the many illustrations found in mail-order catalogs.

Attitude Changes toward Men's Sandals

The question that comes to mind after doing this intensive research is, why has it taken so long for sandals to become popular with men in North America? On one hand, men had the choice of cool and comfortable footwear, especially in warmer climates, but on the other hand, there was a general reluctance of many men to try something different. Women appeared to have no inhibitions regarding the wearing of sandals or new fashions as men. Barbara Shaum (2010), a shoe designer who operated a boutique in New York, observed footwear trends for fifty years. Shaum has produced some fifty sandal types that cater to a clientele equally divided between men and women. She maintains that clothing and footwear styles have become more casual since the 1990s, when people started "to wear loose clothing and sandals," and she believes that casual Fridays had a lot to do with this change.[13] Another influence on shoes occurred in the 1960s and 1970s with the advent of the Flower Children movement that resulted in a more unisex look to clothing and footwear.

In the twenty-first century, men wear earrings, long hair, and short pants, which during most of the twentieth century would have been unheard of. But, when it comes to sandals, there has been reluctance by most men to wear them. Beryl Wing, image consultant, makes the point that wearing sandals may be a question of "power" for men:

Sandals cover less of the foot; therefore, mak[ing] a man feel vulnerable; not a happy state for most men. Men don't ever want to be laughed at which indicates a loss of power.

Sandals have the hint of the artist in them, and while women love the artistic and being different, men tend to follow the leader and shun the creative [at least with regard to footwear]. Men are practical in that they wear what is functional. [Thus,] a pair of sandals that comes out only on weekends during the summer months is not usually a smart buy. Men don't want 1,000 pairs of shoes like Imelda Marcos, or even a closet full like the women in their lives. They do want functional, versatile footwear for multiple duty.[14]

The wearing of sandals never seemed a problem with the Romans, even with power issues, but their slaves could not wear any type of footwear to show class distinctions. And few people know the heat Thomas Jefferson took when he was the first US president to wear lace-up shoes in the White House, which at that time was considered a feminine style.

Because of the controversy associated with men and sandals, it was helpful to ascertain how people actually feel about this subject. Polls about men's usage of sandals with comments from around the world were found on the internet. One called "Men Wearing Sandals" appeared on the Mister Poll site in 2008 and addressed the question "Should men wear sandals?" A total of seventy-nine men said yes, and forty-one women in the sample agreed with the statement (see Table 8-A).

SHOULD MEN WEAR SANDALS?				
GENDER	YES		NO	
	#	%	#	%
MEN	79	81%	19	19%
WOMEN	41	73%	15	27%
TOTALS	120		34	

Table 8-A
Source: Mister Poll, 2008

In this poll a question was also asked whether a man should wear socks with sandals, and out of a total of 106 respondents, 69 percent felt socks should never be worn with sandals.[15]

Another internet poll on the subject of mandals was found, but fewer than twenty people responded, hardly a representative sample. This poll was originally placed on the internet in 2003 when the term "mandal" was not well known by the public. Most respondents in the poll, all of whom were men, said they had seen a significant increase in mandal popularity over the years. When asked if they had "ever [been] ridiculed by others for wearing mandals," approximately three-fourths replied they had *not*, while 25 percent *had* been ridiculed. Seven respondents said they wore mandals because "they are cool."[16]

Besides some men being ridiculed as adults for wearing mandals, there could also be some reluctance by men wearing them because of an unpleasant experience with sandals when they were boys.

Another poll called "Boys in sandals—Were you forced to wear sandals?" shows some interesting facts. Only men were asked to respond to this question, and thirty-five out of a total sample of eighty-six said they *were* forced to wear sandals against their wishes, while fifty-one said they were not forced to wear sandals (see Table 8-B).

BOYS IN SANDALS— WERE YOU FORCED TO WEAR SANDALS TO SCHOOL?				
	YES		NO	
	#	%	#	%
MEN	35	41%	51	51%

Table 8-B
Source: Mister Poll, 2004.

On the other hand, girls were asked, "Do you like to see boys wearing sandals?" Of the thirty-one female respondents, twenty said, "Yes," three said, "Sometimes," and two said, "Some guys look great in sandals." Only one of the girls said, "No."

Jimmie, the teenage boy who created the poll in 2004, said:

I was always embarrassed to wear sandals in public especially around friends. My mother made me wear sandals from my earliest memories and still makes me wear them in public on most every occasion. I always felt that sandals were for girls, not boys. I am one of the only boys in my Jr. High who wears sandals to school. The guys sometimes tease me but a lot of the girls think it's "cute" to see a guy in sandals. Sometimes it can be embarrassing.[17]

Richard Swanson, a Michigan man, said that he loved wearing his brown barefoot sandals in the 1940s when a boy. He had no problem wearing them to school until the first day in fifth grade, when boys who had previously worn sandals suddenly found them infantile and began to tease him. As a result, he persuaded his parents to buy him monk-strap Oxfords for school wear.[18] Barefoot sandals were still available in children's sizes at that time for those boys or girls who wished to wear them before being eventually "sized out." In fact, Sears catalogs for the late 1940s had the twin T-strap style revived in adult sizes for a few years, but it was listed as "ladies" footwear. Thus, girls who had outgrown the children's sizes could continue to wear the style in ladies' sizes. For boys it was a different story, since they would not wear girls or ladies shoes, which to them was worse than to wear infantile sandals.

Unpleasant Sandal Experiences

From what has been uncovered in this study, shoes seem to have been a common target to bully and tease young boys no matter their age. Could this bullying and teasing affect how adult men perceived the wearing of sandals when they became adults? One seven-year-old boy described an unpleasant experience at school where he was bullied because his mother made him wear white sandals with a single strap and buckle with a cutout "daffodil design" on top between the toe and strap. He hated these shoes "with a passion."[19] There was a boy seen in a Valley Stream, New York, class photograph wearing similar white sandals to school. There was no date on the picture, but it appears to be from the early 1940s, as judged by the clothing style. Since other children in the class picture had on sandals, teasing was probably not a problem for him. It was only after the wearing of sandals and short pants fell into disuse that one could be teased for continuing to wear them. Geography could have played a role for children who wore sandals in urban cities like New York, Boston, and Philadelphia, which had more sandal wearers because of the large numbers of immigrants from southern Europe, where they were more commonly worn.

Paul said in 1999 that in the UK boys who wore sandals after the age of eight or nine created a certain "stigma." He recalled being with a group of friends in the early 1970s between the ages of twelve to fifteen when they saw another boy a few years younger who wore shorts and was "still wearing sandals." They said the boy must be a "baby" or "mummy's boy." Paul also recalled boys aged fourteen or fifteen who continued to wear sandals regardless of the teasing they received. When Paul entered secondary school, he still had a fairly new pair of sandals but wore them around the house or in the garden, where none of his friends would "catch" him with them on.[20]

A German contributor to Historical Boys' Clothing stated that when he was thirteen years old he felt that to wear sandals was in some way "exciting," but he was also "embarrassed" because of his age. This German youth and his friends began to view sandals as "girlish" or "uncool." One day his mother took him to a shoe store to buy sandals, but when he returned home with the sandals on and stepped out of the car, he saw that his friends playing in the street were definitely looking at his feet. To this young man's relief, not one of them said a word about his sandals.[21]

Another example is from Henery Busum, an eleven-year-old in 1946. Busum was forced to wear a short-pants Little Lord Fauntleroy suit with shiny black shoes as a ring bearer at a wedding, but was extremely embarrassed by the event. Henery stated that he "wouldn't be caught dead wearing short pants, knee socks, [and sandals or Mary Janes] which he considered a totally sissy look." The reaction to his clothing from wedding guests was, "The gals thought I looked just too cute for words and the men smirked and tried to keep from bursting out laughing."[22] One might wonder if the men at the wedding in 1946 would have worn similar Fauntleroy-type suits and footwear when they were boys twenty years earlier, a time when this clothing style was popular.

By the last half of the twentieth century, sandals and short pants had virtually disappeared from the fashion scene, except for very small boys or those required to wear this clothing during formal occasions like weddings. As such, there is probably a reluctance of many men who remember them when they were children to wear them now that they have come back in vogue. But the attitude of men to not wear sandals has changed, as judged by the increase of men who wear mandals.

Decline of Sandals for Men

One might wonder why sandals fell out of fashion even in warm-climate countries like Italy and Spain. Weidner said in 2008 that it was not sandals that became unpopular but "that fashion is often more important than comfort." Italy was an example, he reported, whereby the 1980s sneakers became more popular than sandals. The reason was that sneakers were both fashionable and comfortable. Teenagers started this trend, which was then picked up by younger boys because they were more practical than sandals for sports, particularly soccer. In fact, one could tell where a person lived based on his clothing and shoes in the first half of the twentieth century, but "by the 1980s this [clothing distinction] had ended, and both boys and girls [wore] an American-influenced pan-European fashion with both jeans and sneakers a very important part of that look." Weidner went on to state that "sandals never disappeared" completely; they just were no longer the principal type of footwear.[23] Sandals were still popular in 1973 in Italy for boys and girls, but sneakers started to be worn, which eventually became the dominant footwear fashion for children in all of Europe as well as North America.

According to Kippen (2004), an authority on sandals, throughout much of history "footwear did not differ according to sex," although women might adorn their sandals with jewels more than men.[24] And, in ancient Rome, sandal color was more important in differentiating rank and authority rather than gender. Until the 1900s most boys dressed in kilts, tunics, or dresses with the same shoes and sandals as girls did with no thought of being the same. So, why is there such a strong feeling about clothing and footwear with respect to gender today? Why are there boy shoes and girl shoes? These points will be addressed in the next chapter in more detail. Suffice it to say that many men, until recently, considered sandals to be more a female style and to be avoided at all costs.

Marketing Influences

Roberts (2002) states that shopping malls played a big role in affecting gender choices with respect to clothing. She says:

By making constant male/female associations with certain products and activities [because] they create and reinforce the notion that gender is something innate that comes from within, [companies can] target certain people. [The] constant linkage of products with gender . . . is seen throughout our entire lives, [and] contributes to the unconscious internalization of gender. Malls tell us what is and is not masculine and feminine by making connections between products and gender which certainly does not come from within. [People think] there is a need to display gender [which] can only be done with and through accessories, items and products.[25]

By the separation of a boys section of clothing from the girls for generations, each sex unconsciously accepts the colors, patterns, styles, and shapes displayed within a particular section as either masculine or feminine. Actually, the only major difference between a man's and woman's feet is the size, with the man's generally longer and wider.

Shoes in and of themselves are gender-neutral because they can be worn by either sex, as was the case throughout most of history.[26] So, with both sexes having been conditioned to the traditional roles of men and women, it is no wonder boys objected and continue to object to wearing certain so-called "female" items of clothing, including footwear that they believe to be infantile and feminine. To change this thinking, it might help to label footwear as unisex, which would eliminate this situation so people could wear what they like without fear of criticism.

Dr. Martens is labeling many of its styles with male and female sizes printed on the inside of the shoe as well as on the outside of the box. This company collaborated with the designer Raf Simons to produce some new men's fisherman-style sandals as part of its Spring/Summer 2011 shoe collection. As yet, these shoes are sized only for men, so it will be interesting if they will also put women's sizes inside the sandals as well as on the box.

The research shows that strap shoes, once worn only by men as soldiers or royalty, are now avoided by the majority of men because of the name "Mary Jane" that has become associated with the style in the US. The author wonders if there could be an element of fear or a potential loss of manliness as a form of anxiety to wear sandals which are a form of the strap shoe even though the Roman Empire was built by men wearing them. Coker states that in 2006 "some guys, obviously having doubts about their masculinity, made fun of other guys who wear flip-flops or sandals, or as they call them, Mandals during the warmer months."[27] Turner (2006) believes "there is nothing even remotely feminine about sandals or flip-flops. If flip-flops were more commonly called thongs, then maybe! But no."[28] Thus, the name applied to an object is very significant with respect to gender identity. The term "mandal" may help those men who have had hang-ups to feel more at ease with sandal usage. Thus, the concept of mandals was a marketing tool to attract men and boys to a return to wear sandals.

There is a myth that a boy or man who may wear a shoe that has been labeled by the manufacturer as feminine may make that person gay. No evidence was found to link the wearing of sandals to make an individual gay. In fact, girls in the 1970s often shopped for jogging shoes in the male section because the kind of shoe they wanted was not available in the girls' department. Girls also felt that the girls' versions of jogging shoes were not as well made as those for boys and men.

Traditionally, certain colors were considered more masculine or feminine, like red or pink for females. No boy would wear red shoes or sandals. But, when Michael Jordan started to wear red basketball shoes, it suddenly became acceptable for boys and men to wear that color. During the 2010s one can view different-colored shoes for men and boys quite frequently on sports teams at both the college and professional levels and at the local shopping malls. And football players have also worn pink shoes and gloves in support of a cure for breast cancer. If enough male celebrities, like rock singer Marc Bolan, wear Mary Jane–type shoes, who can predict if the strap shoes will again become a male accessory, or at least unisex, as it was in days past? However, gender perceptions are still strong and are difficult to alter.

Divito wrote in 2006 for the Associated Press that "men's sandals remain, in a weird way, controversial, eliciting strong feelings on one side or the other."[29] As a result of this statement, the author checked the internet for public opinion on "gayness" and sandal use. A poll in 2006 under the title "The Sandal Debate: Gay or Nay?" indicated that of the 105 participants, 46 percent said that sandal use was "Not Gay," 7 percent said, "Maybe a little Gay," and only 20 percent felt, "Yes, Gay."[30]

THE SANDAL DEBATE: GAY OR NAY?		
	Number	Percent
Yes, Gay	21	20%
Maybe a Little Gay	8	7%
Not Gay	48	46%
Jesus Wore Sandals	28	27%
Total	105	100%

Table 8-C

Source: Poll. Xbox360&Xbox Forums. "The Sandal Debate: Gay or Nay?" 2006.

An example of an extremely negative attitude about men who wore sandals was illustrated by a British reader who posted a comment at Fashion156.com in 2008. This individual stated that all the men in her family did not and would not wear sandals, and "look[ed] down" on other men who wore them. If she brought a boyfriend home to meet her parents he must never wear sandals or her father would not "take him seriously" nor would he "trust" him.[31] Another internet reader in 2006 responding to the question "What do you think of Mandals?" stated that while he didn't want to offend anyone, he felt a guy who wore sandals was branded as "wimpy" and not "capable of taking charge and very much in touch with his feminine side."[32] With such attitudes toward men who wear sandals, it is no wonder it has been difficult and an upward struggle for men to wear them.

Additional Sandal Questions

Comments presented above from polls on the internet about mandals have been tame compared to the controversy that occurred with a high-profile individual, President Barack Obama, in 2010. This event with the president became known as the "Obama Mandal Scandal!"

On July 31, 2010, President Barack Obama wore a pair of open-toe sandals with jeans to the International Spy Museum in Washington, DC. Unbelievably, simply wearing sandals and jeans resulted in a flood of headlines on the internet. The comments were either pro or con and ranged from "Awful sandals and ugly jeans" to "Where can I get some Obama sandals?"[33] Closed-toe sandals would have drawn less attention because the president's feet would have been largely covered, but he should have been able to wear what he wanted, like Thomas Jefferson did when he wore his controversial lace-up shoes, or George W. Bush wearing his Crocs and presidential-seal socks. It may be as a result of the publicity and internet reaction that the president may have actually encouraged more men to wear sandals.

Wilkinson posted pictures on the internet of the actor Mel Gibson and other celebrities wearing mandals in 2010, and this only "heated [up the] controversy of well-known people wearing these sandals."[34] On the other hand, some people maintained that sandals should be worn only by men at the beach or in the shower.[35]

Mohn (2010) raised the question "Should men be *allowed* to wear sandals?" which gendered a significant debate on this subject on the internet. He questioned why there were such:

harsh opinions about men wearing sandals [and asked]: Are sandals unattractive, feminine or out of style? The plain truth is they are in fact comfortable, low maintenance footwear, and for the most part, not expensive to buy; all reasons which have contributed to the sandal's increased popularity.[36]

However, controversy still exists and will continue until people accept the phenomenon that men once again can and will wear sandals, or get tired of debating the subject.

Another reason sandals may have been slow to be worn by men is a reluctance to show their feet and toes in public. There have been many postings on the internet alluding to unsightly (ugly) toes and feet on men who wear open-toe sandals, especially those men who wear such footwear in the workplace. Kay (2005) says *Fortune Magazine* called mandals the "SUV of footwear: bold, paradigm-shifting, slightly disingenuous, and dangerously popular" that appeals to many men. But she says that if you are going to invest in a pair of mandals, you should get a pedicure and not display toenails that are crumbling and yellow. More and more men are following this advice and getting pedicures. Kay says her husband refused to get a pedicure until she talked him into it. When he finally got one, he "loved it," and then decided he wanted to get sandals. He bought a pair which he wore with slacks to business meetings, and sat "across from people with his bare toes exposed." She tried to dissuade him from doing this, but "he wouldn't listen."[37]

Another big issue regarding mandal use is whether to wear socks with them. How this notion about socks started is not clear, since even many Romans wore a form of sock under their sandals in cold weather. Currently, the consensus is that socks and sandals *do not mix*. However, many disregard this unwritten "rule" and continue to wear socks with this footwear. In Europe socks worn with sandals appear to be more acceptable than in North America. And, as more sandal/sneaker hybrids become available to consumers, it may become more acceptable to wear socks with sandals for those who so desire. This is because many hybrid sandal/sneakers look more like athletic shoes, and since one can wear socks with sneakers without criticism, it may be an easy transition to wear socks with this hybrid.

In the article "Socks and Sandals: On the front lines of the style war," fashion lover Sally Ho stated in 2008 that the look of socks and sandals was unattractive, but often something unattractive can be interesting so that "what was once ugly may not stay that way forever."[38] Actually, the concept of no socks with sandals may already be changing, based on models seen on different runways who wore socks with sandals. On the internet one can see hundreds of people who wore socks with sandals in all types of settings. There was even an ad for an "Outdoor Sandal Sock" in 2004, designed specifically to go with sports sandals with the claim that they have "optimum moisture transport."[39]

Sandals and Foot Health

As the increase in sales of mandals has occurred, so has the rise in men's foot problems. The American College of Foot and Ankle Surgeons saw an increase in heel and big toe pain, Achilles tendonitis, aches in the legs and back, and even breaks and fractures in the foot's twenty-six bones, related to the wearing of improper sandals and flip-flops with little or no support. Their recommendation in 2009 was to buy mandals with padded straps and cushioned sturdy soles.[40] Problems related to aches in the legs and back are also linked to improper footwear.

Dr. Rock Positano (2007), who wrote "Mandal with Care" for the *New York Post*, states that wearing open-toe sandals could make a person susceptible to foot injury, as well as expose the feet to insect bites and sidewalk hazards. Stubbed toes that result in fractures or ingrown toenails are a constant problem with exposed toes in open-toe sandals. And, with more skin exposed to the sun in sandals, there has been an increase in the cancer cases that involve the feet.[41] Closed-toe sandals, while not as cool as their open-toe cousins, cover most of the foot and, thus, could prevent some of these foot problems.

Finally, it has been observed that mandals keep up with the fashion rule that adults are the first to start a footwear style and later that same style is downsized to be worn by children. Mandals seem to be no exception to this rule of fashion. An example of this rule was a picture of Ben from Berkeley, California, that appeared in *Superhero Journal*, March 2008, with his first pair of mandals, made by See Kai Run Shoe Company.[42]

Although Ben's mandals have hook-and-loop straps rather than the older-style buckles, the basic sandal was similar to the barefoot sandals worn a hundred years earlier. One could then question if the word "mandal" will continue to be used as more and more men wear sandals, as the term may no longer be needed.

Since there are still hang-ups as to a sandal being feminine or juvenile that could prevent more men from adopting the mandal style, there will be an in-depth discussion in the next chapter on this concern.

Chapter 8 Notes

---

1. O'Keeffe, *Shoes*, 240, 434.

2. Young, Emily, "Making their Mark: It's all about Comfort as Sandals for Men Gain Ground," *Eagle Tribune* (July 16, 2006), eagletribune.com/lifestyle/local.

3. "Do Men Wear Sandals?" AskMen.com, eds. (September 6, 2008), askmen.com.

4. Larson, C., quoted by Emily Young, "Making their Mark," *Eagle Tribune.*

5. Habib, J., quoted by Emily Young, "Making their Mark," *Eagle Tribune.*

6. Blackman, M., quoted by Emily Young, "Making their Mark," *Eagle Tribune.*

7. Divito, N., "Father's Day Fashion: The Rise of the Mandal," Associated Press (June 10, 2007), recordonline.com/apps/pbcs.

8. "Jay-Z Helps Bring Sandals Back," *Chronic Magazine* (2009), chronicmagazine.com/archived/public.php?level=1&page_id=2030.

9. The NPD Group, "Sandals Continue to Lead Sales Growth for Independent Footwear Retailers, Reports NPD," The NPD Group, Inc., June 25, 2015, www.npd.com/wps/portal/npd/us/news/press-releases/2015/sandals-continue-to-lead-sales-growth-for-independent-footwear-retailers-reports-npd/.

10. Sears, Roebuck and Co. Spring/Summer catalog (1950), 386.

11. Sears, Roebuck and Co. Spring/Summer catalog (1971), 255.

12. O'Keeffe, *Shoes*, 290.

13. Shaum, B., quoted by Isabel Wilkinson, "Men's Sandals Called Mandals," *Daily Beast* (August 5, 2010), thedailybeast.com/blogs-and-stories/2010-08-05/mens-sandals-called-mandals.

14. Wing, B., quoted by Jessica Jones in "Do Real Men Wear Sandals?" *Fashion Worlds* (June 2004), fashionworlds.blogspot.com/2000.

15. "Men Wearing Sandals," Mister Poll Enterprises (April 7, 2008), www.misterpoll.com/polls/81641.

16. ———, "Mandals," Mister Poll Enterprises (August 10, 2003), misterpoll.com/polls/126762/results.

17. ———, "Boys in Sandals – Were you Forced to Wear Sandals?" Mister Poll Enterprises (December 9, 2004), misterpoll.com/polls/188845/results.

18. Swanson, Richard, mail correspondence (October 1, 2010).

19. Zarocostas, M., "My Dainty Little Shoes," *City Writers Review*, vol. II (September 2002), web.archive.org/web/20020928151026/http://www.citywriters.com/shoes.html.

20. Weidner, D., "English School Sandals: Paul," Historical Boys' Clothing (November 10, 1999), www.histclo.com/schun/gar/shoe/sandal/su-sandale9601.html.

21. ———, "German Sandals: Personal Experiences," Historical Boys' Clothing (July 4, 2000), www.histclo.com/style/foot/sandal/cou/ger/gsand-pe01.html.

22. ———, "Ring Bearer Memories: America, 1946," Historical Boys' Clothing (October 1, 2000), www.histclo.com/act/rel/wed/ring2-us4601.html.

23. ———, "Italian Footwear Chronology – The 20th Century," Historical Boys' Clothing (June 19, 2008), www.histclo.com/country/it/gar/foot/chron/igfc20.html.

24. Kippen, C., "The History of Footwear – Sandals," Curtin University of Technology, Department of Podiatry (Perth, Australia, December 2004), web.archive.org/web/20030701025947/http://podiatry.curtin.edu.au/sandal.html.

25. Roberts, K., "Shopping Malls and Their Role in the Gender System in America," paper for Senior Seminar: Rethinking Sex and Gender, Prof. Bernice L. Hausman (Spring 2002), filebox.vt.edu/users/bhausman/pastcourses/rethink/roberts.

26. Ibid.

27. Coker, M., "Why I'll Wear Vans This Summer," *OC Weekly* (June 22, 2006), www.ocweekly.com/why-ill-wear-vans-this-summer-6371646/.

28. Turner, L., "Theology & Geometry," *Blogger* (2003–08), theogeo.blogspot.com/2006/08.

29. Divito, "Father's Day Fashion."

30. "Poll: The Sandal Debate: Gay or Nay?" TeamXbox Forums (August 2006), forum.teamxbox.com/showthread.php?=461244.

31. Solon-Parry, C., "Sandals for Men," Daily Fashion and Style Blog – Fashion 156 (June 29, 2008), fashion156.dsvr.co.uk/blog/index.php?blog=68&PHPSESSID=6d687c51e411f31c.

32. Galeanda, "What do you think of mandals (man sandals)?" Answer Bag (July 25, 2008), answerbag.com/q_view/876781.

33. Neumann, Jeff, "Barack Obama Mandal Scandal," *Gawker* (July 31, 2010), gawker.com/5601449/barack-obamas-mandal-scandal.

34. Wilkinson, I., "Men's Sandals Called Mandals-Mel Gibson's Mandals," *Daily Beast* (August 5, 2010), thedailybeast.com/blogs-and-stories/2010-08-05/mens-sandals-called-mandals.

35. Ibid.

36. Mohn, M., "Should Men Be Allowed to Wear Sandals?" The Campus Throne (April 7, 2010), googleusercontent.com/search?q=cache:NEuZUW2kzIUJ:thecampusthron.

37. Kay, A., "No Toes Please," Workplace Trends (2005), andreakay.com/workplacetrends/art_6015 (membership required to access).

38. Ho, S., quoted by Monica Pak, "Socks and sandals: on the front lines of the style war," *Toronto Observer* (October 12, 2008), torontoobserver.ca.

39. "Outdoor Sandal Sock," The Sturdy Soapbox (April 22, 2004), sandalsandsocks.typepad.com/soapbox/2004/04/page/2.

40. "Are Popular Sandals Causing Foot Problems in Men?" American College of Foot and Ankle Surgeons, *Foot & Health Facts: Healthy Feet For An Active Life* (2009), www.foothealthfacts.org/article/are-popular-sandals-causing-foot-problems-in-men.

41. Positano, R., "Mandal With Care," *New York Post* (June 26, 2007), www.hss.edu/newsroom_hss-sandels-for-men-foot-health-mandal.asp.

42. "Ben Mandals and Other Pleasures," *Superhero Journal* (March 2008), www.andreascher.com/2008/03/ben-mandals-and-other-pleasures/.

CHAPTER 9

SHOES AND GENDER IN PERSPECTIVE

Previous chapters have focused on closed-toe sandals, including Mary Jane shoes, from an historical perspective. This final chapter, although more controversial and thought-provoking, addresses how people *feel* about sandal footwear from a phenomenological perspective, and how this perspective influences who wears them. It was the Romans who conquered the world wearing sandals and kilt-like uniforms. And it was the Egyptians who wore flip-flop-style sandals for thousands of years without giving them a second thought.

With such a distinguished past, why did sandals and strap shoes fall out of favor, and why has it taken so long for them to be rediscovered as a mainstream fashion by men? Moreover, why were sandals, including the Mary Jane style, once worn by soldiers and military figures, known as sissy footwear? To ascertain the answers to these questions, polls on the internet and questionnaires were used to collect primary source information to augment information found in the literature and photographic records.

Sandals and Gender

Footwear and clothing are powerful symbols of gender. And the fear of being identified with the wrong gender is so strong it

221

has transcended clothing and footwear to other items, such as bicycles, toys, and even some foods. This extreme gender consciousness has occurred because the public is constantly bombarded by mass media to reinforce existing values. Statements such as the title of Feirstein's 1982 book, *Real Men Don't Eat Quiche: A Guidebook to All That Is Truly Masculine*, continue to perpetuate gender differences and reinforce gender inequalities.[1] Sexist comments in advertisements contribute to the long-held view that women are inferior to men. Ads that include women are used by advertisers and manufacturers to increase overall sales because empirical data has found that sex sells, and who does this better than women? Unfortunately, this emphasis on a specific gender, whether real or perceived, has created serious consequences.

Maglaty (2011) in a *Smithsonian Magazine* article quotes Paoletti that the "more you individualize clothing, the more you can sell." Therefore, the fact of having items like shoes, strollers, or even diapers designed in pink or blue colors results in higher sales.[2] No longer is it possible to hand down clothing attire from one child to another, unless the items are for the same gender. Some parents may be embarrassed if a son is seen riding in a pink stroller or is on a pink bicycle because others may comment that he is a girl. There has also been some effort to change the traditional color-coding by creating unisex styles and making gender-neutral colors available. But feelings pro and con on this subject remain strong, judging by comments found in this research.

Layettes, an assortment of clothing, diapers, and bedding sold for newborn babies, was originally available in gender-neutral colors of yellow and white until marketers began to make separate blue and pink colors for boys and girls so onlookers could more easily distinguish boys from girls. Color identification was also facilitated by prenatal tests and ultrasounds that determined the sex, which has helped to increase the sales of gender-specific items well in advance of a baby's birth.

Likewise, for countless generations, as discussed in previous chapters, boys often wore dress-type garments to the age of four or five, when they were "breeched," or graduated to male garments. The question then arises of why are dress-like garments no longer appropriate for boys and men after thousands of years of use in Western society? There are, of course, some holdouts in the form of kilts that are still worn by Scottish and Greek soldiers. Kilts are also worn by many police departments band members in the US when marching in parades, as in President Obama's 2009 inauguration. Should these men wearing kilts be labeled as "sissies" or "warriors," or does it really matter? And are the boys who are wearing strap shoes because of a more practical reason of not yet knowing how to tie shoes with laces examples of sissies (Figure 9-1)?

In Figure 9-2, a photo from the early 1900s shows two boys and a girl wearing barefoot sandals. The older boy has on a sailor suit, while the younger one is dressed like Little Lord Fauntleroy's style as seen in the comic strip character Buster Brown so popular at that time. The boy's sister is dressed like Buster's sister, Mary Jane, in a typical dress and sandals. No one in the early 1900s raised an eyebrow at children's clothing or footwear styles, because they were considered gender-neutral. In contrast, in May 2010, a picture of an eight-to-ten-year-old boy wearing a pair of the same sandals as in Figure 9-2 in the 1900s was advertised on eBay where the seller listed the item as "Tommy-Boy in Shorts and Girl Shoes." Correspondence to the seller for clarification on why she listed the sandals this way was, "They *looked* like girls' shoes."

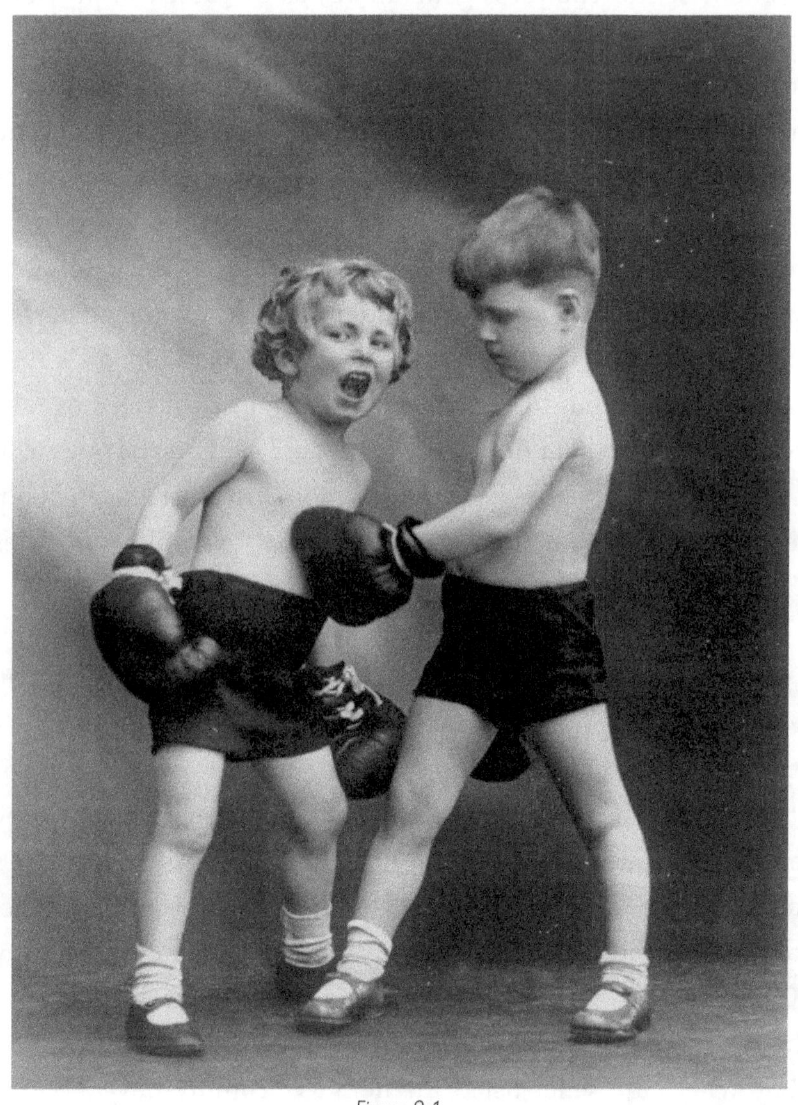

Figure 9-1

20th-century warriors wearing strap shoes, ca. 1935

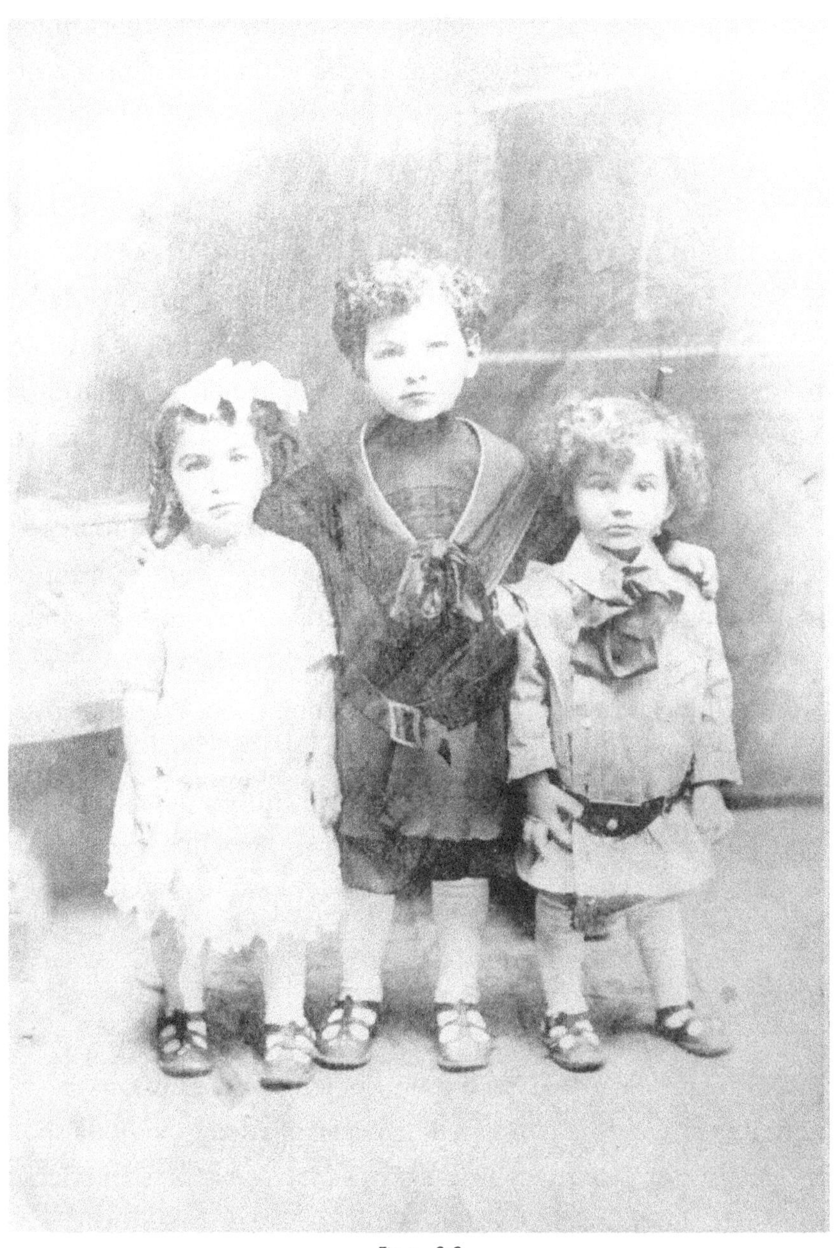

Figure 9-2
Children wearing barefoot sandals, Early 1900s

Sandals of this style were discussed at great length in chapter 4, where it was noted that they had been worn by soldiers in the Balkans. These sandals were actually descendants of similar footwear worn by Roman soldiers two thousand years ago. So, why over the years have they become known as girls' shoes? Even a twelve-year-old boy by the name of Tyson in Michigan in 2008, according to his grandfather, refused to wear to school his new high-top Converse sneakers because girls wore them in his class.[3] William wore these same sneakers in gym class in the 1950s when girls would not be seen dead wearing a pair. Girls at that time preferred low-cut Keds or tennis shoes. So why cannot people go by the old saying "If the shoe fits, wear it?"

Research has shown that many footwear types first appeared in history as men's footwear and subsequently were "appropriated" by women, which eventually became feminine styles or at the least unisex when men continued to wear them. Crocs are a twenty-first-century example of this phenomenon. While the process by which various footwear has been identified with one gender or the other is very complex and not fully understood, the following discussions may acquaint the reader with some of the factors involved with footwear and how many people *feel* about them.

Differences between *Girl* Shoes and *Boy* Shoes

During the early twentieth century there was a move to *genderize* footwear with male or female names assigned to various shoe styles. Current shoe ads with any styles that have straps and buckles, with the possible exception of monk-strap Oxfords, are labeled as "Mary Janes," regardless of the fact they originated as a masculine style. For marketers, straps of any kind equate "feminine" footwear. A notable exception was the German Finn

Comfort Company that sold several shoe styles as "Men's Mary Janes." An inquiry was sent to the company asking whether the shoes were being bought by men with the name "Mary Jane" attached to them. A response was not received. However, the name "Mary Jane" in subsequent advertisements was changed to "Men's Adjustable Strap Shoes" while the style remained the same.

The public, through the help of marketers or manufacturers, has become conditioned to recognize a difference between masculine and feminine footwear and believe that there *is* some innate quality built into a shoe or sandal that makes it appropriate only for one gender and not the other. From an historical perspective based on evidence provided in the previous chapters, this concept is actually a myth. Over the centuries, there has been little difference between men's and women's footwear except for size, with the exception of footwear worn by the upper classes, who could afford more decorative embellishments.

Footwear advertised to children has been sold in children's sizes over the years rather than separate sizes, until the twentieth century, when the shoes were sized smaller to look like adult styles. This change was born out by the photographic records and research. The only case for real gender differences in footwear was whether the shoe leather came from the hide of a cow or a bull. However, when names of shoe styles were given to shoes in the early 1900s, it was to help guide consumers to specific children's styles, even if the names were arbitrarily assigned by advertisers. Notwithstanding the assigning of gender names, manufacturers learned to produce more men's and boys' footwear, because they knew that many women buy men's shoes in addition to their own for comfort and freedom of movement. So it is not often clear whether it is the manufacturer, the advertiser, or the retail store that assigned a name to a shoe, as the classic Mary Jane–style shoe listed in 2010 on the internet as "Little Eric." If this was a girls' shoe, why was it called "Eric" rather than "Erica"? It could be that the name "Eric" may be in the process of becoming a girls' name, as have other former masculine names. After further investigation it was found that the company who made the shoe was itself called "Little Eric," rather than the shoe.

Rubinstein (1995) believes a "new direction" is occurring in men's clothing, as there is a translation of some feminine styles for men appearing in their designs.[4] This could account for the strap shoe styles that appeared at fashion shows in the first decade of the twenty-first century by designers like Dior, Givenchy, and Telfar, who had male models wear them on the runway. And, in the case of Telfar, some male models wore deconstructed (split) pants that resembled skirts. One could speculate if there could be any connection with these fashion shows and the Payless.com strap shoe listed as "Boy's Rugged Mary Jane" or Dr. Martens one- and two-bar shoes listed as "Men's Mary Janes" worn by the male models shown in Figure 9-3. A rather unique single-strap shoe was also marketed in 2010 in Ethiopia and listed as unisex with a sole made from recycled tires.

Are these examples coincidences or trial balloon to see whether the male sex in the US will once again wear strap shoes, as is so common in European markets where they continued to be popular?

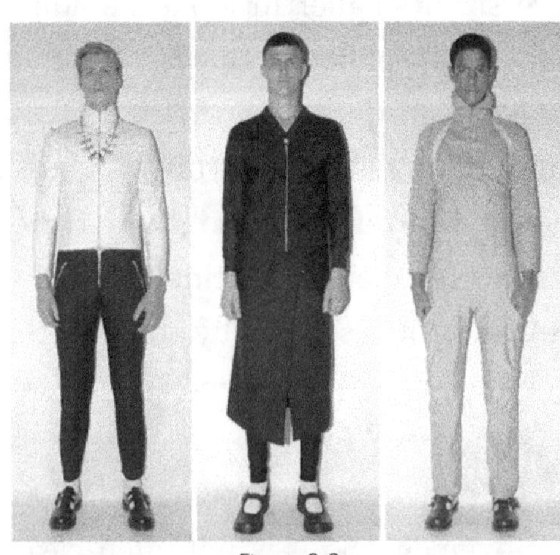

Figure 9-3

Telfar male models wearing Dr. Martens, 2009

In the late 1980s Princess Diana of the UK dressed her two boys in strap shoes to continue the long tradition of royal children wearing this conservative style of footwear. Since strap shoes by this time were considered old-fashioned by most commoners, one wonders if they were worn as a badge to identify the aristocracy. The photographic record shows that mostly wealthy boys wore strap shoes in the late 1900s. Rubenstein (1995) states that *clothing* can act as a "uniform [which] separates the classes and identifies rank."[5] Working-class boys avoided strap shoes, unless the parents wanted their sons to emulate the upper class as part of snob appeal.

On the other hand, girls in all social classes wore Mary Jane–style shoes, as seen in period photos. Much has been written in fashion literature about the snob appeal effect and trickle-down theory for readers who desire more information. In the case of shoes, the trickle-down phenomenon occurs when a small number of trendsetters wear a new style, which is then adopted by the public at large when at this point the trend innovators have moved on to another new fashion. Another reason a child wore button or buckle-strap footwear was that it was easier to fasten than to tie shoelaces. So why would lace shoes be favored over strap shoes for small boys? One explanation might be that most adults at this time period wore lace-up shoes, and since children were considered miniature adults in their clothing attire, they wore laced shoes as their parents did.

Toward the end of the twentieth century the best features of sandals, such as large open areas to ventilate the feet, and sneakers, which have sturdy construction with non-wearing and better-traction soles, were combined to create sandal/sneaker hybrids. An example of this hybrid was the Nike Rift athletic shoe, which has a separate compartment for the large toe but in all other aspects resembles a single-strap Mary Jane with a large open area on top and a strap across the instep. This shoe was popular in the US for women, but was not a winner for men. In the UK the shoe enjoyed popularity with both women and men, as seen by sales on eBay. These Nike footwear are different enough from classic Mary Jane shoes to qualify as a new style that may appeal to the male trendsetter. Nike Rifts may be a positive example of a barrier against men who wear strapped footwear as seen in European countries, which have a single-size system not differentiated by sex as in the US. They even appeared on the feet of men modeling Van Anderson fashions for Spring/Summer 2015.

Gender differences with respect to footwear, except for certain types of high heels, begin to appear less well defined in the twenty-first century than in the twentieth century. Winick (1995), in his book *Desexualization in American Life*, states that "there is a neutral-ization of life going on whereby clothing has become more androg-ynous with more boys going into their sisters' wardrobes and vice versa. Companies are aware of this phenomenon and mak[ing] more boys' clothing and shoes than girls' [because] they know that girls will buy boys' clothing for themselves."[6] Moreover, Rubinstein (1995) says that there is "a new direction in male dress—a masculine translation of female style."[7] Subtle gender differences may also be found in athletic footwear, but for the most part they have become unisex. This unisex footwear can be seen in a larger number of sandal/sneaker hybrids worn by both sexes.

In order to collect information on how people feel about foot-wear and gender, a poll was placed on the internet in 2008 and remained there until November 2009 with the title "Gender and Shoes/Sandals."[8] There were between 129 and 133 responses, since not everyone answered all the questions. There were 110 men who responded and 22 who said they were female.

The results are summarized in Table 9-A.

OPINIONS ON GENDER AND SHOES/SANDALS							
	Yes		No		Not Sure		Total Persons Responding
	#	%	#	%	#	%	
1. Would you wear unisex shoes/sandals?	100	76%	22	17%	9	7%	131
2. Can people wear footwear designated for the opposite sex?	91	69%	29	22%	12	9%	132
3. Do you need a shoe's name to help you buy it?	12	9%	111	83%	10	8%	133
4. Would a guy wearing a "girls'" shoe make him gay?	18	13%	94	71%	21	16%	133
5. Is there a relationship between color and gender?	70	53%	45	35%	16	12%	131
6. Can anyone wear shoes they like without worrying about gender?	105	81%	17	13%	7	6%	129
7. Would a male wearing female footwear be considered "inferior" to other males?	23	17%	97	75%	10	8%	130

Table 9-A

Source: "Gender and Shoes/Sandals," Mister Poll, November 9, 2009.

Three-quarters (76 percent) of the respondents (men and women) said they would have no problem wearing unisex footwear, and 69 percent of those responding said they have no problem with wearing shoes that have been labeled by manufacturers or advertisers as being for the opposite sex. Moreover, 111 of the respondents (83 percent) said they don't need the *names* applied by advertisers to footwear to guide them on which sandals or shoes to purchase. A total of 94 respondents felt that wearing footwear of the opposite sex would not make a person gay.

Although feelings about color and footwear may be diminishing, over half (53 percent) of the respondents felt that there is a relationship between color and shoes, such as pink for women. But 105, or 81 percent, of the respondents did feel that a person should be able to wear whatever footwear they like without worrying about gender considerations. Finally, 75 percent, or three-quarters, of the respondents felt that wearing what are labeled as "female" footwear would not make a man *inferior* to other men. So, based on these findings, there appears to be a relaxing of negative feelings about men once again wearing sandals, which is occurring as discussed in the previous chapter as more and more men have discovered the benefits of wearing sandals, as can be seen in the twenty-first century.

Even after this research, it was still unclear how sandals diffused to North America. In 1903 the *New York Times* reported that factories could not keep up with the demand for T-strap sandals, referred to as the "English barefoot sandals." A movement in Europe that called for more hygienic footwear for health reasons was a possible reason for the rediscovery of the sandal around the turn of the twentieth century. A back-to-nature movement led by Sebastian Kneipp, a Catholic priest, who founded a health center with baths at Worishofen in Bavaria, Germany, got his idea to either go barefoot or wear sandals from Capuchin monks. He wrote that he "sold 60,000 pairs of specially designed sandals each year worn by both people of means and people of low degree."[9]

Eventually, many health centers were built throughout North America and Europe, including the famous sanatorium operated by John Harvey Kellogg at Battle Creek, Michigan. Kellogg was influenced by Kneipp, so it was feasible that the sandal was recommended at these health centers like in Germany. Thus, the term "barefoot sandal" could be derived from Kneipp's concept of walking *barefoot* or in *sandals*. Even the hippie movement of the 1960s and 1970s has been traced to Kneipp and others in the late nineteenth century as part of the back-to-nature movement.

Sandals by Social Status

The sandal was a badge of authority in Roman times, where there existed a strict hierarchy of usage. By decree, Emperor Marcus Aurelius (121–180 AD) stated that only he, as emperor, and his successors could wear red sandals. Roman senators wore black sandals, high-ranking tribunes in the Roman legions wore white sandals, and all others wore brown sandals, while slaves went barefoot. After the fall of the Roman Empire, sandal-making became a lost art in Europe. And, when the sandal was worn, it was identified with lower-class workers that resulted in further decline in usage.

Over hundreds of years it has been common to use clothing and footwear to demonstrate a person's social class. In fact, there has in the past been a tendency for the middle class to copy styles worn by the wealthy, royalty, and the famous. Weidner (2008) maintains that this was especially true in North America, which became the primary reason that clothing like the Little Lord Fauntleroy suit became so popular for boys.[10] It was this style, perhaps more than any other, that received the most ridicule and bullying from older boys toward younger children, especially young boys. Children do not want to play with other kids who do not wear the same or similar style of clothing and shoes, as it can make them feel inferior.[11] Numerous accounts are available of boys who were forced to wear the Fauntleroy suit, including ring bearers at weddings. William remembered seeing a child dressed in a Little Lord Fauntleroy outfit with Mary Jane shoes in the Sunday comics during the 1940s. He assumed the character was a girl. But, in fact, the character was a boy named Perry Winkle. Perry was dressed as a boy of the late 1800s or early 1900s, when such clothing was common. Girls during this same time never wore Fauntleroy suits because it would have exposed their legs, but they did wear the strap shoes. Research found that Howard Hughes's mother made him dress this way to be "better" than the other boys his age in Texas. His suit was the typical Fauntleroy style made of dark blue/black velvet with lace collar, cuffs, hat, and tie, plus long socks with Mary Jane shoes. An example of a

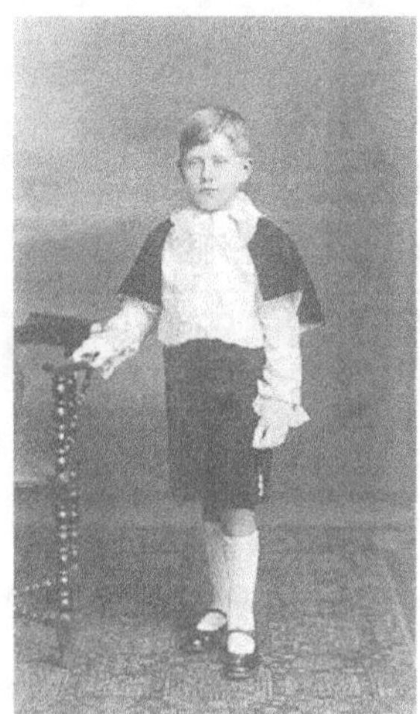

Figure 9-4
*Scottish boy in modified
Fauntleroy suit, 1910*

Scottish boy wearing a modified Fauntleroy suit about 1910 is shown in Figure 9-4. Paoletti (1991) maintains such clothes were "effeminate to modern eyes, but signified nascent masculinity to Victorian parents."[12]

The Fauntleroy suit was also known as a "cavalier-style" velvet suit. By the 1920s the suit had begun to decline in usage, but even today one can still see boys, and even men, like Laurel and Hardy, wear them in movies and television shows. Kippen (2005) writes that these suits "soon were regarded by boys as sissy and effeminate."[13] This concept of being effeminate could have been reinforced when the book *Little Lord Fauntleroy* became a movie, with the main character, Errol, portrayed by a pretty curly-haired girl. In 1921, the movie was remade with Mary Pickford as the little boy, which further established the person as a girl. However, subsequent films made in 1936 and 1980 did have boys playing the part of Errol.

As upper- and middle-income mothers dressed their boys in elaborate clothing styles and strap shoes to imitate royalty or boys of affluent families, these little boys looked different in dress than their peers. As a result, many young boys became the object of bullying and name-calling, maybe not so much for the clothing style, but because they tried to imitate their social betters or the upper class. Today, most people think of the Mary Jane shoe as a little girls' shoe. One could argue that strap shoes are unisex because they were in the past and continue to be in the twenty-first century on both sexes and even some soldiers. The current Mary Jane is marketed under the headings of "buckle brogues" or "strap and buckle" shoes in the UK. A pair auctioned on eBay in August 2008 in a men's size UK 10 (US men's size 11) had a write-up that stated, "These brogues are worn by the officers and sergeants of the Highland Regiments." Buckle brogues are considered the correct footwear for a kilt-type uniform and are available from thistleshoes.com in Scotland. Another firm, Kintail House Ltd., also sells buckle brogues to size UK 14 in New Zealand as an accessory for its line of kilts. The company states that "many consider the Scottish Strap and Buckle Brogue to be the most attractive men's footwear ever made."[14]

In this context, the Scottish boy in Figure 9-4 does not look effeminate or sissy when compared to the Highland Soldiers' footwear, and further, he could be classified in a warrior category.

However, one could question the white knee socks worn by the boy in contrast to the colorful plaid Highland socks worn by the soldiers.

While the sandal once showed class rank in Roman times, a *New York Times* article states that "sandals no longer signify class because they are worn all year by all types of people just as was the case for much of the clothing in the twenty-first century."[15]

Sandals by Color

As discussed previously, color was an important criterion to distinguish and influence class authority and gender choices. But footwear color continued to be a significant factor to label a shoe as either male or female. In the mid-1950s, a general rule was that boys wore brown or blue sandals while girls wore red or white ones.

Crocs, discussed in chapter 7, are a modern example of how color may still be important for gender association. Crocs started out in the 2000s as a men's boat shoe at the Fort Lauderdale, Florida, boat show, but quickly began to be worn by women and children. When a simple strap across the instep was added to create the Mary Jane Croc, a female shoe emerged and became a best seller. So, to counteract a decline in sales to boys, the company added a Spider-Man logo on the rear strap and sides of the Crocs to make it appeal to boys. And a male shoe was born.

Does this sound confusing? Just wait, as there is more to come. Brittany posted on the Yahoo! Issues blog, December 8, 2007, that Crocs are really unisex: "You just have to choose the right color for the appropriate gender." Another person who calls herself New Momma stated on the same blog, on March 12, 2007, that Crocs are for both girls and boys, but, "if you want to make sure, [the shoes] are definitely a boy's version to appease your hubby, they have blue and green camo ones." She stated that she planned on getting her "son a pair this summer [2007], probably just [the] blue ones." Natalie wrote on April 21, 2007, at the mormonmommywars.com blog that at the turn of the twentieth century, "pink was a color for boys. It's even coming back in style now."

Busse states that "most people have been taught that certain colors should only be worn by females [like pink and purple], but that is changing as a result of the influences by hip-hop boys and rappers on TV who've really been into all colors, especially pink." Pink may be making a comeback for boys and men, as exemplified by pink shirts, ties, suits, and even footwear. But some color/gender relationships are still taboo. Robyn Jody (2007) notes that "it's not always the style. If a guy wears ice skates or classic 'quad' roller skates with white boots, even though the boot style for men and women is identical, they're *sissy* shoes."[16] Technically, white is the *absence* of color, but it can also evoke personal feelings and memories. If football and basketball players wear white high-top shoes or boots, why not ice or roller skaters? Perhaps this barrier of color is beginning to shatter, as professional hockey players have some white details on their otherwise black skates.

In Warner's (2006) book, *When the Girls Came Out to Play: The Birth of American Sportswear*, there are numerous photographs of men and women wearing identical dark-colored skates in the 1800s. It was difficult to determine from the details on the pictures whether they wore shoe boots or they just fastened the skates to their normal, dark high-top boots. When did white shoe skates first appear? These skates became popular in the 1920s when Olympic gold medalist Sonja Henie began wearing them.

In 2011, a thirteen-year-old boy on the internet stated he needed a pair of ice skates, and asked whether he could use his sister's hand-me-down skates. The only problem he saw was that the skates were white. People who responded said it was okay to use his sister's skates, but some emphatically stated that white was for girls only. Only one person indicated he had dyed his sister's skates black to make them masculine, but when they got scratched, the white showed through and he felt embarrassed. Another person stated that "the whole men wear black skates, women wear white thing is so, so, stupid . . . they're just colors."[17] More research in the area of color and gender is needed to clarify questions with respect to personal feelings and footwear color. However, when shoes are identical except for color, why should color make a difference?

The color red in footwear is an interesting topic that has been referred to in previous chapters of this book. Red has always been considered a hot color favored by men, since in the past it denoted rank and power (i.e. only the emperor was permitted to wear red sandals in ancient Rome). Louis XIV of France wore red high-heel shoes that increased his height but also became a symbol of authority and power, as in the case of the Roman emperors. Another use of red was in the footwear and tunics worn by Spartan soldiers to conceal from their enemies any blood from wounds. But, when Spartan youth began to wear red footwear as a fad, officials stopped this behavior through a decree that only soldiers could wear the red boots when they went to war.

Today, red footwear and jerseys have made a comeback with men on different professional and college sports teams. Football players in the 2010 National Football League wore hot-pink shoes to support Breast Cancer Week. And one can go to any local mall and see men and boys wearing red athletic shoes.

Color in clothing and accessories, including footwear, has been used as a social marker to indicate a person's sex. Many people still feel uneasy if a child's sex is unknown, as it could cause socially awkward situations. So the introduction of pink and blue solved this problem, but it also raised other issues. The convention of girls dressed in pink and boys in blue has become so entrenched in our society that to vary from this norm was and is to run the risk of hostility of many peers. Many women would never be seen in colors deemed appropriate only for men, no matter the age, even though they may like and prefer such colors. The paradox is that certain clothing styles and footwear once viewed as masculine are now considered feminine.

Renkl (2000), on her Nashville Scene blog, relates that her three-year-old son said in a shoe store that he wanted a pair of shiny red patent-leather shoes. His father's comment to the request was, "Those shoes are for girls." And the boy responded, "They will be *my* shoes, and I'm not a girl." After some urging by his older son and wife, the father relented and said the boy could have the shoes. But his final comment was, "These red shoes are as close as you get to *pink*."[18] On the subject of color and footwear, data from the internet poll taken during the period from 2008 to 2009 (see Table 9-A), shows that 70 respondents, or 53 percent of the total of 131, felt that color is related to gender.[19]

In 2011, an extreme incident occurred related to color in Sweden where a six-year-old boy named Oskar was stabbed in the neck by a bully who didn't like that Oskar preferred pink clothing, nail polish, and ballet. Oskar "complained to his parents that classmates taunted him, calling him gay and a girl." Fortunately, the bully used a dull knife and Oskar wasn't seriously injured in the attack.[20] Instances of gang violence have also occurred because individuals wore the wrong-color clothing in the wrong part of town.[21]

There have been many instances where women have not been satisfied with footwear available to them in store displays and mail-order catalogs so they have turned to wearing more masculine styles. Women in the last half of the nineteenth century demanded high-top boots to replace the flimsy thin-soled slippers they were expected to wear. One of the primary reasons for this shoe change was to allow women to be in the outdoors and participate in sports. According to Rexford (2008), "A new world was about to open up for women: the world of the outdoors, of sports, of business, and public action. The Cinderella age of the slipper was over. The age of the boot had begun."[22]

More and more women began to wear boot styles that had previously been considered masculine or unisex. But, with boots, there was not much likelihood of men abandoning the style as more and more women wore them because men had to wear them for work or perform their duties in the military. Yet men had worn strap shoes from Roman times but wanted nothing to do with them once they became known as "Mary Janes." So it would appear that the *name* rather than the physical characteristics of the shoe affected its popularity.

The shoes Nike Rifts and FiveFingers with straps across the instep were discussed, but *never* termed "Mary Janes." These shoes went on to become popular with male runners, even in shades of pink and white. And fashion shows like the one Dior did in 2006 and Telfar in 2009–2010 presented male models who wore strap shoes and kilt-like garments on the runway, which may have begun the reversal for males to wear footwear with straps.

For this phenomenon to occur, many men and boys will have to cross the perceived gender lines with strap shoes and sandals, which may take some time, as it appears that hang-ups and fears are well entrenched from early childhood, and culturally reinforced. In the case of the model in the 2009 Telfar show who is wearing Mary Jane shoes and deconstructed pants that resemble a skirt, it would be a difficult and challenging new fashion context. It is important that one should view these styles within a *changing and evolving* fashion context. Mary Jane shoes and deconstructed pants may be for menswear a novel idea, but it is not a novel idea, as it came from a Japanese designer for women's wear and was introduced to the public in the mid-to-late 1980s. It should be noted that women often borrow male styles that represent not only comfort, but also male status, authority, or a means to achieve societal equality. The Telfar model's attire is a representation of a gender blending that crosses cultural and geographic boundaries to become acceptable to both female and male fashion experimenters of fashion for both sexes. And, according to the author's observations, twenty-first-century men appear more willing to adorn themselves in feminine attire, as evidenced in clothing styles and accessories that include shoes and colors. This so-called "feminine" look is consistent with the more relaxed and casual appearance.

Negrin (2008) states that "the blurred difference between casual and work clothing has tended to lessen the distinction between gender and class, and also has lessened regional and ethnic variations between city and countryside."[23] Agins (2000) has gone even further to say that fashion has become "out of style," as most firms allow casual dress any time rather than just on "dress down Fridays."[24] This is in sharp contrast to the instance that William recalled when a fellow office worker was sent home in the early 1960s because he came to work wearing a Bermuda shorts suit complete with tie and jacket. The pendulum in fashion acceptance has definitely shifted in the last fifty years.

The Historic Boys' Clothing website has an account of a boy required to wear a very fancy velvet outfit until the age of eight to church or at Sunday dinners. The clothing consisted of short pants, a collarless short jacket, frilly white blouse with collar worn outside the jacket, knee socks or anklets, and either saddle shoes or double-bar, closed-toe T-strap sandals. Another boy on the site recalls similar formal attire he had to wear as a ring bearer at a wedding. He writes, "I still remember the trepidation felt as mother unwrapped the tissue [from] what I would be wearing every Sunday." He really dreaded going out in public in these clothes, but at the same time he really enjoyed all the attention he received.[25]

Finally, a third boy who was twelve years old at the time reports he had to wear a sailor outfit to his sister's Confirmation at the end of fifth grade. He was sure that the blouse was a girl's because the one he had to wear the previous year no longer fit and he had to accompany his mother to the local children's store the Saturday before the Confirmation to buy another one. As his mother could find no acceptable shirt in the boys' section, she bought a blouse in the girls' section. He states, "I did not try anything on, but somehow we went home with two blouses. One was the sailor collar with short puffed sleeves, the other was a ruffled round collar back button, and short puffed sleeves. The latter one I wore only once [and] it was horrible." And his mother told him he looked very cute in the clothes.[26]

Why is there such deep-seated fear or uneasiness when boys wear a girls' blouse, as in the previous example, or when they wear shoes like Mary Janes that are perceived as feminine, which are nothing more than stitched pieces of leather? Actually, the clothing described earlier was considered in fashion for the well-to-do boys, like the Little Lord Fauntleroy suits so popular for mothers, but not necessarily popular for the young boys who had to wear them.

However, one must see things in proper perspective and

juxtaposed in time and space. An illustration that appeared in 1907 in the *Ladies Home Journal* presents a boys' fashion at the turn of the twentieth century, featuring a Napoleon military-style hat and a kilted Fauntleroy outfit, which was a boys' garment for that time. Queen Victoria, as discussed previously, popularized the kilt for boys by requiring her sons to wear them for visits to Scotland. Long hair and strap shoes were part of the attire. But strap shoes and long hair, even with ringlets, can be found on both sexes during this time period. People thought this look very stylish. But a problem began when the image was superimposed into the mid-1950s and beyond. Girls, who had previously covered their legs for modesty reasons, began to wear clothes similar to what was worn exclusively by boys. Additionally, boys had abandoned strap shoes in North America, where they became known as "Mary Janes," worn almost exclusively by girls, except for the very well-to-do boys. This change in children's fashions certainly is an example of a gender shift, as fashion cycles and social conventions and perceptions of strap shoes changed over time.

Weidner (2005) maintains that a style did not "become old fashioned as much as it became juvenile."[27] And being thought of as childish, in addition to the perception of the clothes being girlish, may account for why the boys discussed earlier rejected the clothes they were forced to wear by their mothers. It appears that using movies, television, magazines, and newspapers, the advertising industry accelerated this process of change over the last one hundred years as they constantly offered new styles with gender differences accentuated.

Now, contrast this with garments worn by the sixteenth-century soldiers in Figure 9-5. These soldiers are both carrying weapons, but the one on the left appears to be in a dress, while the other one wears a variation of a tunic. Both have fancy headwear,

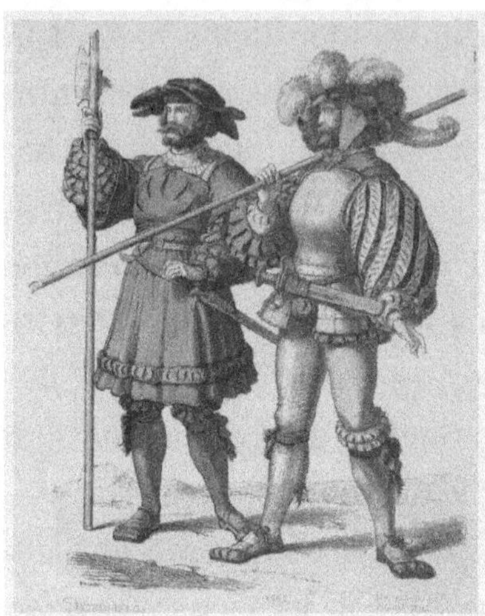

Figure 9-5
Soldiers, 1500s

garters, tights, and Mary Jane–style shoes. Living at that time, one would not say the soldiers looked effeminate, at least not to their faces. But if someone in the twenty-first century wore these clothes and shoes other than as a costume, what would people think? Present-day rules and social taboos allow women the liberty to adorn themselves this or any other way if they so choose, but men and boys generally cannot.

Even in the latter half of the 1900s children could be attired in traditional-style clothes for formal dress-up occasions, like the ring bearers' costumes at weddings. The 1969 edition of *Emily Post's Etiquette* recommended that "pages may be dressed in quaint old-fashioned . . . suits of white silk or satin, [while] ring bearers and train bearers are most often dressed in white suits, preferably with short pants. Tiny boys and girls [also] wear slippers with a strap and white socks." In the 1970s *McCall's* magazine, in its engagement and wedding guide, it recommended that:

The ring bearer's costume usually is a white suit with short pants or short white pants worn with a ruffled white blouse, a colored sash, socks and strapped patent leather shoes which may be either black or white. Page boys, though slightly older, are generally dressed like the ring bearer.[28]

Twenty years later, Letitia Baldrige's *Complete Guide to the New*

Manners for the '90s recommended that the ring bearer wear satin or velvet shorts, or knickers, with white knee socks and, where possible, *all* children in a wedding party "should wear black patent leather or white Mary Jane shoes and white socks."[29] The updated edition in 2003 still has the same Mary Jane shoes recommendation.

A shift from strap shoes to saddle shoes occurred in the latter part of the 1900s in North America as strap shoes became old-fashioned or too "sissy" for most boys to wear, even for formal occasions. But, in the UK, pictures from the 1980s show royal weddings in which the boys wore strap shoes, as had been done for hundreds of years. However, even in the UK, this practice could be changing, as the May 2011 wedding of Prince William and Kate Middleton had page boys wearing pumps just like the older grooms, but with no strap shoes.

Figure 9-6 shows a boy and girl dressed in traditional Austrian folk costumes. Would the boy be seen as a sissy, or is he wearing footwear that has been worn for centuries? If boys and men dressed as warriors with strap shoes in the past, why are these shoes considered sissy like in today's culture when girls are dressing more and more like boys? Most comments read during this research state that it is all right for women to wear male shoes, but it is not appropriate for men to don female attire and shoes. Ulrich (2002) states that footwear has played an important role in the feminist movement with women appropriating men's styles for themselves, an important step in their quest for equality. This is because in the past women have traditionally been seen as second-class citizens and inferior to men. She further writes that the "footwear industry deliberately did their best to keep [women] right where they were thought to belong in society."[30] Therefore, today's women are not about to give up the gains they have made, which include the wearing of men's clothing and footwear.

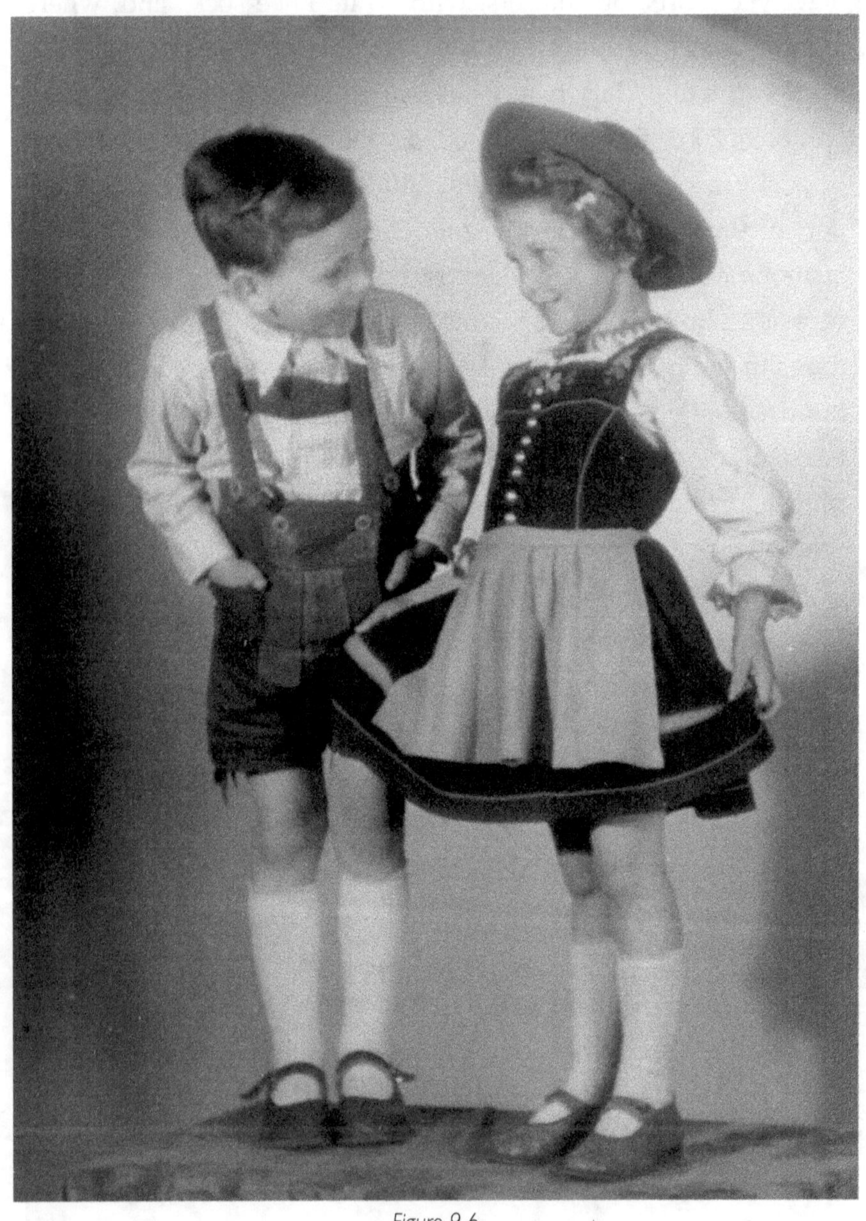

Figure 9-6
Traditional dress for Austrian children, 1930s

With the rise of the feminist movement in the 1960s and 1970s, more unisex styles appeared in retail and specialty stores. Dr. Martens made several examples of unisex shoe styles, with both men's and women's sizes printed inside the shoes and on the outside of the box. Many Dr. Martens were so similar that it was often difficult to tell the difference between a men's and a woman's shoe except by size.

As a result of women assuming male clothing and footwear to dress in, men have avoided the so-called "unisex" styles, particularly in shoes, which has resulted in fewer styles available to men. And, unless more new styles in shoes are created for men, they will eventually run out of men's fashions to wear. Chuck (2006), on an internet blog, complains about women wearing men's footwear because "guys don't have much left . . . Leave our shoes alone!"[31]

Besides the feminist influence on shoes, there is the reluctance of many men and boys to wear something *new*. Boys who wear what their peers consider girls' shoes run into the problem of being bullied, called sissies, or being beaten up after school. While this concept is not unique to Europe or North America, it is becoming more common throughout the world. Jemanda (2007), speaking of Afrikaans schools in South Africa, notes if a male child showed up at his school with his "sister's Mary Jane or T-bars on his feet, the other children would have had a lot of derogatory names for [him] plus he would have been sent packing with bruises and a re-arranged nose."[32] What has happened to the concept of gender equality and the pursuit of happiness? Why are there still such strong feelings and emotions on this subject?

Sissy Defined

The terms "sissy" or "girly" have been used numerous places

in this book. Now, it is time to examine exactly what these terms mean, and more specifically what is meant by the phrase "sissy shoes." On WordNet, the definition of "sissy" is "a timid man or boy considered childish or unassertive."[33] Wikipedia adds the word "effeminate" to their definition, and that person "fails to behave according to the traditional male gender role."[34] With reference to shoes, Lindsey (2007) says that "sissy shoes are the kind your mother might have put you in as a kid and would have made you feel like a sissy. In other words, kids' or adult shoes that look like kids' shoes."[35]

Robyn Jodie (2007) is more technical and proposes a formula to define a sissy shoe. The formula is $S = J + f$, in which S = sissy shoe, J = Juvenile, and f = feminine. According to this definition, for a shoe to qualify as a sissy shoe, it must contain *both* a juvenile and feminine component. He capitalizes the "J" to indicate that juvenile is more important than the "f" or feminine characteristics. He further states that saddle shoes qualify because they are worn more often by young children off the golf course, and have a high "J" (juvenile) component. On the other hand, high heels have a high "f" score and still are *not* sissy shoes because they are virtually never worn by young children.[36] Regardless of whether one agrees with this formula, the concept is rather intriguing. Using the formula with Crocs, which were originally a men's boating shoe, and now are worn by men, women, and children, the shoes are not considered sissy. But, with the introduction of the new Mary Jane Crocs in 2010, will they be worn largely by women and girls and thus qualify as a sissy shoe if men or boys wear them in the future?

Traditional Mary Jane shoes with the single strap over the instep, once commonly worn by adults and children of both sexes, were not considered a sissy shoe in the past. But with the name

"Mary Jane" attached to the shoe just before World War I, things began to change, and fewer and fewer men wore them. Now, Mary Janes are considered a sissy shoe, at least for men to wear them in North America. However, there are indications, as reported in previous chapters, that the pendulum may swing back as men begin to rediscover the style, which will result in the strap shoe no longer being in the sissy category. This will more likely occur in Europe, where the Mary Jane name has not generally been used. This phenomenon may be occurring in the 2010s in Germany, where the CP Shoes Co. made historic strap shoes in the Mary Jane style in men's sizes as part of the reproductions of soldiers' footwear from the period 1250 to 1500 AD. The Finn Comfort Company, also in Germany, advertised men's adjustable strap shoes in its 2012 line of shoes on the internet.

T-strap sandals referred to as "Mary Janes," both single and double bar, are much harder to assess with respect to gender factors. The double-T-bar style, originally termed "barefoot sandals," discussed in chapter 5, and the single-bar T-straps date back to Roman times in one form or another, but reappeared in North America only at the turn of the twentieth century. At that time, they were advertised as shoes for the "entire family," possibly as part of the health movement then occurring. But, as men stopped wearing the double-bar T-strap, they became a child's sandal and only occasionally seen in women's sizes. T-strap shoes became very popular in Europe during the 1900s, especially in the UK, where they became part of prep school uniforms. And, in North America after the 1920s, the strap shoe was available only up to size 3 or 4 for little boys. So, even if boys wanted to wear them, larger sizes were not available without going to women's sizes.

The term "sissy" came into use during the 1840s as an affectionate name for a female sibling. By the 1880s, it became associated with men and boys then considered as helpless, spiritless, or weak. And, around 1900, the term "sissy" started to be applied to effeminate-looking men. At the time, men believed women to be inferior to men by referring to them as the weaker sex.

When Teddy Roosevelt, in the early 1900s, stressed that boys needed to be "real boys," the term "sissy" was just starting to be used more as people became more gender-conscious, with companies starting to advertise clothing and footwear specific to boys or girls. In fact, Teddy Roosevelt as a child was dressed in skirts, and when president, one of his small sons wore a dress-like or tunic garment without anyone giving it a thought. Likewise, Franklin D. Roosevelt, in 1884 at the age of two and a half, wore a dress, hat, and strap shoes with long, curly hair as seen in Figure 9-7. Certainly, neither of these presidents could be considered a sissy, nor other presidents pictured in skirted garments as small boys.

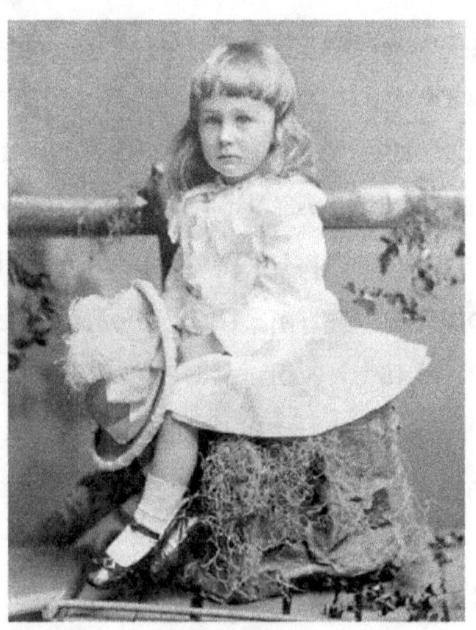

Figure 9-7
Franklin Delano Roosevelt at age two, 1884

Boys Dressed as Girls?

It must be emphasized that contrary to the type of clothing and footwear boys wore in old pictures, as seen through present-day eyes, it does not appear to have been a conscious effort on the part of most parents to dress them as girls, or have them wear what are now considered feminine shoes. Boys wore what was popular for boys at that time period, which followed advice found in fashion magazines, newspapers, and catalog ads. Children were very aware of what was appropriate for each sex in the past, just like today. Illustrating this point is a comic strip from the 1900s in which Richard Outcault, creator of Buster Brown as well as the comic strip in 1903, had Buster and his girlfriend Florence exchange clothes and in the process cut Florence's hair to look like Buster's hair. Both children wear strap shoes, typical for children at that time, but the comic strip was not about shoes, rather the clothes worn by each child. Buster's mother reacts violently to his wearing Florence's clothes.

However, there are instances when mothers did deliberately dress their sons in female clothing long after the age when most boys were breeched or began to wear pants instead of the customary baby dresses. In these cases, the reason was because either the mother wished for a girl rather than a boy, or there was a superstitious held belief.

Weidner (2006) feels these outfits, made of lightweight cotton, would have been very comfortable to wear before the invention of air conditioning.[37]

Further, Historic Boys' Clothing reports that in certain parts of Ireland it was customary for boys to the age of twelve to wear "long flannel dresses so that they would intentionally look like girls [as] their mothers feared that the *banshees*, a type of fairy, would steal their wee boys." This dress for boys was also a common practice well into the twentieth century by some Dutch mothers who lived in isolated areas of the Netherlands.[38] Passarelli (2009) also reports that the practice of dressing boys to look like girls up to two years of age was practiced by certain Romani women to keep evil spirits from stealing them.[39] And boys wore dress-like garments in English workhouses in the 1800s and early 1900s, presumably for economic reasons, because the dresses were cheaper to make and easy to keep clean.

Kippen (2005), a podiatrist and shoe historian at the University of Perth's Department of Podiatry, reports that until World War I, everyone dressed very young boys and girls in similar-style dresses, often referred to as petticoats, until the age of five or six. However, boys could still be forced to wear dresses long after this age even into their teens or early twenties, to correct behavioral problems. Using dresses on boys who misbehaved was called "petticoat discipline." These boys had to suffer the indignity of wearing bows, short pants, velvet fabric, curled hair, and even girl's underwear. If this attire failed to curb abhorrent behavior, then more lace and ruffles were added. As part of the punishment, lads were (further) paraded in front of their family and friends, who in turn were expected to demean and degrade them as part of the behavior control. Kippen (2005) also states that:

> Bed wetting often resulted in punishment which required boys [to be] dressed in nappies [diapers] and baby clothes ... practices common among the middle and upper class families. Naughty boys in mixed [sex] schools might be required to sit in the girls' section of a class.[40]

A poll on the internet created in September 2001, called "Does petticoating really happen?" revealed the following information: Out of 443 male participants in the poll, 362 (81 percent) revealed they had been punished by petticoating discipline. Of these, 240 boys (over 61 percent) felt the practice did improve their behavior, while 73 (19 percent) said it did not improve their behavior, and 78 (20 percent) were not sure.[41]

Jimmy (2004) states he was forced to wear sandals as a boy and felt embarrassed when he had to wear white girly sandals with short pants. He says when he misbehaved his mother would put white sandals on him, especially in the summer, and then take him to numerous stores so other people could see them. He felt he "could see other mothers and kids pointing at [his] feet and giggling." Even when he visited his cousins, he "always was teased and embarrassed by [the white sandals]." In any event, Jimmy admits that it did eventually improve his behavior.[42]

There have been instances in recent times when boys have submitted voluntarily to wearing girls' clothing and footwear, besides for a Halloween costume or stage performance. An example is Lei Lydia, who operated the AtlantaBridal.com site, which reports she had been outfitting bridal parties for twenty-eight years and during that time had seen a few instances, although extremely rare, when boys dressed as flower girls or bridesmaids at formal weddings.

A perusal of the AtlantaBridal.com site further showed that others also had witnessed cross-dressing of boys, so it may be more common than expected. Some boys felt humiliated by the experience while others thought it was novel. And some readers saw no problem with cross-dressing as long as the boy approved, while others were hostile in their disapproval, as evidenced in their comments.

One person from London, England, in 2005 posted in the

AtlantaBridal.com site that he had substituted as a flower girl for his cousin, Rachael, age twelve plus, at a wedding in 1962, when he was ten years old. Four days before the wedding, Rachael came down with the measles. The boy thought he would have to wear an outfit similar to the one worn by his seven-year-old brother, who was to be the ring bearer and dressed in a "white blouse, pale blue velvet knickerbockers and black Mary Janes." But, after much persuasion by his mother, the ten-year-old agreed to wear the clothes Rachael was going to wear. In spite of comments from the women on how fantastic he looked, the boy felt terrified as he walked down the aisle trying to keep his legs from trembling:

> I was dressed in a pale blue satin, knee length dress with all the trimmings, and I mean all! Paper nylon petticoat, lipstick, eye shadow; I even had to wear frilly nylon panties! The worst part was being required to wear stockings.
>
> Because Rachael was nearly 13, she was to be allowed to dress more grown up, and as I was her same size, I wore what she had intended to wear. The only thing that kept me going was the older bridesmaid whispering words of encouragement the whole time.
>
> As a ten-year-old I had no ill effects from the experience and [even though] it was nerve wracking at that time; I lived to tell the tale.

While teasing his older brother about wearing a dress, the seven-year-old brother did not object to wearing a velvet outfit with Mary Jane shoes, because they were still being worn by boys in the UK at the time.[43]

Kristen of Naestved, Denmark, commented in 2005 that her husband's cousin, a seven-year-old boy, "stepped in for another cousin, a girl nine years old who had to go into hospital at the last minute. Now, in his mid twenties, married with a daughter of his own, he treasures his memories of our wedding and the photographs of him in his dress. No harm done."[44] Walter of Pasadena, California, wrote in October 2005 that there are pictures of him "in a flower girl's dress in the late forties" in which everyone said he looked "cute." He grew up to be an Army Ranger with two combat tours in Viet Nam and never wore girls' clothing again. "Guess it didn't bother me or change my sexual identity. So, if a boy will wears a dress, let him . . . [it]may make him tougher," he said, which is reminiscent of the boy in the Johnny Cash song "A Boy Named Sue."[45]

Warrior or Sissy

The question of whether footwear that includes Mary Janes or other closed-toe sandals falls into the warrior or sissy category was and is difficult to assess. This depends on the circumstance in which the shoes are worn, such as in the case of the boy who substituted at the wedding for the girl who went to the hospital at the last minute. It can also depend on the time period in history, such as when soldiers wore and in some instances continue to wear a Mary Jane variation of buckle brogues as part of their uniforms, like the Scottish Highlanders. Finally, it can depend on styles favored by mothers who wish to copy the fashions worn by royalty, or those perceived to be their social betters, even when the fashion footwear has become outdated at that time. Currently, many boys wear junior-sized tuxedos as ring bearers. Thus, the time lag is an example seen over and over in this research where:

1. Children originally dressed as their elders.
2. As adults take on new styles, children continue to wear the old styles.
3. Children abandon the old-fashioned styles and begin to

adopt the new fashions that adults currently wear, or risk being called a sissy.

One can wonder that boys who wear tuxedos like their elders will continue to wear them if and when the adults switch to another style, such as formal kilt suits. With the entire female sex, no matter their age, now wearing pants even as part of school uniforms, is it possible that boys who wear pants like the girls will be called "sissies" in the future because they look like the girls? This whole phenomenon may seem farfetched, but this has happened before in fashion. So where does it stop? It doesn't and won't, since fashion styles go in cycles and are retro but made to look modern.

Carrying things to an extreme, in early 2011, a Toronto, Canada, couple decided to conceal the sex of their four-month-old baby named Storm until the child was old enough to decide for itself what gender it was. The couple had two older boys, aged two and five, who were free to wear dresses or pants according to their current whim. The older boy's favorite color was pink and both boys had their hair in whatever style or length they wished. Further, the boys were homeschooled to protect them from adverse comments and possible bullying. While the couple was fine with this way of raising their three children, 90 percent of people on the internet disapproved of their parenting style.[46]

Mary Beth (2005) of Dover, New Jersey, sees no issue with a boy who wears girls' clothing, since it was the custom for either sex in the past. She maintains that "if enough moms began to raise their sons that way, the custom would be reinstituted, and no little boy dressed as the flower carrier would need to feel embarrassed or out of place."[47] Is this trend beginning? The *New York Times* reports that men marched up Fifth Avenue in New York City on

March 2009 proclaiming their right to wear kilts. There was also a man who wore a he-skirt with boxers or wrestlers' shoes, as seen in an advertisement from *Selections from the Dorcus Collection* that appeared in the 1970s (Figure 9-8).

Will calling a skirt a "he-skirt" make it legitimate for men to wear skirts? Is this the same as encouraging men to again wear sandals by calling them "mandals"? Will men again don the single-strap Mary Jane–type shoes by calling them "buckle brogues" like Scottish Highlanders?

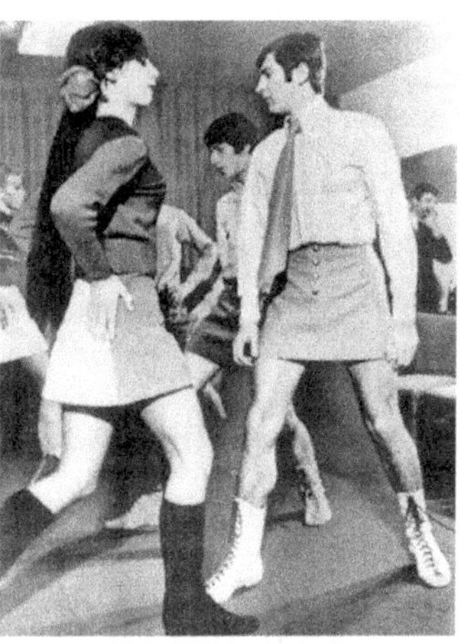

Figure 9-8
Dorcus he-skirts, 1970s

The boy in Figure 9-9 who makes what appears to be a military salute definitely would not fall into the category of sissy, even though he has on strap shoes, which the seller of the photo on eBay stated were girl shoes.

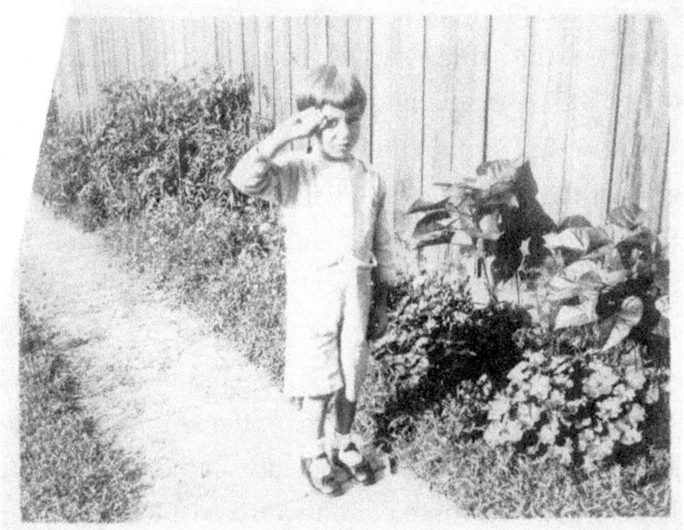

Figure 9-9
Boy saluting, Early 1900s

In Scotland, the term "jessie" is more common than the word "sissy." Jenkins (1979), in his novel *Fergus Lamont*, relates how a seven-and-a-half-year-old boy was required to wear a kilt while visiting his grandfather. This young boy felt self-conscious about the experience and feared being called a jessie, not because he thought kilts were a girls' garment, but because none of his friends wore kilts. Actually, what he feared most was that someone would lift up his kilt to see what was underneath. To alleviate this fear, his mother told him that soldiers who wore kilts normally wore nothing underneath. She suggested that her son kick in the shin anyone who lifted his kilt and "exposed his backside to the lassies."[48]

With respect to Mary Jane shoes, opinions may even be changing. In a Yahoo! Answers blog in 2007, a person responded to the question "Why is it that boys look better than girls wearing these shoes? I have seen plenty of boys wearing them, and [they] are way better looking than on girls' feet."[49] Most other people answering the same question didn't agree with this opinion. In response to the question "What do you think of men wearing Mary Jane shoes?" at the same blog, Alexia stated: "Mary Jane shoes + Men = Gay!"[50] Of course, a person is not gay simply because of the clothes they wear. And, in any event, change in fashion, or anything else for that matter, is inevitable in a postmodern society.

In postmodernity, change occurs over time whether anyone likes it or not. For example, one of the major sartorial changes occurred when Thomas Jefferson wore long pants in the White House as opposed to the clothing style worn by his predecessors George Washington and John Adams. Jefferson was also criticized when he wore corset shoes with shoelaces rather than buckles, because shoelaces in that time period were considered feminine.

Another blogger by the name of Mary Beth questioned why

being dressed as a woman is such a problem. This challenge "implies that clothing and activities generally considered feminine are inferior to those considered masculine, which they aren't."[51] It should be noted that the Romans, who wore kilts, viewed men who wore britches as barbarians. The author of this book does not advocate that men wear skirts, or strap shoes, or anything else; rather, an individual should support the right of anyone to wear whatever he/she chooses to wear. On the other hand, people *should* be more concerned with the connotation of implied inferiority of women as it relates to the terms "sissy" or "girly."

Sissy Equals Inferior Females?

To many, the terms "sissy" or "girly" have taken on a strongly negative connotation. The implication is that girls are not as good as boys, and a boy must avoid anything female because he will catch the plague. If boys and men are perceived to wear anything remotely considered feminine or to participate in any female activity, they are branded a "sissy" and subjected to bullying or worse. Natalie (2007) writes that several people express themselves this way on the Mormon Mommy Wars blog: "People are still reinforcing problematic gender stereotypes, and being girly is equated to being weak. It's just so dangerous to frame the world in [terms of] masculine/feminine, strong/weak." Amber, in the same year, blogged that we "teach gender equality, but we still need to teach children to be proud that they are boys [or] girls."[52]

Once started, it is difficult to modify or stop the reference to negative words. Currently, there may be less use of the term "sissy" within a negative context, as fashions have become more androgynous and unisex.

In 2011, interviews were conducted with sixty students at Georgia Tech University in Atlanta, Georgia, of which seventeen were male and forty-three were female, to canvass opinion on gender and shoes/sandals. The students were enthusiastic about a book on sandals and thought the subject was "cool." Table 9-B summarizes the findings of selected questions from the questionnaire.

RESULTS OF INTERVIEWS ON SANDALS (MEN)							
	Yes		No		Not Sure		Total
	#	%	#	%	#	%	Men
1. Is it acceptable for females to wear male footwear, but not vice versa?	11	64%	3	18%	3	18%	17
2. Can males wear sandals they like even if they look like female footwear?	12	70%	3	18%	2	12%	17
3. Do manufacturers place names on shoes to condition people to believe there are gender differences in footwear?	11	65%	5	29%	1	6%	17
4. Would calling a sandal a mandal make it acceptable to males regardless of its appearance?	2	12%	14	82%	1	6%	17

Table 9-B

Source: V. Bolen, information from questionnaires, May 2011.

RESULTS OF INTERVIEWS ON SANDALS (WOMEN)							
	Yes		No		Not Sure		Total
	#	%	#	%	#	%	Women
1. Is it acceptable for females to wear male footwear, but not vice versa?	20	47%	19	44%	4	9%	43
2. Can males wear sandals they like even if they look like female footwear?	28	65%	9	21%	6	14%	43
3. Do manufacturers place names on shoes to condition people to believe there are gender differences in footwear?	29	67%	6	14%	8	19%	43
4. Would calling a sandal a mandal make it acceptable to males regardless of its appearance?	6	14%	31	72%	6	14%	43

Table 9-C

Source: V. Bolen, information from questionnaires, May 2011.

The data show 64 percent of the men (eleven) and 47 percent of the women (twenty) agree that it is acceptable for women to wear male attire but not vice versa. Fully 70 percent (twelve) of male respondents and 65 percent of women (twenty-eight) agree that men can wear sandals even though they may look feminine. Finally, 82 percent of men (fourteen) and 72 percent of women (thirty-one) believe that calling a sandal a "mandal" would not make it acceptable to men, regardless of its appearance. One of the findings was that boys still will not wear shoes like exercise Mary Janes because the name implies they are girls' shoes, even though many admired the style. It was determined during the research the term "sissy" was not being used as much as in the past because the word "girly" is now preferred, and without a negative connotation among college students. But a fear still exists on the part of men to wear something where they might be laughed at and lose a degree of power. Actually, mandals could be seen as a reversal of the trend, which O'Keeffe (1996) says happens when footwear is first worn by men and subsequently appropriated by women.[53]

As shoe preferences have changed over time into the postmodern era, there is a definite trend toward androgyny in the perception of shoe styles. Hopefully, a degree of equality among the sexes will occur as a result. Yet, when one looks at shoe advertisements in catalogs, magazines, or on the internet, many shoe ads have gendered names assigned to the various styles. Will this practice continue? And why would people need the help of advertisers that give a male or female name to a shoe style so people can better select the footwear they may like? Is this naming of shoes to better identify male or female footwear? Is this *help* of gendered shoe names needed more in children's footwear, where the sizes for both sexes are the same?

For adults, it is easier to tell a male from a female shoe in North America because the women's sizes are different from those of men, while in the United Kingdom and the rest of Europe the use of a standardized series of sizes is truly androgynous. Why are shoe manufacturers in the US so adamant to keep the antiquated shoe-sizing system as opposed to the rest of the world? Could the sizing of shoes be like the metric and Celsius system of temperatures that was tried in the US but failed to win approval by the populace who prefer the status quo?

Winick (1995) notes that men spend more on fragrance than do women. Men also wear jewelry, have long hair, and have other attributes that traditionally only women had a few years ago. He refers to this taking of traditional female things as "gender bending." As a result, unisex clothing and footwear has become so common that it may finally be time to retire the term "sissy" as it relates to clothing items, particularly shoes.[54]

Shoe Names Make a Difference

In the research for this book, an attempt was made to collect firsthand information on the question of the need to assign names to various shoe styles. In response to the question "Do you need a shoe's name to help you buy it?" only 12 men and women, or 9 percent of the 133 total, thought such names were useful (see Table 9-A). Moreover, information collected from questionnaires indicated that eleven men (65 percent of the male sample) and twenty-nine women (67 percent of female) believe that manufacturers/advertisers use names to deliberately condition people to believe there is a connection between gender and shoe styles. In fact, Payless ShoeSource Inc. outlets must agree, because a visit to several of their stores in 2010 revealed that boys' and girls' shoes were grouped by size and listed as kids' shoes. On the other hand, men's and women's shoes were still located in separate areas, as each gender still has its own sizes.

To name a sandal "mandal" for men was not necessary according to fourteen men (82 percent of men) and thirty-one women (72 percent of women) in 2011 obtained from the questionnaire. Women commented that it made no difference what a shoe was called, as they were *still sandals*. "Mandals" could have been the name used by shoe manufacturers to encourage men to wear sandals, but the term could eventually be discarded once a majority of men wore them. In this way, the term "mandal" could be considered a transition word which will eventually disappear from the shoe vocabulary.

Unlike mandals, an instance where a shoe name has continued to have a major impact on the sales of strap shoes and sandals previously worn by both sexes, but now largely marketed to women, is the name "Mary Jane." However, both men and boys may wear strap shoes in the future like the buckle brogues, but probably not with this name attached to them. As noted earlier, the Finn Comfort Company in Germany actually changed its ad from "Men's Mary Janes" to "Men's Adjustable Strap Shoes" to make them more acceptable to male purchasers.

The National Bellas Hess Company offered a pair of Mary Jane–type sandals in its September 1950 sale catalog as "Men's Cool Sandals – Cowboy Buckle." This name undoubtedly attracted more male buyers than the name "Mary Jane." It was not possible to get sales information since the company filed for bankruptcy in 1971 and went out of business shortly thereafter.

Advertisers' Role

Advertising companies began to differentiate shoe styles by gender on a much larger scale about the time of World War I by assigning male or female names to various styles. This assigning of names was done arbitrarily. Swanson (2008) recalls when he joined the Boy Scouts in the 1940s that his parents bought him a pair of brown moc-toe-type Oxfords that were advertised as Boy Scout shoes, while girls during this same the time period were wearing Girl Scout shoes just like his.[55]

It would appear that having two separate lines of shoes with only the name different is an example of companies setting artificial norms for their own gain and profit. And the different shoe lines for one's sex resulted in people becoming conditioned to shoe gender, to such an extent that it has approached a social taboo to wear the wrong type. This same process has occurred with the colors pink for girls and women and blue for boys and men. Fortunately, these color barriers are being broken as people begin to be color-blind with respect to gender and color. But there are still strong feelings by some individuals regarding color and gender, as discussed in this book.

A woman posted a question at the Parents Center Forum in 2007 asking who decides what is female clothing and what is male clothing:

Is it the manufacturers? The retailers? The fashion gurus? Or is it the individual wearers? What right have women to dictate to the male sex what is and is not appropriate for them to wear?[56]

These are very valid questions but beyond the scope and purpose of this study on closed-toe sandals.

Katie Roberts (2002), in her paper "The Shopping Malls and Their Role in the Gender System in America," writes that from infancy a child sees gender displayed in certain ways for boys and girls:

In America going against the societal norms of how to properly display maleness or femaleness is often negatively viewed. Malls, by displaying products and activities reinforce the notion that gender is something innate that comes from within. People begin to think there is an internal male and female characteristic [that] actually creates the desires for the objects, not society or the institutions themselves. One learns to buy products that society prescribes are for their gender.

This pattern tends to be true for adults as well as children. Further, in shoe stores, certain styles, according to Roberts (2002):

are directed toward men [while] others are meant to reach women. It is the way that each sex is *lured* into believing a product is "meant" or designed for them. Things like the color pink, floral patterns, and dresses are commonly known to represent little girls in our culture. Blues, animals, sports activities, cars, and darker colors are typically associated with little boys. Tags and pictures often target the sex of the wearer thus making boys and girls feel like these clothes are meant for a particular sex. [After generations] each sex has unconsciously accepted the colors, patterns, styles, and shapes displayed within the section as being somehow innately masculine or feminine.[57]

Such patterns and perceptions are not easily broken. Roberts (2002) has reminded us there are also men's and women's sections in shoe stores; however, children's shoes "appear to be a bit more neutral or genderless, because some of the shoes meant for little boys could be worn by little girls, and vice versa without much social criticism."

Roberts notes that handbags and other accessories are often placed in locations where they can be matched with the shoes. Pocketbooks, an accessory, are larger than men's wallets in order to make women feel it is *okay* for them to buy more because they believe that all women need many things to "properly display their gender and their personalities." Roberts carries this division a step further by stating that "separating the sexes allows people to rationalize why men and women are in different [unequal] jobs, and why men and women are treated differently in society."[58]

Regarding this same question, Bob (2011), a man, mentions that:

It is probably better [for] businesses to sell girl's and boy's shoes [separately] than to have a good selection of gender neutral shoes, because it means that families have only half the scope for hand-me-down shoes. Little kids' shoes rarely wear out before they are grown out of, and if they can be passed onto little brothers or sisters regardless of gender that reduces the need for new shoes by fifty percent.[59]

Kippen (2005) writes that the basic Mary Jane shoe represents the:

first example of sexualized footwear for children based on commercialism. In the 1930s the shoe style took a quantum leap in worldwide sales when Shirley Temple wore them on screen with her dancing outfits. [Moreover,] she helped establish Mary Janes as the shoe style for little girls. Her management missed no commercial opportunity and sold *Shirley Temple Mary Janes* by the millions.[60]

The female name "Mary Janes," plus strap shoes advertised as little girls' shoes, could be the reason men and boys, at least in North America, developed a phobia toward wearing this shoe.

This feeling has also occurred with fisherman sandals and bare-foot sandals, but not with monk-strap shoes, which have remained primarily a male shoe. But even with a strap across the instep, the monk strap is more of an Oxford style than a sandal. Is it any wonder that strapped sandals were avoided and caused much uneasiness to many boys and men for so many years?

With the arrival of the mandal, men began to rediscover the benefits of a sandal style, as shown by its increased sales in the twenty-first century as discussed earlier in chapter 8. This change in men wearing mandal sandals could be considered a paradigm shift in footwear for men, especially with respect to sneaker/sandal hybrids as a wave of the future in men's footwear. New shoe styles, according to Wilson (1969), are worn first by younger people because of fads and to copy celebrities or sports figures.[61] Only after some time passes are newer footwear trends taken up by older people. This is a 180-degree turn from the past when adults were the first to wear new-style clothing and footwear.

As the colors pink and red are seen more and more on men and boys, in addition to short pants and different types of sandals, this could be seen as an emancipation of men's fashion. Men may wear short pants and sandal styles in the summer to keep cool, but one wonders if wearing this attire year-round is an attempt by them to capture a sense of youthfulness or reclaim a feeling of innocence similar to that of women who wear Mary Jane shoes, according to Thompson (2003), to "feel like little girls again [and] evoke a retro time of innocence" in a postmodern society.[62]

With examples of men and boys starting to wear Mary Jane–type shoes in the movies and on television, this style may be reclaimed or rediscovered by the mainstream male wearers. These same men would probably need to have the name "Mary Janes" changed to another perceived masculine term like "mandals" to assuage fears, hang-ups, or uneasiness to overcome the many years of advertised conditioning. Alexander (2009) reports that H&M in their 2009 spring collection had made skirts available to mainstream men who could walk into any of their stores and buy one designed just for men, without a fuss. She further believes that this change is just part of a fashion revolution and emphasizes that men have worn skirts long before they wore pants.[63]

In 2012, the Stride Rite Company, which has made children's shoes since 1919, offered a two-strap boys' sandal on sale that was listed simply as TT TY. It was rugged in appearance with a closed-toe and gel-cushioned tennis-shoe sole to permit durability and maximum comfort, but with the added openness of a sandal to keep the feet cool during summer months. Since the sandal was a marine-style shoe it could be used in or out of water.[64] There was also a very similar men's sports PDQ Trail Walking Closed-Toe Sandal on eBay in 2012 listed by the Shoeshoebedo Co. located in the UK. Both the TT TY boys' and the men's PDQ Trail Walking sandals had two straps that crossed the instep, reminiscent of two-strap Mary Janes. With no gender-associated name, shoe manufacturers are again marketing straps to boys and men. One could wonder if these closed-toe sandals are an example of a crack in the gender barrier for strap shoes after almost one hundred years. And Carrie Bartley (2014) listed on eBay a pair of preowned youth "Unisex Doc. Martens Red Patent Leather Mary Janes" that had both US men's and ladies' sizes printed inside the shoe, since most Dr. Martens are listed as unisex in this way. When asked if a boy had actually worn these shoes, Bartley was not sure but said it was "certainly possible since [she] lives in a fairly progressive metropolitan area [Portland, Oregon]."[65]

Hopefully, the discussion in the foregoing pages has provided an historical overview of closed-toe sandals and Mary Jane shoes over the centuries, to place them in proper perspective for a post-modern society. Mary Jane and other sandals could also impact trends of the future in the evolution of perceptions, styles, and current societal values of footwear for both genders.

Chapter 9 Notes

1. Feirstein, B., *Real Men Don't Eat Quiche: A Guidebook to All That Is Truly Masculine* (1982).

2. Maglaty, J., "When Did Girls Start Wearing Pink?" Smithsonian.com (April 8, 2011), smithsonianmag.com/arts-culture.

3. Swanson, email correspondence (August 26, 2008).

4. Rubenstein, R. P., *Dress Code* (1995), 102.

5. Ibid., 149.

6. Winick, C., *Desexualization in American Life* (1995), 239.

7. Rubinstein, *Dress Code*, 102.

8. "Gender and Shoes/Sandals," Mister Poll (November 9, 2009).

9. Young, S. and Sebastian Kneipp, *Sue Young Homeopathy* (May 28, 2008). Also, Kneipp, S., *My Will: A Legacy to the Healthy and the Sick* (1886), 34, www.sueyounghistories.com/2008-05-28-sebastian-kneipp-and-homeopathy/.

10. Weidner, D., "American Constitution: Modern Critics," Historical Boys' Clothing (May 21, 2008), histclo.com/country/us/hist.

11. Rubinstein, *Dress Code*, 208.

12. Paoletti, J. B., "Little Lord Fauntleroy and His Dad," *The Transformation of Masculine Dress in America, 1880–1900* (Sally Queen & Associates, 1991), sallyqueenassociates.com/Fauntleroy (domain no longer active).

13. Kippen, C., *Foot Talk* (July 3, 2005), 4.

14. "Strap and Buckle Formal Brogues," Kintal House Ltd. (2008), www.kintailhouse.com/shop/highland-dress/brogues.

15. "Curb Appeal: Seduction From the Ground Up," *New York Times* (June 17, 2003), www.nytimes.com/2003/06/17/nyregion/curb-appeal-seduction-from-the-ground-up.html.

16. Jody, R., "What Exactly is a Sissy Shoe?" Goody2Shoes (May 13, 2007), organek.net/forums/Goody2Shoes (domain no longer active).

17. "Is it ok to get and wear a pair of hand-me down ice skates from my sister?" Yahoo! Answers (November 21, 2010), ph.answers.yahoo.com/question/index?qid=20101108064559AAJMsfC.

18. Renkl, M., "Shiny Shoes," *Nashville Scene* (March 6, 2000), www.weeklywire.com/ww/03-06-00/nash_cl-home_brood.html.

19. "Gender and Shoes/Sandals," Mister Poll (November 2009).

20. "Boy Stabbed in Neck at School Because He Likes Pink," *AOL News* (February 11, 2011), aolnews.com/2011/02/11/boy-6-stabbed-in-neck-at-school. Also at www.reddit.com/r/atheism/comments/fje3w/6year_old_boy_stabbed_in_the_neck_for_wearing/.

21. Thompson, M. J., correspondence (May 21, 2013).

22. Rexford, N. E., "Teensy-Weensy, Itty-Bitty Shoes," *Humanities*, vol. 29, no. 2 (March/April 2008), www.neh.gov/humanities/2008/marchapril/feature/teensy-weensy-itty-bitty-shoes.

23. Negrin, L., *Appearance and Identity: Fashioning the Body in Postmodernity* (2008), 16.

24. Agins, T., *The End of Fashion* (2000), 282.

25. "Modern Velvet Suits: Personal Experiences — America, 1963," Historical Boys' Clothing, www.histclo.com/style/suit/other/vpeu601.html.

26. Ibid.

27. Weidner, D., "Fashion Transformations: Cycles in Boys Clothing," Historical Boys' Clothing (September 18, 2005), www.histclo.com/chron/cycle/cycle-trans.html.

28. ———, "Ring Bearer Etiquette," Historical Boys' Clothing (March 30, 1998), www.histclo.com/act/rel/wed/ring1.html.

29. Ibid.

30. Ulrich, M., "One Step at a Time," *Women's History Then and Now-Footwear* (2002), cwrl.utexas.edu/~ulrich/femhist.

31. Chuck, "Girl wearing boys' shoes?" Yahoo! Answers (June 22, 2006), answers.yahoo.com/question?qid=20080920182419AAkTDZF&cp=2.

32. Jamanda (November 4, 2007), mary-janeshoes.com/phpbb/viewtopic.php?f=2&t=177.

33. "Sissy," WordNet (June 9, 2011), wordnetweb.princeton.edu/perl/webwn?s=sissy.

34. "Sissy," *Wikipedia* (June 6, 2011), en.wikipedia.org/wiki/Sissy.

35. Lindsey, "The Whole Idea," Goody2Shoes (January 10, 2007), organek.net/forum/goody2shoes.

36. Jody, R., "What exactly is a sissy shoe?" Goody2Shoes (May 13, 2007), organek.net/forum/goody2shoes.

37. Weidner, D., "American Boy Dresses: Styles — Seasonality," Historical Boys' Clothing (November 11, 2006), www.histclo.com/country/us/gar/skirted/dress/style/usds-sea.html.

38. ———, "Irish Kilts: Chronology," Historical Boys Clothing (July 24, 2009).

39. Passarelli, L., "Gypsy Wedding," *Reminisce* (February/March 2009), 12.

40. Kippen, C., "Petticoat Discipline and Mary Janes," Foot Talk (December 21, 2005), foottalk.blogspot.com/2005/12/petticoat-discipline-and-mary-janes.html.

41. "Does Petticoating Really Happen?" Mister Poll (September 26, 2001), misterpoll.com/polls/40969/results.

42. "Boys in Sandals – Were you forced to wear sandals?" Mister Poll (January 19, 2005), www.misterpoll.com/polls/188845.

43. Lydia, L., "Dressing the Ring Bearer," AtlantaBridal.com (June 3, 2006), bigclosetr.us/topshelf/system/files/Boys%20as%20bridesmaids.pdf.

44. Ibid.

45. Ibid.

46. "Meet the parents who are raising a 'genderless' baby," Yahoo! Lifestyle (May 25, 2011), uk.style.yahoo.com/blogs/yahoo-lifestyles/meet-parents-raising-genderless-baby-105402289.html.

47. Marybeth, comment on "Dressing the Ring Bearer," AtlantaBridal.com (August 12, 2005), bigclosetr.us/topshelf/system/files/Boys%20as%20bridesmaids.pdf.

48. Jenkins, R., *Fergus Lamont* (1979), 4.

49. Atreyu, "Why is it that boys look better than girls wearing Mary Jane shoes?" Yahoo! Answers (June 23, 2007), answers.yahoo.com/question/index?qid=20070623145943AAwcbxy.

50. Alexia, "What do you think of men wearing Mary Jane shoes?" Yahoo! Answers (June 7, 2007), answers.yahoo.com/question/index?qid=20070607120417AAzpPik.

51. Marybeth, "Dressing."

52. Natalie and Amber, comments on Mormon Mommy Wars – Pretty in Pink (April 2007), web.archive.org/web/20070514050325/mormonmommywars.com/?p=663.

53. O'Keeffe, *Shoes*, 434.

54. Winick, *Desexualization*, 19.

55. Swanson, email correspondence.

56. Fox, K., "School uniforms-generally," Parents Center Forum (June 8, 2007), parentscenter.gov.uk/forum/messageview.

57. Roberts, K., "Shopping Malls."

58. Ibid.

59. Bob, email correspondence (July 28, 2011).

60. Kippen, C., Foot Talk (July 3, 2005), 4.

61. Wilson, *History of Shoe Fashion* (1969), 2.

62. Thompson, "Mary Janes" (2003), 5, 12.

63. Alexander, H., "H&M Skirts for Men Hit the Mainstream" (2009), hubpages.com/hub/-HM-Skirts-for-Men-Hit-The-Mainstream.

64. "Toddler Sandals TT TY Marine Navy," Stride Rite of Toledo by Curavo Shoes Inc. (2011), webcache.googleusercontent.com.

65. Bartley, C., email correspondence (August 2014).

ACKNOWLEDGMENTS

The author gratefully acknowledges the assistance and encouragement of many people and educational institutions in the research project culminating in this book. First and foremost was the manuscript's editorial critique by Dr. Mary J. Thompson. Others who offered suggestions and peer reviews of the text include Dr. Jo B. Paoletti, Dr. Kristine Runberg Smith, Dr. Cameron Kippen, and Dr. Elizabeth Mellish. The author also thanks Dr. Alexandra Shumaker, Richard Swanson, Jonathan Walford, Bill Busse, Brandon G. Gingerich, Alan J. Bevan, Preston Dunn, Patricia L. Cosby, and Razvan Prunea for their input. Dennis Weidner, who maintains the Historical Boys' Clothing website, provided valuable historical insight. The staff at the libraries of the Fashion Institute of Technology, the New York Public Library, the Bata Shoe Museum, and the Rutgers Special Collections and University Archives also were most helpful and encouraging, as was the staff of the Chesters Roman Fort and Museum in Hexham, UK. The author also wishes to acknowledge Valerie Bolen for her inspiration, travel guidance, and ongoing encouragement, along with Anita Collins for her technical expertise and editorial assistance in helping to make this book a reality.

ABOUT THE AUTHOR

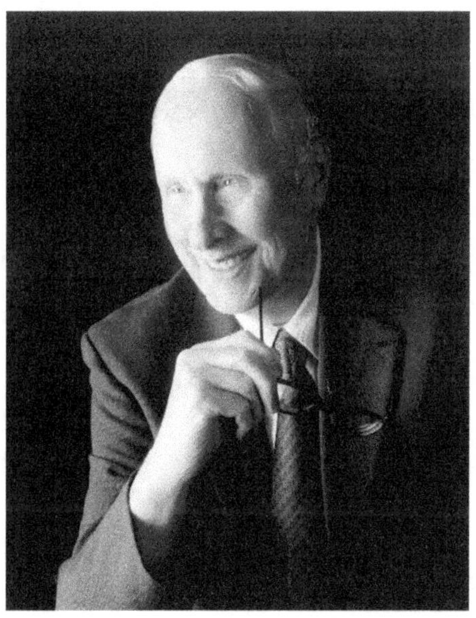

William J. Bolen earned a Ph.D. in cultural geography from Rutgers University. He completed his dissertation on the impact of Italian immigrants in transforming the US cultural landscape, including a detailed analysis of the Italian Ironbound colony in Newark, New Jersey, at the turn of the twentieth century.

Dr. Bolen has spent the past twelve years researching cultural biases and gender differences in footwear. In the years to come, he anticipates a trend toward gender-neutral shoes and clothing.

Also by William J. Bolen, Ph.D.

*The Changing Geography of Italian Immigrants in the United States:
A Case Study of the Ironbound Colony, Newark, New Jersey*

www.ingramcontent.com/pod-product-compliance
Lightning Source LLC
Chambersburg PA
CBHW051756050726
47598CB00006B/2306